THE WORLD'S
HEALTHIEST FOOD

THE WORLD'S HEALTHIEST FOOD

Recipes by
ANNE MARSHALL

Nutrition Text by
CAROLYN KELLY

Recipe Photography by
PETER JOHNSON & PHIL WYMANT

General Editor
MARGARET OLDS

STEWART, TABORI & CHANG
NEW YORK

Library of Congress Catalog Card Number: 96-69258

ISBN: 1-55670-493-3

Publisher: Gordon Cheers

Managing Editor: Margaret Olds

Editors: Charles Pierce and H.D.R. Campbell

Senior Editors: Kate Etherington and Susan Page

Art Director: Stan Lamond

Text: Anne Marshall and Carolyn Kelly

Food Photographers: Peter Johnson and Phil Wymant

Food Stylists: Ann Creber and Lucy Mortensen

Nutritional Analysis: Carolyn Kelly

Scenic Photography: Random House (Australia)
International Picture Collection

Printed in Hong Kong

First Edition
10 9 8 7 6 5 4 3 2 1

Page 1: *Young Buddhist monks collecting donations
of food in Yunnan Province, China.*

Pages 2–3: *A field of sunflowers in Russia, where
their cultivation as an oilseed crop began.*

Page 4: *Minestrone, Barbecued Garlic Shrimp and
Avocado Salad.*

Pages 6–7: *A village girl collecting melons in
Rajasthan, India.*

CONTENTS

❧

CONTENTS

WE ARE WHAT WE EAT

GOOD NUTRITION BUILDS HEALTH

It's usually easy to spot healthy people in a crowd. They look good! Healthy people have lots of vitality and an aura of well-being. They are not too fat, not too thin, have shiny hair, a clear complexion and bright eyes. This appearance can be attributed to the foods they eat.

Healthy people practice good nutrition—the science of adequately nourishing the body by choosing a variety of foods low in fat, salt and sugar and high in complex carbohydrate and dietary fiber.

To achieve overall good health, good nutrition must be combined with exercise and stress management. Alcohol consumption should be moderate and smoking should be avoided.

The body needs six major nutrients to maintain health. These are carbohydrate (including dietary fiber), protein, fat, vitamins, minerals and water.

CARBOHYDRATE

Carbohydrate provides the body with 4 calories of energy per gram. It is the most efficient fuel that the body uses for energy. Carbohydrates are classified into two groups: simple and complex. *Simple* carbohydrates include sugars such as those found in fruit, milk and honey. *Complex* carbohydrates are obtained from bread, cereal, pasta, rice, fruits, vegetables and legumes. Food sources of complex carbohydrates also provide dietary fiber. Fifty to sixty percent of energy (calories) consumed should come from carbohydrate.

Left: *Rice drying in northern India. Rice is a good source of carbohydrate.*
Below: *One of the most brightly colored field crops, rape is the source of canola oil. Canola oil is a monounsaturated oil.*

Dietary fiber

Dietary fiber is divided into two groups: soluble and insoluble. Foods rich in dietary fiber contain a mixture of these fiber components, some higher in one type of fiber, some in the other. *Soluble* dietary fiber, obtained from oats, legumes, fruits and citrus peel, helps to control blood sugar levels and assists in lowering cholesterol levels. *Insoluble* dietary fiber, obtained from vegetables, nuts, seeds, fruits and grains, slows down the emptying of the stomach. This makes us feel fuller longer and helps prevent constipation by making the feces softer and bulkier. Insoluble fiber helps in the prevention of bowel cancer, because cancer-causing substances spend less time in contact with the bowel wall. It is recommended that individuals have an intake of 25–30 grams of dietary fiber from a variety of sources each day.

PROTEIN

Protein provides the body with 4 calories of energy per gram. Besides providing energy, it promotes the growth and maintenance of body tissue including muscles, skin, blood cells, nerves, hair and nails. Proteins consist of building blocks called amino acids, of which there are twenty-two. Eight essential amino acids cannot be made by the body. They must come from the food we eat. Essential amino acids are obtained from animal products that include lean meat, fish, poultry, milk, yogurt, cheese and eggs. Vegetable protein sources such as cereals, legumes, nuts and seeds lack one or more of the essential amino acids and are called "incomplete" proteins. To make a "complete" protein certain types of vegetable protein products need to be eaten together, such as beans and rice. This is the principle of a successful vegetarian diet. (See page 217 for more detail.)

FAT

Fat provides the body with 9 calories of energy per gram, twice as much energy as carbohydrates or proteins. Fats are made up of fatty acids, some of which are essential (they cannot be made by the body), such as linoleic (omega-6) and linolenic (omega-3), and some which act as a carrier for the fat-soluble vitamins A, D, E and K. Fats are also important as they provide texture to food, give a feeling of fullness in the stomach, are part of the membrane structures and also act as messengers for prostaglandins (hormone-like substances). Sources of fat include margarine, oils, butter, cream, visible fat on some cuts of meat and chicken skin. Other less obvious sources of fat include cookies, pastries, cakes, potato chips, chocolate and French fries—all of which have a high percentage of energy derived from fat. There are three main types of fat present in most foods: *saturated, polyunsaturated* and *monounsaturated*. These fats predominate in particular foods and have different effects on the level of cholesterol in the blood. (See page 213 for more detail.) The calories from fat intake should not exceed 20–30 percent of the total daily calorie intake.

VITAMINS

Vitamins are essential organic nutrients needed by the body to carry out chemical reactions. There are two classes of vitamins, *fat-soluble* vitamins, A, D, E and K, and *water-soluble* vitamins, which include the B group and C. An adequate intake of vitamins can be obtained from eating a balanced diet. Vitamin supplements are therefore unnecessary, even harmful to the body if taken in excess. Further information on each vitamin follows.

Vitamin A (Retinol)

This vitamin is required for normal vision. A deficiency of vitamin A may result in "night blindness," a loss of black-and-white vision. Vitamin A also helps with growth and reproduction and keeps the tissues lining the lungs, digestive and reproductive tracts moist and healthy. Good sources are liver, fish liver oils, milk, cheese and yogurt. Food sources of beta-carotene (converted to vitamin A in the body) include dark green and yellow-orange vegetables and fruits such as carrots, sweet potatoes, spinach, broccoli, cantaloupes and apricots.

Vitamin D

Vitamin D works in conjunction with calcium and phosphorus to form strong bones and teeth. A lack of vitamin D may result in a condition of bone density loss known as rickets in children or osteomalacia in adults. A deficiency of vitamin D is rare in countries such as the United States since it is also manufactured by the body when sunlight shines on the skin (for at least 15 minutes each day). People exposed to sufficient sunlight do not need vitamin D from food. However, it does occur in some foods, including fish liver oils, fatty fish such as herring, mackerel, salmon and sardines, dairy products and margarine.

Vitamin E

This vitamin protects certain fats and fat-soluble substances such as vitamin A from being damaged by oxygen. It is especially important for the cell membranes of the

lungs and blood cells since they are in contact with large amounts of oxygen. Vitamin E is found in vegetable oils (especially wheatgerm oil), nuts, seeds, whole grains, fish, avocados, margarine and eggs.

Vitamin K

Vitamin K helps blood to clot and therefore stops bleeding. Approximately 60 percent of vitamin K is made by bacteria in the intestine. A deficiency is rare but can cause excessive internal bleeding, especially in newborn babies, whose intestines are not yet inhabited by bacteria. This is also applicable to people who take large doses of antibiotics that contribute to the destruction of intestinal bacteria. Leafy green vegetables such as spinach, broccoli, cabbage and lettuce, as well as liver are good sources of vitamin K.

Above: *A customer enjoys the freshly prepared hot food from this Japanese food stall.* Top: *Vegetable sellers and their produce add color to a street market in Udaipur, in northwestern India.*

Although some rice is grown on dry land like other grains, most rice is grown in paddy fields flooded with water, such as those shown here in Indonesia.

Vitamin B₁ (Thiamin)

This vitamin makes energy available to the body. It is also required to make the brain, nervous system and heart work properly. A deficiency of vitamin B_1 is rare in Western countries since it is found in such a wide variety of foods. However, if a large amount of alcohol is consumed, vitamin B_1 will not be absorbed properly and severe damage to the brain—a condition known as Wernicke's encephalopathy—can occur. Vitamin B_1 is found in yeast extract, pork, nuts, legumes, wholegrain cereals and cereal products such as bread, pasta, oats and flour.

Vitamin B₂ (Riboflavin)

This vitamin also makes energy available to the body as well as aiding in the growth and repair of body tissues. A deficiency of vitamin B_2 results in sore eyes, cracked lips, a swollen tongue and stunted growth in children. Vitamin B_2 is found in yeast extract, milk, cheese, yogurt, liver, kidney and fortified breakfast cereals.

Vitamin B₃ (Niacin)

This vitamin makes energy available to the body. A deficiency of niacin, which is rare in Western countries, may result in pellagra, and can be associated with dermatitis, diarrhea, dementia and death. Vitamin B_3 is found in yeast extract, peanuts, peanut butter, fish (especially canned fish), liver, lean meat, chicken and wholegrain cereals.

Vitamin B₆ (Pyridoxine)

Vitamin B_6 is needed for essential chemical reactions involving protein and for the formation and growth of red blood cells. It is also used by the body to make niacin from tryptophan. A deficiency of this vitamin can lead to convulsions, anemia, dermatitis and a swollen tongue. Vitamin B_6 is found in yeast extract, bananas, lean meat, fish, bran, walnuts, wheat germ, lentils and avocados.

Vitamin B₁₂ (Cyanocobalamin)

This vitamin works with folic acid (see next entry) in the formation of red blood cells. It also assists in manufacturing DNA and RNA and the covering around the nerves. A deficiency of vitamin B_{12} results in anemia, but can also cause nerve damage. Children whose diet does not include any animal foods run a higher risk of developing a vitamin B_{12} deficiency. This vitamin can be stored for 5 to 10 years in the body. Foods of animal origin, especially liver and kidney, are the best sources. Vitamin B_{12} is also found in mushrooms, sauerkraut, fermented soy products such as tempeh and tofu and some fortified soy drinks (check the label to be sure).

Folic Acid (Folacin)

This is required for the formation of red blood cells and the growth and repair of tissues. Deficiencies may result in anemia. The need for folic acid is increased during pregnancy and deformed babies may result if the need is not met. It is found in yeast extract, liver, lentils, chickpeas and green leafy vegetables.

Other B Group Vitamins

Biotin and pantothenic acid are also members of the B group. However, a deficiency of these vitamins is rare in most Western countries since they are found in a wide variety of foods.

Vitamin C (Ascorbic Acid)

Vitamin C is necessary to make and maintain connective tissue. It also protects against infection and assists in iron absorption. Since it is not made or stored by the body, vitamin C must be included in the daily diet. A vitamin C deficiency may result in anemia, nausea, infection, bleeding gums, bruising, depression and failure of wounds to heal. Vitamin C is contained in many fruits and vegetables: oranges, lemons, grapefruit and other citrus fruits; cabbage-type and dark green vegetables like broccoli; strawberries, bell peppers, tomatoes, potatoes, papayas and mangos.

MINERALS

Minerals are inorganic substances which perform a variety of functions such as the formation of bones and teeth, protein and genetic material. They are also involved in passing the nerve impulses, and are part of the enzymes which allow chemical reactions in the body to take place. Further information on specific minerals follows.

Calcium

Calcium is required for the growth and development of bones and teeth. It also assists blood to clot and facilitates normal nerve and muscle activity. Calcium requirements increase during pregnancy, adolescence and lactation and are very important during infancy and childhood. A calcium deficiency can be partly responsible for osteoporosis in older women, causing the bones to become porous and break easily. Milk, cheese and yogurt are the best sources of calcium, but it is also found in almonds, sesame seeds, canned salmon, fortified soy-bean milk, broccoli, cabbage, legumes and oranges.

Phosphorus

This mineral is essential for the formation of bones and teeth and helps in the release of energy from proteins, fats, carbohydrate and some of the B-complex vitamins. A deficiency of phosphorus is rare as it is present in a wide variety of foods. Problems with bones and teeth, blood cells and muscle weakness can occur if phosphorus is inadequate in the diet. It is found in lean meat, poultry, fish, eggs, milk, cheese, yogurt, wholegrain cereals, legumes, nuts and vegetables.

Sodium

Sodium is needed for normal nerve and muscle function, and, with potassium, for the proper balance of water inside and around body cells. The requirement for sodium can easily be met by a balanced diet, without the need to add extra salt or take a salt supplement. (Salt is 40 percent sodium and 60 percent chloride.) Meat, milk, seafood and some vegetables contain sodium. It is also present in baking powder, self-rising flour, monosodium glutamate and bicarbonate of soda. Processed foods contain an abundance of sodium and should be avoided. These include snack foods such as chips, salted nuts and "fast foods" like pizza and hamburgers. Other processed foods like canned vegetables, canned and dried soups and sauces, yeast extracts, butter and margarine are also high in sodium.

Potassium

Potassium helps regulate the balance of fluid inside and around the body cells. It also assists in proper muscle and nerve function. Potassium deficiency is quite rare but can be caused by taking diuretics and

Right: *One of the armada of fishing boats that supplies Indonesians with their main source of protein.*
Below: *Beef and dairy cattle are raised at Myrtleford, in southeastern Australia.*

steroids or by vomiting and diarrhea. It occurs in vegetables (especially potatoes), milk, fish, nuts, lean meat, wholegrain cereals, legumes, fresh fruits (especially bananas) and dried fruits (especially prunes).

Iron

Iron is necessary for the formation of hemoglobin in red blood cells, which carries oxygen to every cell in the body. If there is a lack of iron in the diet, less oxygen will reach the body cells and tiredness and anemia may occur. Iron occurs in liver, kidney, some shellfish, lean meat, canned fish, wholegrain cereals and wholegrain bread, legumes, dried fruits, including nuts, green vegetables, fortified milk, tomato juice and raisins. There are two forms of iron, *heme* and *non-heme*. Heme is present in animal tissue and is generally better absorbed by the body than non-heme iron, which is present in plant foods.

Zinc

Zinc is needed for growth, wound healing, good vision, taste and reproduction. It also forms part of many enzymes which cause reactions to take place in the body. Zinc deficiency is quite rare in Western countries, but can occur in heavy drinkers and in those whose diet is mainly vegetarian. Symptoms include slow wound healing, stunted growth, poor taste sensation and low sperm count. Oysters, lean beef, liver, crab, shrimp, rolled oats, dried beans and nuts are good sources of zinc.

Iodine

Iodine aids in the proper functioning of the thyroid gland. An iodine deficiency results in a condition known as goiter, where the thyroid gland becomes swollen in an attempt to make larger quantities of thyroxine, the hormone that controls the body's metabolic rate. Goiter used to be common where the soil lacked iodine, although it is rare today since people are no longer limited to food grown in the poor soil of a particular area. Iodine is found in fish,

shellfish, mollusks and kelp. Some plants are good sources of iodine, provided the soil in which they are grown contains good quantities of iodine. Dairy products such as milk and cheese are also sources of iodine, as the sterilizing solutions used in dairies contain traces of it.

Magnesium

Magnesium helps with the formation of bones; acts as a co-factor in many enzyme systems; is involved in the transmission of nerve impulses; and assists in the relaxation of muscles. It is found in broccoli, spinach, cabbage, seafood, wheatgerm, wholegrain cereals, bread, legumes, nuts and oats.

Selenium

Like vitamins C and E, selenium acts as an anti-oxidant to protect cell membranes from damage by oxygen. Selenium is also needed in small quantities to boost the immune system as well as to protect the heart, liver and muscles. Wholegrain cereals, lean meat, cheese and eggs are good sources.

WATER

Although water does not provide the body with energy (calories), it makes up about 60–70 percent of the body's composition and is vital for all the cells of the body to work properly. The amount of water needed

Left: *The spicy aromatic rhizomes of the ginger plant may be used fresh, dried and ground, crystallized, preserved and pickled.* Below: *Goods on sale at a produce market in Asiago, in northern Italy.*

varies per individual; it is usually between four to eight 8-ounce glasses each day. Water aids in digestion, regulates body temperature and lubricates our joints. Obtain water from many sources: milk, fruit juice, club soda, tea, coffee and other beverages. Water is also found in foods such as spinach (94 percent water), potatoes (82 percent water), apples (85 percent water) and bread (38 percent water). Drink water regularly throughout the day, along with other beverages and food to ensure proper hydration.

CURRENT TRENDS VS. IDEAL RATIOS

The typical American diet is high in fat, salt and sugar and low in carbohydrate and dietary fiber. Nutritionists and dietitians would like to change it to a diet high in carbohydrate and dietary fiber and low in fat (especially saturated), salt and sugar. Some people believe this is difficult to achieve and that food will also be less enjoyable. This could not be further from the truth. This book is full of recipes that are good for you and taste good, too.

Consuming a healthy, balanced diet can be simply achieved in accordance with the American Dietary Guidelines and the pyramid approach to eating. These are discussed in detail throughout the following pages and provide ideas on how to adopt a diet with more carbohydrate and dietary fiber and with less fat, salt and sugar.

Putting the American Dietary Guidelines into practice can prevent many health problems from developing. The common health problems related to poor eating habits include obesity, coronary heart disease, hypertension (or high blood pressure), some forms of cancer, diabetes and diseases of the large intestine.

THE AMERICAN DIETARY GUIDELINES

Eat a variety of foods

"Variety is the spice of life" is a well-known phrase that emphasizes the importance of choosing a variety of foods to maintain good health. It is evident from the previous discussion of vitamins and minerals that a number of different foods are required to obtain the many different nutrients necessary for normal, healthy body functioning. *The World's Healthiest Food* uses a wide variety of foods, including fresh fruits and vegetables, cereals, grains, breads, legumes, seafood, chicken, lean meat, nuts, eggs and dairy products, to produce a selection of delicious and nutritious recipes from all over the world.

Balance the food you eat with physical activity to maintain or improve your weight
"Energy In = Energy Out + Stored Energy" is the basic energy equation. Food provides the body with energy to be used for metabolic processes and to perform activity. When more energy is taken in than is needed by the body, it is stored and excess body weight results. This is a common problem in Western society where diets are high in fat and low in dietary fiber and a sedentary lifestyle predominates. Weight loss results when more energy is used than is taken in. Clearly, balancing the food you eat with physical activity is important to maintain or achieve a healthy weight. Page 210 shows tables for ideal calorie intake based on height, frame and activity level.

A tool used to determine if an individual is at a healthy weight is the Healthy Weight Range (HWR) chart. The HWR is based on the Body Mass Index (BMI) which is equal to:

$$\frac{\text{weight (kilograms)}}{\text{height (meters)}^2}$$

A worked example is outlined below:

Weight = 65 kilograms

Height = 1.7 meters (170 centimeters)

Body Mass Index = $\dfrac{65}{1.7 \times 1.7}$ = 22.5

Note: 1 kilogram = 2.2 pounds
      1 meter = 39 inches

Farmlands in southern France: a tranquil rural scene in shades of green and gold.

A BMI of 20–25 is associated with good health. A BMI above 25 is considered overweight and a BMI below 20 is considered underweight. Both are associated with poor health states.

Choose a diet with plenty of grains, vegetables and fruits

The recipes in this book incorporate a variety of grains, fresh fruits and vegetables. These foods are important because they are rich in dietary fiber (both soluble and insoluble forms), full of vitamins and minerals and contain negligible fat.

Choose a diet low in fat and cholesterol

Fat is very energy dense, providing the body with 9 calories per gram. Health-related diseases associated with the overconsumption of fat include coronary heart disease, obesity, diabetes and various forms of cancer. It is recommended that the number of calories supplied by fat be reduced to 20–30 percent of your daily diet.

Saturated fat, found mainly in animal products, is associated with raised blood cholesterol. In particular, saturated fat raises "bad" LDL cholesterol while reducing "good" HDL cholesterol. LDL (low density lipoprotein) cholesterol is often termed the bad cholesterol because it accumulates along arterial walls, and thus increases the risk of heart disease. HDL (high density lipoprotein) cholesterol does not accumulate along arterial walls and is not retained within the body.

Polyunsaturated fat, found mainly in vegetable oils such as sunflower oil and polyunsaturated margarines, as well as nuts, seeds and soy beans, is associated with decreased blood cholesterol. It reduces bad LDL cholesterol, but also reduces good HDL cholesterol. Omega-3 polyunsaturated fats found in some fish like mackerel, tuna and salmon have been associated with a low incidence of coronary heart disease and low blood pressure.

Monounsaturated fat, found mainly in almonds, avocados, olives, olive oil, canola oil, peanut oil and macadamia nut oil, is also associated with reduced blood cholesterol. It has the most beneficial effect on the lipoprotein fractions, lowering bad LDL cholesterol but increasing good HDL cholesterol. Monounsaturated fat is the fat of choice for health's sake and has been used in appropriate recipes in this book. However, it must be remembered that fat is still fat, containing twice the energy per gram as protein or carbohydrate. This is why a diet needs to be kept low in all fat.

Cholesterol is a fatty substance that may accumulate along arterial walls and result in a heart attack. However, cholesterol is not a totally undesirable substance, as it is a vital part of cell membranes and certain hormones and aids in the digestion of fats. The body makes its own cholesterol. There are also dietary forms of cholesterol found in eggs, liver, seafood and chicken. However, medical practitioners and nutritionists agree that if you are trying to lower your blood cholesterol it is more important to reduce total fat and saturated fat intake than to reduce intake of dietary forms of cholesterol.

Choose a diet moderate in sugars

Sugar provides little or no nutritional value aside from energy and is to be consumed in moderation. Research has shown that it

NUTRITION NOTES

Using a computer dietary database, the recipes in this book have been analyzed for energy (measured in calories), protein, fat, saturated fat, monounsaturated fat, polyunsaturated fat, carbohydrate, dietary fiber, sodium, iron and cholesterol. These nutrients were chosen according to the American Dietary Guidelines issued by the National Center for Nutrition and Dietetics, so that the user of this book can become familiar with foods that are good sources of carbohydrate and dietary fiber and are low in fat and sodium. The percentage of calories from the different types of fat is also given.

Nutritional information is provided per serving for each recipe, with the serving size shown at the top of the recipe. If a recipe is served to fewer or more people, simply re-calculate the nutrients based on the number of servings given in the book. If an ingredient is specified as "optional" or as a "garnish," it has not been included in the nutritional analysis. If an option is given for a monounsaturated or polyunsaturated margarine or oil, the analysis is based on the monounsaturated option.

Above: *Young Chinese boys trying to keep some of the local sugarcane crop.*
Top: *Vitamin-C-rich mandarins tolerate China's cold winters better than oranges.*

is associated with dental decay and contributes to excess weight. However, there is little evidence to link sugar directly to heart disease, diabetes and other disease.

Sugar takes many different forms including fructose (in fruits and honey); lactose (in milk); sucrose (in sugar cane or sugar beet); maltose (in malted products) and glucose (in honey, fruits and vegetables). It is evident from this list that a "sweet

tooth" can be satisfied with foods such as fruit and milk, which provide other valuable nutrients in addition to the sugars they contain. The desserts and cakes in this cookbook use many fresh fruits and low-fat dairy products to provide sweet-tasting yet nutritious alternatives to traditional sugary desserts.

Choose a diet moderate in salt and sodium

Excess sodium has been linked to high blood pressure in Western society and this is why it needs to be reduced in the diet. Enough sodium exists in foods naturally to satisfy the recommended dietary intake of 2300 mg per day. Unfortunately, many people do add salt to food during cooking and again at the table. In addition, many processed and fast foods, like hamburgers, pizzas, canned vegetables and soups are very high in sodium. The recipes in this book use low-salt, reduced-salt or salt-free products where appropriate.

If you drink alcohol, do so in moderation

High alcohol consumption is associated with a lowered metabolism—hence weight gain and raised blood pressure. Excessive alcohol consumption is also linked to liver and brain damage, cancer, ulcers and heart disease. A standard drink contains approximately 10 g of pure alcohol and equals an 8-ounce glass of regular beer, a 4-ounce glass of wine, a 2-ounce glass of port or sherry, or a 1-ounce jigger of spirits. Alcohol in moderation (1–2 drinks per day) is beneficial as it has a relaxing effect on the body and has been shown to reduce the formation of blood clots and the risk of heart disease. Children and adolescents, pregnant women and those trying to conceive, and those who have difficulty in keeping their alcohol intake within moderate limits should not drink alcohol.

THE PYRAMID APPROACH TO EATING

The food pyramid illustrates graphically that a balanced diet means eating more of some foods and less of others. Think of the pyramids of Egypt! Just as a pyramid has a strong base to support it, the bottom part of the food pyramid contains the most important foods upon which the diet is built to support the human body.

The USDA Healthy Diet Pyramid (illustrated opposite) was launched by the US Department of Agriculture and the Department of Health and Human Services in the United States in April, 1992. It is a smart educational tool that uses colorful models of food to show just how easy it is to select the right foods and follow a well-balanced diet. The USDA Pyramid is divided horizontally into four sections, from the base upwards. Eat most of those foods in the bottom section and eat least of those in the top section.

The bread, cereal, rice and pasta group (6–11 servings per day) is important. One serving equals 1 slice of bread, 1 ounce of ready-to-eat cereal or ½ cup of cooked cereal, rice or pasta. These foods provide energy-giving complex carbohydrates, are a good source of dietary fiber and are low in fat and sugar. The vegetable group (3–5 servings per day) and the fruit group (2–4 servings per day) provide a wide range of vitamins and minerals, dietary fiber and contain little fat or sugar. One serving of vegetables equals 1 cup of raw leafy vegetables, ½ cup of other vegetables, cooked or raw, or ¾ cup of vegetable juice. One serving of fruit equals 1 medium apple, banana or orange, ½ cup of chopped cooked or canned fruit or ¾ cup of fruit juice. The milk, yogurt and cheese group (2–3 servings per day), although a source

of fat (in varying amounts), also supplies other valuable nutrients, especially protein, calcium and phosphorus. One serving equals 1 cup of milk or yogurt, 1½ ounces of natural cheese or 2 ounces of processed cheese. The meat, poultry, fish, dry beans, eggs and nuts group (2–3 servings per day) is valuable for its protein, iron and zinc content, although it also supplies some fat (again, in varying amounts). One serving equals 2–3 ounces of cooked lean meat, fish or poultry (½ cup of cooked dried beans, 1 egg, ⅓ cup of nuts and 2 tablespoons of peanut butter each count as 1 ounce of meat). Fats, oils and sweets should be used sparingly since they provide little nutritional value. Many processed and prepared foods contain large amounts of fat, sugar and salt. Consume only occasionally.

Other Dietary Pyramids
The Mediterranean and Asian food pyramids not only give an idea of proportion of foods, but also indicate how often a particular food should be eaten. Meat—a

source of saturated fat—is situated at the top of these food pyramids and is assigned a low monthly consumption level. High-carbohydrate, high-fiber, low-fat foods (rice, noodles, bread and potatoes) make up the base of the pyramids and should be consumed daily, along with fruits, vegetables, legumes and nuts. The fact that the Asian and Mediterranean diets are low in saturated fat and contain a recommended moderate amount of either vegetable oil (polyunsaturated) or olive oil monounsaturated), may account for longevity and the low incidence of coronary heart disease in these countries.

It is evident from the overview of the food pyramids that each of the food groups supplies different nutrients in varying amounts. It is necessary to eat foods from these food groups in the proportion and frequency suggested for a healthy, balanced diet. The following recipes use healthy ingredients and meet the nutritional criteria for healthy eating to help you to achieve this goal.

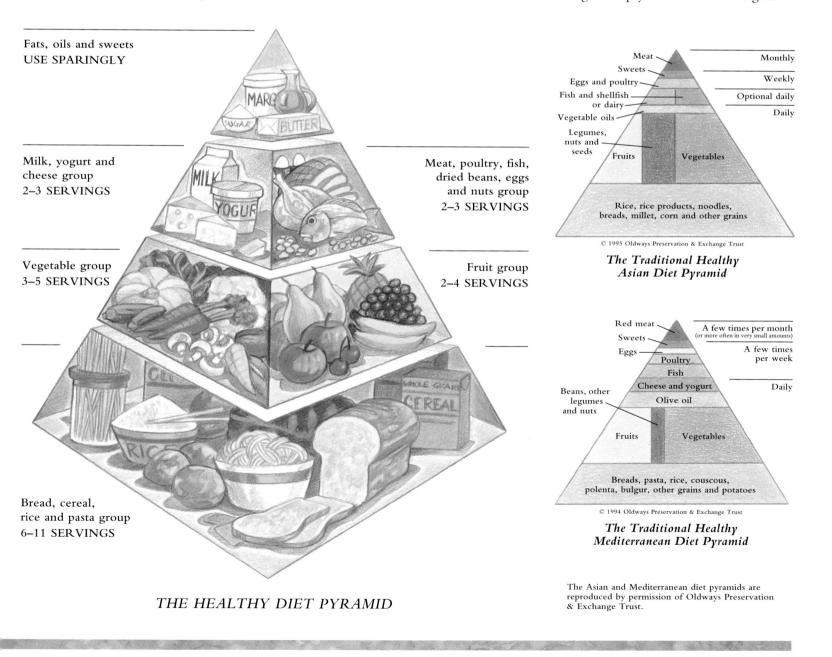

Fats, oils and sweets
USE SPARINGLY

Milk, yogurt and cheese group
2–3 SERVINGS

Vegetable group
3–5 SERVINGS

Meat, poultry, fish, dried beans, eggs and nuts group
2–3 SERVINGS

Fruit group
2–4 SERVINGS

Bread, cereal, rice and pasta group
6–11 SERVINGS

THE HEALTHY DIET PYRAMID

Meat — Monthly
Sweets — Weekly
Eggs and poultry — Optional daily
Fish and shellfish or dairy —
Vegetable oils — Daily
Legumes, nuts and seeds
Fruits   Vegetables

Rice, rice products, noodles, breads, millet, corn and other grains

© 1995 Oldways Preservation & Exchange Trust

The Traditional Healthy Asian Diet Pyramid

Red meat — A few times per month (or more often in very small amounts)
Sweets —
Eggs — A few times per week
Poultry
Fish
Cheese and yogurt — Daily
Beans, other legumes and nuts
Olive oil
Fruits   Vegetables

Breads, pasta, rice, couscous, polenta, bulgur, other grains and potatoes

© 1994 Oldways Preservation & Exchange Trust

The Traditional Healthy Mediterranean Diet Pyramid

The Asian and Mediterranean diet pyramids are reproduced by permission of Oldways Preservation & Exchange Trust.

BREAKFASTS & BRUNCHES

This chapter introduces some fascinating and healthy breakfast dishes from different countries and cultures around the world.

How often have you been told that breakfast is the most important meal of the day? We've all heard this repeatedly and some of us recite it to our children. How many of us put it into practice and make a good breakfast a daily event? We all should!

People of all ages and all occupations need a healthy breakfast to refuel the body after the night's fast. If we skimp on breakfast, we usually run out of energy and start to feel irritable late in the morning.

Breakfast should be a well-balanced combination of carbohydrate and protein with some vitamins and minerals. The food should be selected according to the climate—light and refreshing in hot weather, warm and sustaining in cold weather. The same rules apply to brunch, a later, more relaxed version of breakfast usually enjoyed on weekends.

The recipes which follow all highlight healthy ingredients that are wonderful for starting your day. There is a fairly equal balance of dishes from hot and cold climate countries. There is plenty of inspiration here to help you start your day well, no matter what the weather holds in store.

Breakfast is the meal which varies more than any other around the world. It can range from the American style of enjoying sweet treats such as Pear and Strawberry Muffins or stacked Blueberry Banana Buttermilk Drop Scones, to soft-textured Scrambled Eggs with Herbs, or comforting warm Gourmet Porridge and traditional Oatcakes from Britain, to the refreshing tropical fruit breakfasts like Banana and Mango Lassi from India and Tropical Morning Papaya from Indonesia.

Perhaps the healthiest breakfast dish of all is homemade muesli, an idea specifically created to provide a nutritionally balanced breakfast as part of a healing diet based on raw foods. This was the challenge that Dr Max Bircher-Benner of Switzerland set for himself, and accomplished, over one hundred years ago. Those of us who breakfast regularly on muesli should be eternally grateful! Muesli is a nourishing and energising mixture of grains, dried fruits, nuts and seeds. Additionally, it is an extremely good source of fiber.

Another valuable and equally irreplaceable healthy breakfast food is yogurt. This versatile dairy product has a heritage which goes back thousands of years in eastern Europe. The herdsmen there stored milk in large clay pots. In the warm climate, the milk developed a culture and turned

Left: *Grapes are a popular food, both fresh and dried as golden raisins (sultanas) and currants.*
Below: *A bakery in Russia; bread is one of the most common staple foods worldwide.*

naturally into yogurt. Yogurt is an easy-to-digest, perfect breakfast food that goes well with muesli. It is also a valuable source of calcium and phosphorus.

Fruit is another favorite breakfast food. It can be enjoyed in a number of ways—fresh, by itself, juiced or puréed, poached or stewed or dried. Fruit gives a boost of fiber and adds vitamins and minerals to muesli, yogurt or porridge.

In Breakfasts and Brunches, the first chapter in this book of healthy foods from around the world, you will note that we are already focusing on food that is high in fiber and low in fat. Other notable high-fiber breakfast dishes here feature legumes or beans and wholegrain cereals.

Lovers of beans should try the Fava Bean Omelet from Morocco or sustain themselves with a portion of protein- and fiber-rich Boston Baked Beans spooned over hot toasted rye bread from the United States, or Refried Beans with Scrambled Eggs on Tortillas from sunny Mexico.

If you wish to increase your fiber intake with wholegrain cereals, try brunching on Buckwheat Pancakes and Smoked Salmon, from Russia; Homemade Chapatis topped with cottage cheese, mangos and broiled bananas, from India; or Banana Millet Pancakes served with papaya and passionfruit, from Indonesia.

Busy people, who often survive on breakfast-on-the-run, will obtain important sustenance from Tiger's Juice, a favorite breakfast drink in the United States. For a no-cholesterol cooked breakfast, try Grilled Tomato and Mushrooms on Toast from Australia. High-fiber vegetables are combined with protein-rich eggs in Eggs with Spicy Tomatoes from Morocco, and with tofu in the delicious Scrambled Tofu with Vegetables from the United States.

This selection of breakfast and brunch recipes provides you with a wide and exciting variety of suitably nutritious, delicious dishes to start your day well.

Top: *Luscious and refreshing fruit is laid out to tempt passersby at Bombay's Chowpetty Beach, India.*
Above: *Tiers of colorful fruit are lovingly arranged and displayed for temple offerings on the fertile island of Bali, Indonesia.*

TOMATOES AND LEMON MUSHROOMS ON WHOLEGRAIN TOAST

Australia

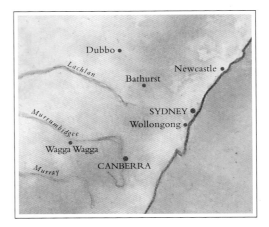

Vegemite is the brand name given in Australia to a sticky brown spread made from a yeast extract. Similar to Savita of the United States and Marmite of the United Kingdom, it is an excellent source of vitamins in the B group— thiamin, riboflavin, niacin and folate. Many Australians love its distinctive flavor and won't travel overseas without it.

TOTAL TIME: 15 MINUTES

SERVES 2

Line the broiler pan with aluminum foil to save cleaning. Although the Savita spread adds extra flavor it can be omitted if it is not available.

2 cups mixed button and small cap
   mushrooms, brushed clean and stalks
   trimmed
juice of 1 lemon or 2 limes
1 tablespoon finely chopped parsley or
   snipped chives, optional
freshly ground black pepper, to taste
2 large, vine-ripened tomatoes
4 warm slices wholegrain toast, sliced
   ¼ inch (6 mm) thick

2 teaspoons margarine
1 teaspoon Savita (Vegemite) yeast extract
parsley sprigs, for garnish

◆ Place the mushrooms in a small, non-stick frying pan. Add the lemon juice. Cover and cook over medium heat until tender, about 5 minutes.
◆ Stir in the chopped parsley, if using. Season to taste with pepper.
◆ Preheat the broiler. Adjust the rack so that the pan is 4–6 inches (10–15 cm) from the source of heat (or preheat the grill on High). Line the broiler pan with foil.
◆ Cut the tomatoes in half and sprinkle the cut surfaces with pepper. Place the tomatoes cut side up on the broiler pan and broil until hot and starting to soften, about 5 minutes.

◆ Place 2 slices of toast on each plate. Spread each slice with ½ teaspoon of the margarine, then with ¼ teaspoon of the Savita. Top each slice with a tomato half, then spoon the mushroom mixture on top, dividing equally.
◆ Garnish with the parsley sprigs and serve immediately.

NUTRITION NOTES

PER SERVING (Analysis uses monounsaturated margarine and includes Savita): 222 calories/ 934 kilojoules; 11 g protein; 6.4 g fat, 27% of calories (1.3 g saturated, 5.5% of calories; 3.3 g monounsaturated, 13.9%; 1.8 g polyunsaturated, 7.6%); 28 g carbohydrate; 7.9 g dietary fiber; 394 mg sodium; 2.4 mg iron; 0 mg cholesterol.

GOURMET PORRIDGE

Britain

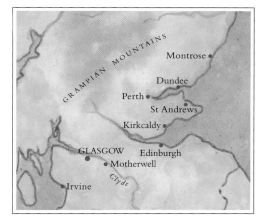

Porridge sustained many a Scottish soldier who fought during the country's bitterly cold winters. This high-fiber, low-fat breakfast dish still fortifies us on a cold winter's morning. The oats are high in complex carbohydrate and, along with the apricots, are an excellent source of fiber. The milk, soy grits and nuts provide protein. The maple syrup may be replaced with molasses to increase the mineral content of the porridge.

TOTAL TIME: 10 MINUTES

SERVES 2

Use kitchen scissors to chop the dried apricots easily.

¾ cup (2½ oz/75 g) quick-cooking
   rolled oats
¾ cup (6 fl oz/175 ml) water
1¼ cups (10 fl oz/300 ml) skim milk
¼ teaspoon ground nutmeg
2 tablespoons soy grits
4 dried apricots, finely chopped
2 teaspoons finely chopped hazelnuts
1 tablespoon plus 1 teaspoon maple syrup
   or golden syrup, optional

◆ Combine the oats and the water in a medium-sized, heavy-bottomed saucepan. Bring to a boil over medium–high heat. Stir in ¾ cup of the skim milk and the nutmeg, reduce the heat to low and simmer, stirring frequently, until the oats are tender, about 2 minutes.
◆ Pour the porridge into 2 warm bowls. Sprinkle half of each of the soy grits, apricots and hazelnuts on top. Add 2 teaspoons of the maple syrup to the center of each bowl, if using.
◆ Serve immediately with the remaining skim milk on the side.

NUTRITION NOTES

*PER SERVING (Analysis includes maple syrup):
311 calories/1303 kilojoules; 15 g protein;
7.8 g fat, 23% of calories (1.3 g saturated,
4% of calories; 3.4 g monounsaturated, 10%;
3.1 g polyunsaturated, 9%); 46 g carbohydrate;
4.6 g dietary fiber; 109 mg sodium; 2.9 mg iron;
6 mg cholesterol.*

OATCAKES AND SCRAMBLED EGGS WITH HERBS

Britain

A good British breakfast used to consist of eggs, bacon, bread, tomatoes and mushrooms—all fried. These days eggs can be served scrambled with herbs for a healthier breakfast. The Scottish oatcake was originally cooked on a griddle or a "bakestone" over an open fire. The oat content is now recognized as a rich source of fiber. Serve this oven-baked version with marmalade or honey.

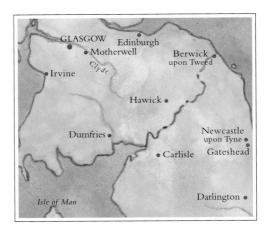

Oatcakes (top) and Scrambled Eggs with Herbs

SCRAMBLED EGGS WITH HERBS

TOTAL TIME: 10 MINUTES

SERVES 2

Vary this recipe by serving with 2 thin slices of smoked salmon; or sprinkling 2 oz (60 g) grated reduced-fat cheese over the egg mixture as the eggs start to set; or use fresh basil instead of parsley.

4 large, free-range eggs
2 tablespoons plus 2 teaspoons skim milk
$\frac{1}{4}$ teaspoon white pepper
pinch salt
2 teaspoons margarine or butter
2 tablespoons finely chopped chives
2 tablespoons finely chopped parsley
2 warm slices wholegrain toast, sliced
    $\frac{1}{4}$ inch (6 mm) thick
chives, for garnish
parsley sprigs, for garnish

◆ In a medium-sized bowl, combine the eggs, milk, pepper and salt. Using a fork, beat the mixture together well. Do not use a rotary beater as the mixture will become too foamy and will not give a creamy texture when cooked.
◆ Melt the margarine in a heavy-bottomed, non-stick saucepan over medium-low heat. Pour the egg mixture into the saucepan and cook, stirring gently with a wooden spoon, until the eggs begin to set. Continue cooking until the eggs are a soft, creamy texture, but not runny, 4 to 5 minutes. Remove the saucepan from the heat immediately, and gently stir in the chopped chives and parsley.
◆ Cut the toast diagonally and place each slice of toast on a warm plate. Spoon the scrambled eggs on top, dividing equally. Garnish with the chives and parsley sprigs and serve immediately.

OATCAKES

TOTAL TIME: 40 MINUTES

MAKES 8

If fine-ground oatmeal is not available, grind some medium-ground oatmeal in a blender or food processor to give a finer texture. Using butter instead of margarine will give a more traditional flavor, but butter has three times the saturated fat of margarine.

1 cup (4 oz / 125 g) medium-ground
    oatmeal
1 cup (4 oz / 125 g) fine-ground oatmeal
$\frac{1}{4}$ teaspoon baking powder

OATS

The oat was originally a weed that grew wild among the fields of cultivated wheat and barley in the countries of northern Europe. A grain that thrives in damp and cold climates, it was first cultivated by Europeans about 3000 years ago. In classical times the oat was also used for medicinal purposes. Later, the oat became important as a rotation crop in northern Europe. Then its primary use was as a food crop for animals, and in particular for horses, and even today the majority of oats grown are used as animal fodder. During the Middle Ages, in Scandinavia, Ireland and Scotland, oats became a part of the countries' cuisine and were used as a bread cereal or ground into a flour. Each of these regions has developed dishes that are associated with the culinary traditions of the country: with Scotland, porridge and haggis spring to mind. Oats are hulled and ground to produce varying consistencies of meal—fine, medium and coarse. Whole oat groats are hulled untreated oats, which are either cooked or ground. When they are steel-cut—the main method of preparing oat groats in Scotland and Ireland— the oats are cut into three or four pieces. Steel-cut oats are used for porridge, scones, oatcakes and the like and give these quintessentially Scottish foods their chewy texture. Rolled oats are groats that are steamed and then flattened. In the United States oatmeal is the term for oats that are used to make porridge, cakes, pancakes, breads and biscuits. Most forms of oats retain a high percentage of the B and E vitamins and minerals found in the grain. Oats are high in polyunsaturated fats making them an excellent source of energy but they should not be stored for long or the fat will go rancid. Oats are available in supermarkets and health food stores.

$\frac{1}{4}$ teaspoon salt
1 tablespoon melted margarine
2 tablespoons plus 1 teaspoon hot water

◆ Preheat the oven to 350°F (180°C).
◆ Sprinkle a quarter of the medium-ground oatmeal over a baking sheet.
◆ Place the fine-ground oatmeal, baking powder and salt in a small bowl. Mix well.
◆ Add the melted margarine and stir with a wooden spoon until absorbed. Add the water and mix well. Form the mixture into a ball.
◆ Sprinkle another quarter of the medium-ground oatmeal onto a wooden board. Roll the ball of dough in the oatmeal until it is completely coated.
◆ Sprinkle the remaining medium-ground oatmeal over the board. Place the ball on this and, with a rolling pin, roll it out carefully into a very thin round shape, 8 inches (20 cm) in diameter. Cut the round into 8 equal triangular wedges.

◆ Slide the triangles carefully onto the prepared baking sheet. Bake until firm, about 15 minutes, then turn the oven off and leave the oatcakes in the oven, with the oven door open, for an additional 5 minutes.
◆ Transfer the oatcakes carefully onto a wire rack. Serve warm or cold.

NUTRITION NOTES

PER SERVING—Scrambled Eggs with Herbs (Analysis uses monounsaturated margarine): 282 calories/1183 kilojoules; 19 g protein; 17 g fat, 54% of calories (5.3 g saturated, 17% of calories; 8.6 g monounsaturated, 27%; 3.1 g polyunsaturated, 10%); 13 g carbohydrate; 2.3 g dietary fiber; 527 mg sodium; 3.1 mg iron; 450 mg cholesterol.

PER OATCAKE (Analysis uses monounsaturated margarine): 129 calories/542 kilojoules; 3 g protein; 4.2 g fat, 30% of calories (0.8 g saturated, 5.7% of calories; 2.1 g monounsaturated, 15%; 1.3 g polyunsaturated, 9.3%); 19 g carbohydrate; 2.2 g dietary fiber; 67 mg sodium; 1.2 mg iron; 0 mg cholesterol.

SPITIKO YIAOÚRTI

Homemade Yogurt — Greece

Yogurt is a "living food" containing bacteria which aid with the digestion of food and with general health. Yogurt is very versatile and can be used in many traditional savory dishes, soups, salad dressings, with desserts, as well as with fruit for a healthy breakfast. Goat's milk or sheep's milk can be used to make yogurt for people who are allergic to cow's milk. This recipe for yogurt uses skim milk so it is lower in fat than yogurt made with whole milk.

TOTAL TIME: 8 TO 11 HOURS

MAKES 4 CUPS

Chilled, chopped fresh fruit or fruit purées may be folded into the yogurt before serving. Sterilize the thermos bottle before using. Electric yogurt makers are available. Follow manufacturer's instructions for best results.

4 cups (32 fl oz / 1 liter) skim milk
½ cup (1 oz / 30 g) skim milk powder
¼ cup (1½ oz / 45 g) low-fat, plain yogurt

◆ Pour the milk into a medium-sized saucepan and sprinkle the skim milk powder over the surface. Whisk gently until the powder is dissolved.
◆ Bring the milk mixture to a boil over medium heat, watching to ensure it does not boil over, then remove from the heat.
◆ Let the mixture cool to 185°F (85°C), then stir in the yogurt.
◆ Pour the mixture into a sterilized thermos bottle. Cover and set aside until it has thickened, 5 to 8 hours. Once the mixture is set aside do not move it until firm.

◆ Transfer the yogurt to a clean container, cover and store in the refrigerator for at least 3 hours before using.
◆ Serve in individual bowls.

NUTRITION NOTES

PER SERVING: 143 calories / 597 kilojoules; 15 g protein; 0.5 g fat, 3% of calories (0.4 g saturated, 2% of calories; 0.1 g mono-unsaturated, 1%; 0 g polyunsaturated, 0%); 20 g carbohydrate; 0 g dietary fiber; 208 mg sodium; 0 mg iron; 15 mg cholesterol.

PAPAYA TROPIKA

Tropical Morning Papaya—Indonesia

Select a naturally ripened papaya for this elegant breakfast. Avoid buying papayas which have been picked green and then artificially ripened, as they are less flavorful. Some lucky people who live in the tropics can pick the fruit fresh from their own trees. The Seed-Nut Mix may be sprinkled on muesli, porridge or salads to add extra protein. Here, the mixture provides a delicious complement to this light, low-calorie breakfast.

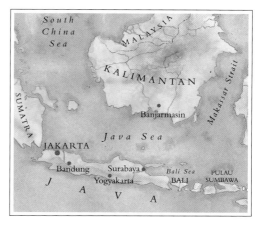

TOTAL TIME: 10 MINUTES

SERVES 2

Store the Seed-Nut Mix in a container with a tightly fitting lid in the refrigerator. The quantities given here will make 2 cups of the mixture.

SEED-NUT MIX

1 cup (5 oz/155 g) sesame seeds
⅔ cup (about 4 oz/125 g) sunflower seeds
  or pumpkin seeds
⅓ cup (about 2 oz/60 g) blanched almonds

1 small papaya (pawpaw) or cantaloupe
  (rockmelon)
juice of 1 orange
juice of 1 lime
1 tablespoon plus 1 teaspoon Seed-Nut
  Mix or sesame seeds

◆ To make the Seed-Nut Mix, place all the ingredients in a blender or food processor and process until evenly ground.
◆ Cut the papaya in half lengthways and, using a metal dessert spoon, remove the seeds and discard.
◆ Place each papaya half on a plate. Mix the orange juice and lime juice in a small pitcher, then pour over the papaya halves. Sprinkle 2 teaspoons of the Seed-Nut Mix on top of each portion.
◆ Serve immediately.

NUTRITION NOTES

PER SERVING: 94 calories/396 kilojoules; 2 g protein; 1.7 g fat, 16% of calories (0.2 g saturated, 1.9% of calories; 0.7 g monounsaturated, 6.6%; 0.8 g polyunsaturated, 7.5%); 18 g carbohydrate; 6.3 g dietary fiber; 17 mg sodium; 1.4 mg iron; 0 mg cholesterol.

KAYLAA BHAGARIKA PURA, KAYLAA AMKI LASSI, CHAPATI

Banana Millet Pancakes, Banana and Mango Lassi and Homemade Chapatis—India

Bananas are versatile and are high in potassium and fiber. Here, banana is added to a pancake batter to make a delightful breakfast. Lassi is nourishing, easy to digest and good for breakfast-on-the-run. The most common Indian bread is the chapati. Here it is served with cottage cheese, banana and mango.

Banana Millet Pancakes (bottom), Banana and Mango Lassi and Homemade Chapatis (left)

KAYLAA BHAGARIKA PURA

Banana Millet Pancakes

TOTAL TIME: 30 MINUTES

SERVES 4

Try to organize your family or guests to be seated at the table and ready for these pancakes as they are best eaten freshly made. Millet flour is available in health food stores.

½ cup (2 oz / 60 g) millet flour
½ cup (2 oz / 60 g) self-rising (self-raising) flour
1 large, free-range egg
1 tablespoon unsweetened coconut milk

1 tablespoon superfine (caster) sugar
1 cup mashed bananas, about 3 medium bananas
½ cup (4 fl oz / 125 ml) skim milk
vegetable oil cooking spray
confectioners' (icing) sugar, for serving
4 wedges papaya (pawpaw)
2 medium passionfruit, halved
lemon wedges or lime wedges, for serving
maple syrup or honey, for serving

◆ Sift the millet flour and self-rising flour into a mixing bowl, then make a well in the center.
◆ Beat the egg with the coconut milk and sugar in a small bowl until smooth. Pour

the egg mixture into the well of the dry ingredients and stir with a wooden spoon. When the mixture starts to stiffen, add the mashed bananas and milk and mix well.
◆ Spray a non-stick or black steel 7 inch (18 cm) crêpe pan with vegetable oil cooking spray.
◆ Heat the pan over medium heat until it is hot enough for a drop of water to sizzle.
◆ Pour one-quarter of the pancake batter into the pan and tilt the pan quickly so that the batter coats the bottom. Cook, shaking the pan occasionally to loosen the pancake until the batter sets, about 1 minute. Turn the pancake and cook the other side until golden, about 1 minute. Slide the cooked

pancake onto a warm plate. Cover with a clean kitchen towel to keep warm.

◆ Continue to cook the batter in the same manner, spraying the pan with oil for each pancake. Stack the cooked pancakes on top of each other, interleaved with strips of waxed (greaseproof) paper to prevent them from sticking together.

◆ Fold each pancake over, then fold over again to form a triangle. Arrange each pancake on a warm plate. Sift a little confectioners' sugar over the top. Add a wedge of papaya, a passionfruit half, some lemon wedges and a drizzle of maple syrup to each plate and serve immediately.

KAYLAA AMKI LASSI

Banana and Mango Lassi

TOTAL TIME: 5 MINUTES

SERVES 2

Lassi can be prepared the night before. Keep covered in the refrigerator. Buttermilk may be substituted for the yogurt.

1 cup (6½ oz/200 g) low-fat, plain yogurt
1 medium banana, sliced
1 medium mango, diced
½ teaspoon ginseng powder, optional
pinch ground cumin
1 cup ice cubes

◆ Combine the yogurt, banana, mango, ginseng, if using, and cumin in a blender or food processor. Purée until smooth.
◆ Divide the ice cubes between 2 tall glasses. Pour in the mixture and serve.

CHAPATI

Homemade Chapatis

TOTAL TIME: 30 TO 35 MINUTES

SERVES 6

If fresh mangos are not available, substitute a small papaya, cut into slices.

2 cups (8 oz/250 g) wholewheat (wholemeal) flour
2 tablespoons plus 1 teaspoon margarine, chilled
¾ cup (6 fl oz/175 ml) lukewarm water
vegetable oil cooking spray
1 cup (6½ oz/200 g) reduced-sodium, low-fat cottage cheese
¼ cup chopped cilantro (coriander)
2 medium mangos, cut into slices
3 medium bananas, halved lengthwise
cilantro (coriander) sprigs, for garnish

PAPAYA (PAWPAW)

Papaya (Carica papaya), also known as pawpaw, is a large tropical fruit with a smooth yellowish skin and juicy flesh which has a cavity of shiny black seeds. Native to Central America, it can now be found in most warm climates. The most popular South American variety has bright yellow flesh while the Fijian variety has peachy pink flesh. When ripe, papaya has a fairly sweet taste and a distinctive aroma. It makes a good dessert, breakfast fruit or garnish. It can also be cooked as a vegetable before it is ripe, and is often used to make jams and pickles. Papaya contains papain, an enzyme used in meat tenderizers. Slightly green papayas can be stored at room temperature until ripe. Ripe fruit should be used as soon as possible but can be refrigerated for up to a week, if well wrapped. Papaya is low in calories, rich in vitamins A and C.

◆ Place the flour in a medium-sized bowl. Add the chilled margarine and cut in with clean fingertips or a pastry blender until the mixture resembles fine bread crumbs. Make a well in the center of the mixture.
◆ Add ¼ cup of the water to the well and mix with a wooden spoon. Gradually stir in enough of the remaining water to form a stiff dough.
◆ Place the dough on a cool, lightly floured surface and form into a ball. Knead the dough until smooth and elastic, but not sticky, about 5 minutes.
◆ Return the dough to the bowl, cover with a damp cloth and set aside at room temperature until the dough has a soft texture, at least 30 minutes.
◆ To shape, divide the dough into 12 equal portions. Knead each piece lightly into a small ball. Roll each ball out on a lightly floured surface, lifting and turning regularly to keep the round shape, until about 5 inches (12 cm) in diameter. Cover the rounds with a damp cloth as you work.
◆ Spray a large, non-stick frying pan with vegetable oil cooking spray.
◆ Heat the frying pan over medium heat until it is hot enough for a drop of water to sizzle.
◆ Add 2 rounds of dough to the pan and cook, shaking the pan until bubbles appear on top of the chapatis, about 1 minute. Turn the chapatis over and cook on the other side, continuing to shake the pan, until cooked, about 1 minute longer.
◆ Slide the chapatis onto a warm plate, cover and keep warm.

◆ Continue cooking in the same manner until all the chapatis are cooked.
◆ Meanwhile, preheat the broiler and adjust the rack so that the pan is 3–5 inches from the source of heat (or preheat the grill on High). Place the bananas on the broiler pan and broil until soft and golden, about 2 minutes.
◆ Combine the cottage cheese and cilantro in a small bowl and mix well.
◆ Place 2 warm chapatis on each plate. Spoon the cottage cheese mixture on top of the chapatis and top with the mango slices. Add a broiled banana half to each plate, garnish with the cilantro sprigs and serve immediately.

NUTRITION NOTES

PER SERVING—Banana and Mango Lassi:
164 calories/685 kilojoules; 10 g protein; 0.4 g fat, 3% of calories (0.2 g saturated, 1.5% of calories; 0.2 g monounsaturated, 1.5%; 0 g polyunsaturated, 0%); 28 g carbohydrate; 2.5 g dietary fiber; 118 mg sodium; 0.6 mg iron; 2 mg cholesterol.

PER SERVING—Banana Millet Pancakes:
182 calories/761 kilojoules; 6 g protein; 2.7 g fat, 13% of calories (1.2 g saturated, 6% of calories; 0.9 g monounsaturated, 4%; 0.6 g polyunsaturated, 3%); 33 g carbohydrate; 3.7 g dietary fiber; 125 mg sodium; 1.2 mg iron; 56 mg cholesterol.

PER SERVING—Homemade Chapatis
(Analysis uses monounsaturated margarine):
262 calories/1105 kilojoules; 9 g protein; 9 g fat, 31% of calories (1.4 g saturated, 4.8% of calories; 5.2 g monounsaturated, 17.9%; 2.4 g polyunsaturated, 8.3%); 37 g carbohydrate; 7.8 g dietary fiber; 35 mg sodium; 2.1 mg iron; 0 mg cholesterol.

FRIJOLES REFRITOS CON HUEVOS

Refried Beans with Scrambled Eggs—Mexico

Because a late lunch is the rule in Mexico, breakfasts tend to be quite hearty. No meal is complete without a dish of beans, and refried beans in one form or another are probably the most popular. This is a hearty nutritious dish enjoyed for breakfast, lunch or dinner. It makes a delicious winter weekend brunch, served with freshly squeezed orange juice. The beans are a good source of dietary fiber.

TOTAL TIME: 2 TO 2½ HOURS

SERVES 6

To save time in the morning, the beans may be cooked the night before and stored, covered, in the refrigerator. Reduced-fat margarine spread has water added and is not a true margarine.

2 cups (15 oz / 470 g) dried red or pinto beans
3 teaspoons virgin olive oil
1 medium onion, finely chopped
¼ teaspoon chili powder
1 tablespoon plus 1 teaspoon reduced-fat
  margarine spread
3 large, vine-ripened tomatoes, about
  1 lb (500 g), coarsely chopped
¼ cup (2 fl oz / 60 ml) water
2 tablespoons chopped parsley or basil
pinch freshly ground black pepper
6 large, free-range eggs
¼ cup (2 fl oz / 60 ml) skim milk
¼ teaspoon freshly ground white pepper
pinch salt
1 tablespoon plus 1 teaspoon margarine
  or butter
6 warm corn tortillas, about 6 inches
  (15 cm) wide

◆ Place the beans in a large, heavy-bottomed saucepan with cold water just to cover. Bring to a boil, uncovered, over high heat. Boil for 2 minutes, remove from the heat and set aside for at least 1 hour.
◆ Drain and rinse the beans, then return them to the saucepan and cover with cold water. Cover and bring to a boil over high heat. Reduce the heat to low and cook the beans until tender, 1 to 1½ hours. (Alternatively, place the rinsed beans with water just to cover in a pressure cooker and cook according to the manufacturer's directions for 20 minutes.) Drain well.
◆ Place the cooked beans in a large bowl and mash well with a fork or potato masher to a coarse consistency.

◆ Heat the oil in a large, non-stick frying pan over medium heat. Add the onion and chili powder and sauté until tender, about 5 minutes. Add the beans and margarine spread, reduce the heat to low and cook, stirring constantly, until heated through, about 4 minutes.
◆ Place the bean mixture in a bowl, cover and keep warm.
◆ Meanwhile, combine the tomatoes, water, parsley and pepper in a small saucepan. Bring to a boil over medium-high heat, then reduce the heat to low and simmer, uncovered, until the mixture has a thick chunky sauce texture, about 5 minutes.
◆ Make scrambled eggs with the eggs, milk, pepper, salt and margarine as directed in the recipe for Scrambled Eggs with Herbs (see page 27).
◆ To serve, place each tortilla on a warm plate. Spoon the bean mixture on top, then the scrambled eggs, dividing equally, and top with the tomato sauce. Serve at once.

NUTRITION NOTES

PER SERVING (Analysis uses monounsaturated margarine): 382 calories/1604 kilojoules; 26 g protein; 13 g fat, 29% of calories (3.5 g saturated, 7.8% of calories; 5.7 g monounsaturated, 12.7%; 3.8 g polyunsaturated, 8.5%); 42 g carbohydrate; 18 g dietary fiber; 221 mg sodium; 5.8 mg iron; 188 mg cholesterol.

RED BEANS

Very similar to red kidney beans, red beans are also like them in flavor but smaller, approximately ⅜ inch (1 cm) long. In Spanish they are known as habas pequeños colorados *or* habichuelas. *The variety known as the red Mexican bean is small and deep reddish brown in color and has a mealy texture. This bean does not fall apart easily and maintains its shape during cooking. Red beans are best cooked over low heat for at least an hour and a half which makes them easier to digest. Red beans have a high nutritional value and are a good, inexpensive source of protein. They are used to add flavor and texture to soups and casseroles or they can be served on their own as a vegetable. They are ideal in mixed bean salads, too. Red beans are a principal ingredient in many Mexican dishes including* chili con carne *and Cajun dishes like spicy rice and beans. Red beans are available dried or canned in speciality food stores and in some health food stores and supermarkets. If they are difficult to find, red kidney beans may be used instead. These are more readily available and also require long, slow cooking.*

EL BIED BIFOULE, BIED B'MATICHA O'LEKAHMA

Fava Bean Omelet and Eggs with Spicy Tomatoes—Morocco

Eggs with Spicy Tomatoes is similar to the French piperade, a reminder that part of Morocco was once a French protectorate. A delicious brunch dish, it is made with eggs and bell peppers and tomatoes. Serve with toasted French bread. Fava Bean Omelet, a popular dish of the Maghreb, makes a wonderful brunch dish, too, and is ideal for picnics, served with salad.

EL BIED BIFOULE

Fava Bean Omelet

TOTAL TIME: 35 TO 40 MINUTES

SERVES 4

Use a 9 inch (23 cm) non-stick omelet pan, non-stick frying pan or a traditional cast-iron omelet pan for making this dish.

2 cups (10 oz/315 g) shelled, peeled fava
    (broad) beans
6 large, free-range eggs
½ cup thinly sliced scallions (spring onions)
juice of ½ lemon
2 teaspoons wholegrain Dijon mustard
pinch freshly ground black pepper
2 teaspoons virgin olive oil

◆ Bring a medium-sized saucepan of water to a boil over high heat. Add the fava beans, reduce the heat to medium-low and cook, covered, until tender, 5 to 10 minutes, depending on the size of the beans. Drain well and set aside.
◆ Break the eggs into a medium-sized bowl. Using a fork, beat the eggs well. Add the scallions, lemon juice, mustard and pepper and mix well. Stir in the fava beans.
◆ Heat the oil in a large, non-stick omelet pan over medium heat. Pour the egg mixture into the pan, reduce the heat to low, cover and cook until the egg mixture is almost set, 12 to 15 minutes.
◆ Meanwhile, preheat the broiler (grill).
◆ Place the omelet pan under the broiler and broil until the top of the omelet is browned, 1 to 2 minutes.
◆ Slide the omelet onto a warm serving plate, cut into wedges and serve immediately. Alternatively, allow to cool and serve cold.

BIED B'MATICHA O'LEKAHMA

Eggs with Spicy Tomatoes

TOTAL TIME: 45 MINUTES

SERVES 4

Traditionally made and served in an ovenproof frying pan, this recipe has been simplified to use a frying pan and an oven-to-table serving dish.

olive oil cooking spray
2 teaspoons virgin olive oil
1 onion, finely chopped
1 medium green bell pepper (capsicum),
    cored, seeded and thinly sliced
1 medium red bell pepper (capsicum), cored,
    seeded and thinly sliced
2 garlic cloves, minced
1 small red chili, seeded and thinly sliced
3 large, vine-ripened tomatoes, about
    1 lb (500 g), coarsely chopped
¼ teaspoon ground cinnamon
pinch salt
5 large, free-range eggs, lightly beaten

◆ Preheat the oven to 350°F (180°C).
◆ Lightly spray a 9 inch (23 cm) oven-to-table serving dish with olive oil cooking spray.
◆ Heat the oil in a large, non-stick frying pan over medium heat. Add the onion and sauté until soft, about 3 minutes.
◆ Stir in the green and red peppers, garlic and chili, and sauté, stirring occasionally, until soft, about 5 minutes.
◆ Add the tomatoes, cinnamon and salt. Cook, stirring occasionally, for 5 minutes.
◆ Pour the mixture into the prepared dish. Carefully pour the beaten eggs over the top.
◆ Bake until the eggs are set, about 15 minutes.
◆ Cut into wedges and serve while warm.

FAVA (BROAD) BEANS

Fava beans (Vicia faba) have been eaten since prehistoric times and were cultivated widely in ancient times, particularly by the Egyptians. They were also a popular food in the Middle Ages. Large, flat, oval-shaped beans, they can be green, brown or beige in color, depending on their age, and have a robust flavor and smooth, creamy texture when cooked. When very young, fava beans can be eaten raw, as is done in Italy; the older beans are best skinned either before or after they are cooked. Fava beans are ideal in purées, soups, casseroles or bean patties but can also be served as a side dish. They are available fresh for part of the year, dried (either whole in their skins or peeled and split), in cans and jars, and frozen, from Greek and Middle Eastern food stores and some supermarkets.

NUTRITION NOTES

PER SERVING—Fava Bean Omelet:
202 calories/848 kilojoules; 17 g protein; 12 g fat, 53% of calories (3.8 g saturated, 17% of calories; 6.2 g monounsaturated, 27%; 2 g polyunsaturated, 9%); 8 g carbohydrate; 6.9 g dietary fiber; 180 mg sodium; 2.7 mg iron; 338 mg cholesterol.

PER SERVING—Eggs with Spicy Tomatoes:
144 calories/603 kilojoules; 10 g protein; 8.8 g fat, 54% of calories (2.7 g saturated, 17% of calories; 4.8 g monounsaturated, 29%; 1.3 g polyunsaturated, 8%); 6 g carbohydrate; 2.9 g dietary fiber; 189 mg sodium; 1.9 mg iron; 225 mg cholesterol.

Fava Bean Omelet and Eggs with Spicy Tomatoes (top)

BLINI S KOPCHIÓNOY GORBLISHEY

Buckwheat Pancakes and Smoked Salmon—Russia

Salmon, fresh or smoked, is used in many Russian traditional dishes. Smoking the fish adds subtle flavor, as well as preserving it. Buckwheat pancakes are the usual accompaniment and together they make a nutritionally well-balanced breakfast. Rich in fiber, protein and vitamins A, D and B, this is appealing and attractive brunch party fare. One could be tempted to eat much too much of it!

TOTAL TIME: 45 MINUTES

SERVES 8

Use a large spoon (about 1 fl oz/30 ml capacity) to measure out the batter for the pancakes.

1 cup (4 oz/125 g) buckwheat flour
1 cup (4 oz/125 g) wholewheat
   (wholemeal plain) flour
2 tablespoons snipped chives
2 teaspoons baking powder
⅓ cup low-fat, reduced-sodium cottage
   cheese or low-fat ricotta cheese
1½ cups (12 fl oz/375 ml) skim milk
1 large, free-range egg, beaten
1 tablespoon margarine or unsalted butter,
   melted
6½ oz (200 g) thinly sliced smoked salmon
8 tablespoons low-fat, plain yogurt
dill or flat-leaf parsley sprigs, for garnish

◆ Mix the buckwheat flour, wholewheat flour, chives and baking powder together in a large bowl. Make a well in the center.
◆ Push the cheese through a very fine mesh sieve into a small mixing bowl. Stir in the milk and egg and blend. Add the cheese mixture to the center of the flour mixture and beat with a wooden spoon until smooth. Pour the mixture into a pitcher.
◆ Lightly brush the bottom of a large, non-stick frying pan with melted margarine. Heat the pan over medium heat until it is hot enough for a drop of water to sizzle.
◆ Pour the batter into the pan to form a neat round, 3 inches (8 cm) in diameter, shaping with the back of a metal spoon if necessary. Continue forming rounds of batter, being careful not to let them touch each other, until the pan is full.
◆ Turn the pancakes over when bubbles appear on the top of the rounds, after about 3 minutes. Cook until the pancakes are

puffed and browned underneath, about 4 minutes. Place the pancakes onto a clean cloth laid over a wire rack, wrap to keep warm.
◆ Continue to cook the remaining batter in the same manner, brushing the pan with more margarine before cooking each batch. Makes about 32 pancakes.
◆ Divide the warm pancakes and the smoked salmon among 8 plates. Add a tablespoon of yogurt to each portion. Garnish with the dill and serve immediately.

NUTRITION NOTES

PER SERVING (Analysis uses monounsaturated margarine and low-fat, reduced-sodium cottage cheese): 181 calories/762 kilojoules; 15 g protein; 4.4 g fat, 22% of calories (1.2 g saturated, 6% of calories; 1.9 g monounsaturated, 9.5%; 1.3 g polyunsaturated, 6.5%); 21 g carbohydrate; 3.7 g dietary fiber; 578 mg sodium; 1.4 mg iron; 44 mg cholesterol.

MUESLI

Switzerland

Muesli was formulated nearly 100 years ago by the Swiss physician, Doctor Max Bircher-Benner. The doctor's aim was to provide patients with a healthy, nutritionally-balanced breakfast as part of an overall healing diet based on raw foods. His ideas were initially rejected but later research confirmed their value. Some mueslis marketed today are based on the original recipe, but many are toasted in high-fat oil and should be avoided.

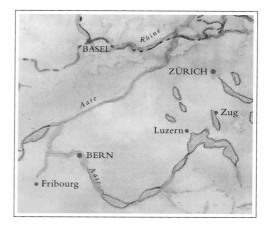

TOTAL TIME: 15 MINUTES

MAKES 8 CUPS

Store the prepared muesli in a cool, dry cupboard and use as required. This recipe contains 10 dry ingredients, based on the original Bircher–Benner formula. For a balanced breakfast, serve the muesli with fruit and low-fat yogurt or milk. Replace the yogurt or milk with fruit juice for a dairy-free breakfast.

MUESLI

2 cups (6½ oz/200 g) rolled oats
1 cup (4 oz/125 g) rolled barley
1 cup (4 oz/125 g) rolled rye or millet
1 cup (4 oz/125 g) rolled wheat
½ cup (about 2 oz/60 g) diced dried apples
    or pears
½ cup (3 oz/90 g) golden raisins (sultanas)
½ cup (4 oz/125 g) turbinado (raw) sugar
½ cup (2 oz/60 g) wheat bran or barley bran
½ cup (1½ oz/45 g) wheat germ
¼ cup (1 oz/30 g) chopped or slivered
    almonds
¼ cup (about 1½ oz/45 g) sunflower
    kernels or pumpkin seeds

⅓ cup (2 oz/60 g) low-fat, plain yogurt or
    ⅓ cup (3 fl oz/90 ml) skim milk

FRUIT SUGGESTIONS

2 pineapple rings, chopped
1 medium banana, sliced
1 small nectarine or peach, sliced
½ medium apple, grated
½ medium pear, grated
½ medium mango, diced
½ cup stewed gooseberries, plums, prunes
    or rhubarb (see page 185)
½ cup seasonal berries or stoneless cherries

DAIRY-FREE SUGGESTIONS

⅓ cup (3 fl oz/90 ml) freshly pressed
    apple juice
⅓ cup (3 fl oz/90 ml) freshly pressed
    grape juice
⅓ cup (3 fl oz/90 ml) freshly squeezed
    grapefruit juice
⅓ cup (3 fl oz/90 ml) freshly squeezed
    orange juice
⅓ cup (3 fl oz/90 ml) freshly pressed
    pear juice
⅓ cup (3 fl oz/90 ml) prune juice

◆ Combine all the muesli ingredients in a large bowl. Transfer the mixture to a large, clean, glass jar with a tightly fitting lid.

◆ Pour ½ cup of the muesli into a cereal bowl. Add the yogurt (or fruit juice) and your choice of the fruits listed.

NUTRITION NOTES

PER SERVING (includes yogurt): 219 calories/ 920 kilojoules; 9 g protein; 4.9 g fat, 20% of calories (0.8 g saturated, 3% of calories; 2 g monounsaturated, 8%; 2.1 g polyunsaturated, 9%); 36 g carbohydrate; 3.5 g dietary fiber; 51 mg sodium; 1.9 mg iron; 3 mg cholesterol.

TIGER'S JUICE AND SCRAMBLED TOFU WITH VEGETABLES

The United States

Scrambled Tofu with Vegetables looks and tastes very similar to traditional scrambled eggs. Tofu is a good source of protein, is low in fat and contains no cholesterol. Tiger's Juice is an excellent breakfast-on-the-run. The origin of its exotic name is not certain—perhaps the name simply reflects the drink's color. This thick orange drink contains lots of vitamin C, a valuable antioxidant.

Tiger's Juice (right) and Scrambled Tofu with Vegetables

NUTRITION NOTES
─────────────────

PER SERVING—Scrambled Tofu with Vegetables:
(Analysis uses monounsaturated margarine): 334
calories/1404 kilojoules; 22 g protein; 14 g fat,
39% of calories (2.4 g saturated, 7% of calories;
5.1 g monounsaturated, 14%; 6.5 g polyunsatu-
rated, 18%); 30 g carbohydrate; 6.1 g dietary
fiber; 505 mg sodium; 6.9 mg iron; 0 mg cholesterol.

PER SERVING—Tiger's Juice:
153 calories/639 kilojoules; 9 g protein; 0.6 g fat,
4% of calories (0.2 g saturated, 1.3% of calories;
0.2 g monounsaturated, 1.3%; 0.2 g polyunsatu-
rated, 1.3%); 26 g carbohydrate; 1.7 g dietary
fiber; 105 mg sodium; 0.4 mg iron; 2 mg cholesterol.

ORANGES

Oranges are native to Southeast Asia and are grown in warm regions across the
world. There are three important categories of oranges: sweet (Citrus sinensis),
mandarin or loose-skinned (Citrus reticulata) and bitter or sour
(Citrus aurantium). Of the sweet oranges, one of the best
known and most popular is the navel orange, a cultivar
from Brazil called "Washington Navel." It has thick
orange skin and a distinctive taste. Also popular is the
blood orange with its reddish flesh. All sweet oranges
are ideal for juicing. The mandarin oranges can be sweet
or tart-sweet. They are good to eat fresh as their skins
slip off the fruit easily. Among the most widely known
is the tangerine from Morocco which has a sweet taste but
thick, rough skin. The bitter orange has a variety of cul-
inary uses: the fruit is used in the making of marmalade and
orangeade; the peel is used to
make candied peel; and
essential oils are ex-
tracted from the peel
and used as a flavor-
ing in liqueurs as
well as sauces and
relishes. Oranges
are available all year
round according to the
varieties in season.

SCRAMBLED TOFU WITH VEGETABLES

TOTAL TIME: 20 MINUTES

SERVES 2

If cholesterol is not a problem, add 2 beaten
eggs (or 1 egg plus 1 egg white, beaten
together) to the saucepan when adding the
tofu and cook as directed until set. The eggs
help to bind the ingredients together.

2 teaspoons margarine
1 small onion, finely chopped
1 small carrot, grated
12 oz (375 g) soft tofu, crumbled
2 teaspoons reduced-sodium soy sauce
¼ cup finely chopped parsley
4 warm slices toasted wholegrain bread,
* sliced about ¼ inch (6 mm) thick*
parsley sprigs, for garnish

◆ Melt the margarine in a large, heavy-
bottomed, non-stick saucepan over medium-low heat. Add the onion and carrot
and sauté, stirring frequently, until soft,
about 5 minutes.
◆ Add the crumbled tofu and cook gently,
stirring and pressing down on the tofu with
a wooden spoon, until the tofu is a golden
color, about 3 minutes.

◆ Stir in the soy sauce and parsley and remove the saucepan from the heat.
◆ Place 2 slices of the toast on each warm
plate and spoon the tofu mixture over the
toast. Garnish with the parsley and serve
immediately.

TIGER'S JUICE

TOTAL TIME: 5 MINUTES

SERVES 2

Brewer's yeast, wheat germ, powdered glucose and ginseng powder are available in
health food stores and some supermarkets.

juice of 4 oranges, about 1½ cups
¾ cup (5 oz/155 g) low-fat, plain yogurt or
* vanilla soy drink*
¼ cup strawberries or raspberries, optional
2 teaspoons brewer's yeast
2 teaspoons powdered glucose, honey or
* maple syrup*
2 teaspoons wheat germ
½ teaspoon ginseng powder

◆ Place all the ingredients in a blender or
food processor and purée until smooth,
about 1 minute.
◆ Divide the mixture between 2 tall glasses
and serve immediately.

POTATO TUNA PATTIES AND BOSTON BAKED BEANS

The United States

Potato Tuna Patties make a good start to a cold morning or a tasty dish to serve for brunch. Boston Baked Beans features dried beans, which are rich in protein, high in soluble fiber and low in fat. Beans were an important part of the Native-American diet. European colonists, new to North America, found them a reliable standby, particularly in winter.

Potato Tuna Patties and Boston Baked Beans (top)

POTATO TUNA PATTIES

TOTAL TIME: 1 HOUR

SERVES 4

Chilling before shaping makes it easier to work with the mixture. Serve with a little salad for a more substantial brunch dish.

1 lb (500 g) red-skinned new potatoes
¼ cup rolled oats
finely grated zest of 1 lemon or 2 limes
2 tablespoons finely chopped parsley or
*   cilantro (coriander)*
1 tablespoon chili sauce
1 large, free-range egg, lightly beaten
1 teaspoon light brown sugar
1 teaspoon finely chopped fresh ginger
6 oz (185 g) canned tuna in spring water,
*   drained, or cooked fresh tuna*
⅓ cup (about 2 oz/60 g) sesame seeds
1 tablespoon plus 1 teaspoon virgin olive oil
parsley or cilantro (coriander) sprigs,
*   optional, for garnish*
lemon or lime wedges, for serving

◆ Cut the potatoes into halves and place in a medium-sized saucepan. Cover with boiling water and cook, covered, over medium-high heat until tender, 15 to 20 minutes. Drain well, place in a potato ricer and purée (or mash until smooth).
◆ Place the puréed potatoes in a large bowl. Add the tuna, oats, lemon zest, chopped parsley, chili sauce, egg, sugar and ginger. Mix well.
◆ Spread the mixture over a plate, cover with plastic wrap and chill in the refrigerator until firm, about 20 minutes.
◆ Divide the mixture into 8 equal portions. Working on a cool, lightly floured surface, shape each portion into rounds or patties.
◆ Place the sesame seeds on a sheet of waxed (greaseproof) paper. Dip each pattie into the sesame seeds, turning until evenly and lightly coated.
◆ Heat the oil in a large, non-stick frying pan over medium heat. Add the patties and cook for 3 minutes. Turn over and cook until golden brown, about 4 minutes longer. Drain on paper towels and transfer to a serving platter.
◆ Garnish with the parsley sprigs, if using, and serve at once with the lemon wedges.

BOSTON BAKED BEANS

TOTAL TIME: 5 HOURS

SERVES 8

Dried cannellini beans can be used instead of navy or Great Northern beans. Both types of beans and molasses are available at health food stores and at some supermarkets.

3¾ cups (1½ lb/750g) dried navy (haricot)
*   or Great Northern beans*
3 medium onions
8 whole cloves
1 cup (6 oz/185 g) dark brown sugar
½ cup (4 fl oz/125 ml) molasses (light
*   treacle)*
2 teaspoons dry mustard
½ teaspoon salt
¼ teaspoon freshly ground black pepper
2 cups (16 fl oz/500 ml) water
¼ cup finely chopped parsley
2 tablespoons apple cider vinegar
8 slices warm rye toast, sliced about ¼ inch
*   (6 mm) thick*

◆ Place the navy beans in a large, heavy-bottomed saucepan with cold water just to cover. Bring to a boil, uncovered, over high heat. Boil for 2 minutes, remove from the heat and set aside for at least 1 hour.
◆ Drain and rinse the beans, then return them to the saucepan. Cover with cold water and add one of the onions, quartered. Cover, bring to a boil over high heat.

Reduce the heat to low and cook the beans until tender, about 1½ hours. (Alternatively, place the rinsed beans with the onion and enough water to cover them in a pressure cooker and cook according to the manufacturer's instructions for 20 minutes.) Drain the beans, discarding the onion.
◆ Preheat the oven to 350°F (180°C).
◆ Stick the cloves into the remaining 2 onions and place them in a large casserole dish or special bean pot. Add the drained beans. In a small bowl, place the sugar, molasses, dry mustard, salt and pepper. Mix well. Stir in the water until well combined. Pour the mixture over the beans.
◆ Cover the casserole dish and bake until the beans are tender, about 2 hours.
◆ Stir the vinegar and parsley into the casserole dish. To serve, place a slice of toast on each plate and spoon the beans on top, dividing equally.

NUTRITION NOTES

PER SERVING—Potato Tuna Patties:
298 calories/1248 kilojoules; 21 g protein;
15 g fat, 44% of calories (2.7 g saturated,
7.9% of calories; 7.7 g monounsaturated, 22.6%;
4.6 g polyunsaturated, 13.5%); 21 g carbohydrate
3.9 g dietary fiber; 182 mg sodium; 2 mg iron;
67 mg cholesterol.

PER SERVING—Boston Baked Beans:
488 calories/2043 kilojoules; 25 g protein;
3.1 g fat, 6% of calories (0.7 g saturated,
1.3% of calories); 0.6 g monounsaturated, 1.2%;
1.8 g polyunsaturated, 3.5%); 91 g carbohydrate;
20 g dietary fiber; 355 mg sodium; 7.9 mg iron;
0 mg cholesterol.

CLOVES

Whole cloves are the dried unopened flower buds of an evergreen tree (Syzygium aromaticum) which belongs to the myrtle family. Originating in the Spice Islands in present-day Indonesia, cloves were introduced to China in about 200 BC and became one of the world's most important spices. Reddish brown in color, they have a spicy, pungent aroma and warm, rich flavor. Their name comes from the Latin word clavus meaning "nail" which the clove resembles. Cloves contain an essential oil and are well known for their medicinal properties: they were used in the Middle Ages, just as today, in the treatment of toothache. Sweet-smelling pomanders—oranges studded with cloves—were a great favorite in the Renaissance. Today in India cloves are mixed with cardamom and offered to diners at the end of a meal to refresh their palates. Cloves can be purchased whole or ground and have a range of uses in baking, pickling and in drinks. The whole clove can be used with stewed fruit, in pickles and added to vegetable dishes and marinades. The concentrated flavor of ground cloves means they should be used sparingly. They add a spicy flavor to cakes, jams, and savory dishes.

BLUEBERRY BANANA BUTTERMILK DROP SCONES AND PEAR AND STRAWBERRY MUFFINS

The United States

After years of cultivation, the wild blueberries of North America have become the plump, juicy, blue gems we know today. Here, they are combined with fiber-rich banana and low-fat buttermilk to make these dainty breakfast drop scones. Muffins continue to be a breakfast/brunch favorite. They are especially nourishing when made with wholewheat flour and other high-fiber ingredients.

Blueberry Banana Buttermilk Drop Scones (top) and Pear and Strawberry Muffins

BLUEBERRY BANANA BUTTER-MILK DROP SCONES

TOTAL TIME: 35 MINUTES

SERVES 6

An electric frying pan is ideal for cooking these drop scones. If you have one, adjust the temperature to the same setting for frying eggs (about 300°F /150°C). Use a large spoon (about 1 fl oz/30 ml capacity) to measure out the batter for the scones.

1 cup blueberries
1 cup (4 oz/125 g) self-rising (self-raising) flour
1/4 teaspoon baking soda (bicarbonate of soda)
1 medium banana, puréed
1 tablespoon superfine (caster) sugar
1/2 cup (4 fl oz/125 ml) buttermilk
1 large, free-range egg, lightly beaten
2 tablespoons margarine, melted
confectioners' (icing) sugar, for serving
ground cinnamon, for serving
1 cup (6 1/2 oz/200 g) low-fat, plain yogurt

◆ Cut 1/4 cup of the blueberries in half if they are large. If the blueberries are small, place 1/4 cup of the berries in a small bowl and gently crush with the back of a large spoon. This will allow the juices and color to flow into the batter.
◆ Sift the flour and baking soda into a large bowl. Add the blueberry halves, another 1/4 cup of blueberries, the banana and the sugar. Mix then make a well in the center.
◆ Add the buttermilk and egg to the well and mix together with a wooden spoon until a smooth batter is formed.
◆ Lightly brush a griddle or large, heavy-bottomed frying pan with melted margarine. Heat the griddle over medium heat until it is hot enough for a drop of water to sizzle. Drop a large spoonful of the mixture, from the tip of the spoon, onto the griddle to form a neat round. Continue forming rounds, being careful not to let them touch each other, until the pan is full. Turn the scones over when bubbles appear on the surface, about 2 minutes. Cook on the other side until risen and golden brown on the bottom, about 2 minutes.
◆ Transfer the scones to a clean cloth laid over a wire rack and cover loosely to keep warm. Cook the remaining batter in the same manner, brushing the pan with more margarine as needed. Makes about 18 scones, 2 1/2 inch (6 cm) wide.
◆ To serve, place 3 warm scones on each plate. Sift a little confectioners' sugar and cinnamon over the tops. Divide the remaining blueberries among the plates and add 2 tablespoons of yogurt to each serving.

TURBINADO (RAW) SUGAR

Most of today's sugar is made from sugar cane and sugar beet which is refined and processed to produce a wide variety of textures, flavors and colors. Sugar has been extracted from sugar cane in India for more than 2500 years, but in Europe the main form of sweetener, until the sixteenth century, was honey. Sugar from sugar cane was available from the time of Alexander the Great but was very expensive and originally used to flavor savory dishes. Sugar cane cultivation was eventually taken to the European colonies in Africa and the Americas and from that time the price of sugar fell and it became accessible to the ordinary citizen. In northern Europe sugar beet was not cultivated commercially until the late eighteenth century. The sugars extracted from sugar cane and sugar beet are virtually identical, and both need to be converted to raw sugar as soon after extraction as possible to prevent deterioration of the sugar. Most raw sugar is not considered suitable for use until after considerable refining, but certain raw sugars, such as turbinado, are produced to such high standards that all they require is to be steam-cleaned before marketing. Turbinado has small golden crystals with just a hint of molasses. It is used in baked foods such as cakes and muffins and its large crystals are ideal for decoration. Contrary to popular belief, refined raw sugar is not more nutritious than ordinary white sugar.

PEAR AND STRAWBERRY MUFFINS

TOTAL TIME: 50 TO 55 MINUTES

MAKES 12

These muffins can be frozen for up to 3 months.

vegetable oil cooking spray
1 cup (8 oz/250 g) turbinado (raw) sugar
1/2 cup (4 oz/125 g) margarine or unsalted butter, softened
2 large, free-range eggs
2 cups (8 oz/250 g) wholewheat (wholemeal plain) flour
1/2 cup (2 oz/60 g) oat bran, barley bran or wheat bran
2 teaspoons baking powder
1/2 cup (4 fl oz/125 ml) skim milk
1 teaspoon vanilla extract (vanilla essence)
1 1/2 cups sliced strawberries
1 cup peeled and grated pear
12 small strawberries, halved

◆ Preheat the oven to 375°F (190°C). Spray a 12 cup muffin pan with vegetable oil cooking spray.
◆ Combine the sugar and butter in a large bowl. Beat with an electric mixer until light and fluffy.
◆ Add the eggs, one at a time, beating well after each addition.
◆ Using a plastic spatula, gently fold in the flour, oat bran and baking powder. Alternate with the milk, vanilla, sliced strawberries and grated pear, folding until evenly combined.
◆ Spoon the batter into the prepared muffin pan, dividing equally. Place 2 strawberry halves on top of each muffin.
◆ Bake until a skewer inserted into the center of a muffin comes out clean, 25 to 30 minutes. Transfer the muffin pan to a wire rack and let stand for 5 minutes, then turn the muffins out onto the rack and cool slightly.
◆ Serve the muffins warm for best results.

NUTRITION NOTES

PER SERVING—Blueberry Banana Buttermilk Drop Scones (Analysis uses monounsaturated margarine): 157 calories/661 kilojoules; 4 g protein; 5.2 g fat, 30% of calories (1 g saturated, 5.8% of calories; 3 g monounsaturated, 17.3%; 1.2 g polyunsaturated, 6.9%); 24 g carbohydrate; 1.6 g dietary fiber; 194 mg sodium; 0.5 mg iron; 38 mg cholesterol.

PER MUFFIN—Pear and Strawberry Muffins (Analysis uses monounsaturated margarine): 260 calories/1092 kilojoules; 6 g protein; 10 g fat, 35% of calories (1.7 g saturated, 6% of calories; 6 g monounsaturated, 21%; 2.3 g polyunsaturated, 8%); 38 g carbohydrate; 4.3 g dietary fiber; 113 mg sodium; 1.4 mg iron; 38 mg cholesterol.

SOUPS & APPETIZERS

Soup enjoys a popular place in cuisines from around the world and is a great way to introduce healthy foods into the diet. Soup is a liquid food made from stock and other ingredients. Stock is a liquid flavored with vegetables, herbs and spices, with a base of meat, chicken, fish or vegetables. Soup usually includes vegetables, legumes, grains or pasta and sometimes meat, chicken or fish. This liquid food sustains us with its nutrients, satisfies our hunger, warms us when served hot and cools us when served chilled. It appears in many different forms: one can be served as a light first course, another can be served with bread as a luncheon dish, another may be hearty enough to make a meal on its own.

Soups generally use a prepared stock as a flavor base for additional ingredients. Recipes for Chicken and Vegetable Stocks are included in this chapter because home-made stocks allow us to control the fat and salt levels that can be quite high in commercial stocks. Prepare them when you have some spare time, then store in the freezer until you need them.

Cuisines from around the world provide us with a delicious and exciting range of soups, each country with its own distinctive flavors and style.

Many soups give us the opportunity to combine a variety of fresh vegetables with fiber-rich, protein-enhanced legumes or dried beans. Unusual but delicious Mixed Bean Soup from South Africa and memorable Split Pea Soup from Britain are perfect examples.

Some soups combine fresh vegetables with high-fiber, complex carbohydrate cereal foods. Minestrone from Italy adds pasta to a rich chunky bean and vegetable broth. Scotch Broth from Britain combines barley with vegetables. Light-textured Cellophane Noodle and Vegetable Soup from China is a lovely blend of crisp-cooked vegetables with delicate noodles supplying carbohydrate.

Nourishing soup can include meat, poultry or fish to increase its protein content in an easy-to-digest form. Many of these universal favorites are particularly suitable for anyone whose health needs a little extra boost. Jewish Chicken Soup with Matzo Dumplings and colorful *Bórscht*, a beef and vegetable broth, both from Russia, are great comfort foods. Fish soups are popular in countries with a long coastline and access to a wealth of seafood. Italian Fish Soup is a delicious, colorful blend of fish and vegetable broth. Hot and Sour Shrimp Soup is a fragrant, aromatic soup popular in Thailand. Protein also comes in forms suitable for vegetarians— Adzuki Bean Soup from China uses tofu (made from soy beans) as its protein component, with a variety of spices to add flavor. Many of these soups are inherited from an old culture of peasant cooking, based on local produce available from both land and sea. They are good examples of recipes that have kept people healthy over many generations!

This selection of healthy soup recipes also includes some tasty, colorful vegetable purées which are easy to digest. Pumpkin and Cauliflower Soup from the United States and Red Pepper and Tomato Soup from Mexico are based on purées. Chilled Lettuce Soup, another example, is light and refreshing—ideal for humid climates. The correct temperature is important when serving soups. Chill bowls for cold soups and warm bowls for hot soups.

Corn Chowder, from Mexico, is another delicious vegetable soup—in this case

Cooking methods and utensils vary enormously from country to country—this picturesque pot is from Japan.

Above: *A Paris* fruitier *promotes sales of broccoli and tomatoes from Brittany.*

Top right: *These pumpkins, destined to be made into jack-o'-lanterns for Halloween, make great eating, too.*

Right: *Tomatoes now feature in cuisines around the world—they are displayed here in a market in Jaisalmer, India.*

the mixture is not puréed, so that the texture of the corn can be enjoyed.

There are some healthy soups made from a combination of raw ingredients. Cold Tomato and Avocado Soup from the United States, is relatively new, while Spanish Gazpacho has been popular for many generations. These uncooked soups are a good source of antioxidants and help maintain the health of the digestive system.

Chopped herbs, thin strips of citrus peel and small spoonfuls of low-fat yogurt (or sour cream) make wonderful garnishes for healthy soups. When any of these soups are accompanied by wholegrain bread or rolls, they provide a very well-balanced meal.

The collection of healthy appetizers includes two traditional Lebanese favorites. *Hummus* features the nourishing chickpea and *Baba Ganoush* is made from the plump eggplant, a favorite vegetable in Middle Eastern cuisine. There is also a delicious, delicate green, high-fiber Fava Bean Dip from Lebanon, and a tasty, light-textured Tofu and Avocado Dip from Australia. These dips can be served with vegetable crudités to add more fiber and avoid the "hidden" fat and salt content of chips and crackers.

These healthy soups and dips are fun and easy to make! Follow the directions carefully for best results.

SCOTCH BROTH AND SPLIT PEA SOUP

Britain

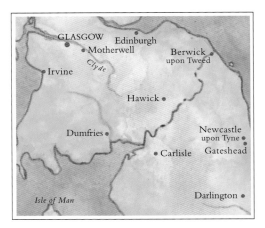

Scotch Broth is one of Scotland's best known dishes. Traditionally made with mutton, nowadays lamb is more frequently used. Barley is rich in complex carbohydrate and dietary fiber and helps control cholesterol levels in the blood. This recipe for Split Pea Soup uses green split peas, which are not as earthy flavored as the yellow. Both are a good source of protein, supply dietary fiber and contain some B vitamins. Serve this soup with bread or croûtons.

Scotch Broth (top) and Split Pea Soup

SCOTCH BROTH

TOTAL TIME: 1 HOUR

SERVES 8

Any surface fat or oil may be removed from a hot soup by floating strips of paper towel on the surface, then quickly and carefully removing them with tongs. The paper absorbs the fat.

1 tablespoon plus 1 teaspoon margarine
2 medium carrots, cut into ¼ inch (6 mm) dice
1 medium onion, finely diced
8 cups (64 fl oz/2 liters) water
1 lb (500 g) lamb shoulder (or neck chops), trimmed of all fat
2 cups (12 oz/375 g) rutabaga (swede) or turnip cut into ¼ inch (6 mm) dice
1 stalk celery, thinly sliced
¼ cup (1½ oz/45 g) hulled barley
2 cups (8 oz/250 g) Brussels sprouts, thinly sliced
½ teaspoon freshly ground black pepper
¼ cup (1 oz/30 g) barley bran or oat bran
¼ teaspoon salt

◆ Melt the margarine in a large, heavy-bottomed saucepan over medium heat. Add the carrots and onion and cover. Cook, stirring and shaking the pan occasionally, until the carrots and onion are tender, about 5 minutes.
◆ Add the water, lamb, rutabaga, celery and barley and bring to a boil over medium-high heat. Reduce the heat and simmer, covered, until the meat and barley are tender, about 30 minutes.
◆ Using a slotted spoon, remove the lamb from the saucepan. Carefully separate the meat from the bones and cut the meat into ¼ inch (6 mm) pieces. Discard the bones.
◆ Remove any surface fat from the broth, then return the lamb to the saucepan.
◆ Add the Brussels sprouts, pepper, bran and salt. Simmer until the sprouts are tender, about 5 minutes. Serve in warm bowls.

SPLIT PEA SOUP

TOTAL TIME: 2 HOURS

SERVES 8

If using Vegetable Stock, allow 1 to 1½ hours additional time if it is not already prepared. Do not stir the split peas during their initial cooking period in water as this makes them stick to the bottom of the saucepan. To reduce the initial cooking time, cook the split peas in a pressure cooker for 20 minutes.

SPLIT PEAS

Split peas are obtained from mature field peas that are dried, mechanically stripped of their cellulose skins, split in two along their seams and often polished. Two very common varieties of the pea (Pisum sativum) are dried and split: the green pea which is smooth and bright green and has a sweetish taste; and the yellow pea which has a more intense and earthy flavor. Dried peas have featured prominently in the diet of humans since Neolithic times—peas were found in the Spirit Cave in Thailand and have been given a rough date of 9700 BC. Peas were also entombed with Egyptian mummies and are believed to date back at least to about 6000 BC. Split peas are a good source of energy and are rich in fiber, vitamin C, iron, some B group vitamins and minerals. Split peas are the main ingredient of the traditional British pea soup and are also used in casseroles and purées. They are often served as a vegetable with smoked ham and in fact cooking them with any type of pork does give them an excellent flavor. Split peas can be purchased very cheaply in supermarkets and should keep for up to a year if stored in an airtight container in a cool, dry place. Choose peas that have a strong color as this indicates freshness when dried. Always wash and rinse split peas well to remove any bits of grit and dirt before cooking.

1¼ cups (8 oz/250 g) dried green split peas, rinsed and drained
6 cups (48 fl oz/1.5 liters) water or Vegetable Stock (see page 52)
2 tablespoons margarine or canola or safflower oil
2 medium leeks, thinly sliced
2 medium potatoes, thinly sliced
1 medium carrot, thinly sliced
2 stalks celery, thinly sliced
1 teaspoon thyme leaves
1 bay leaf
1 cup young green peas, fresh or frozen
¼ cup chopped celery leaves or parsley
¼ teaspoon freshly ground white pepper
¼ teaspoon salt

◆ Place the split peas in a large, heavy-bottomed saucepan and add 4 cups of the water. Cover and bring to a boil over high heat. Reduce the heat to medium-low and cook gently, without stirring, for 1 hour.
◆ Melt the margarine in a large, heavy-bottomed saucepan over medium heat. Add the leeks and sauté, stirring occasionally, until soft, about 5 minutes.
◆ Add the potatoes, carrot, celery, thyme, bay leaf and the remaining 2 cups of water. Cover and bring to a boil over medium-high heat. Reduce the heat to medium-low, add the split peas and their cooking liquid, cover and simmer until tender, about 30 minutes.
◆ Remove the bay leaf and discard. Remove the soup from the heat and set aside to cool slightly. Transfer to a blender or food processor. Process the mixture to a coarse texture, then return to the saucepan.
◆ Stir in the green peas, celery leaves, pepper and salt. Bring to a boil over medium heat. Reduce the heat and simmer, covered, until the peas are tender, about 5 minutes.
◆ Serve in warm bowls or a soup tureen.

NUTRITION NOTES

PER SERVING—Scotch Broth
(Analysis uses monounsaturated margarine):
157 calories/658 kilojoules; 16 g protein; 6.7 g fat, 36% of calories (2.5 g saturated, 13.4% of calories; 3.2 g monounsaturated, 17.2%; 1 g polyunsaturated, 5.4%); 9 g carbohydrate; 4.2 g dietary fiber; 157 mg sodium; 2.4 mg iron; 41 mg cholesterol.

PER SERVING—Split Pea Soup
(Analysis uses monounsaturated margarine):
173 calories/722 kilojoules; 10 g protein; 3.8 g fat, 20% of calories (0.6 g saturated, 3.1% of calories; 2.1 g monounsaturated, 11.1%; 1.1 g polyunsaturated, 5.8%); 24 g carbohydrate; 6.7 g dietary fiber; 93 mg sodium; 2.2 mg iron; 0 mg cholesterol.

Fun See Choy Tong, Adzuki Tong

Cellophane Noodle and Vegetable Soup and
Adzuki Bean Soup—China

Cellophane Noodle and Vegetable Soup features a selection of crisp Chinese vegetables and seaweed. Light in texture, high in fiber, rich in iodine, and low in fat, this is a popular soup for an instant-energy snack. Although native to Japan, adzuki beans are used widely in China. Adzuki Bean Soup is tasty and contains fiber, protein and iron. Serve with a bowl of soy sauce.

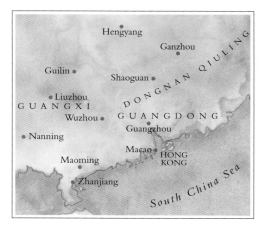

Cellophane Noodle and Vegetable Soup (top) and Adzuki Bean Soup

FUN SEE CHOY TONG

Cellophane Noodle and Vegetable Soup

TOTAL TIME: 35 MINUTES

SERVES 8

Add 1½ to 2 hours additional time if the stock is not already prepared. The Chinese ingredients used here are available from Asian food stores. Use the Japanese giant radish (daikon), if the Chinese one is not available.

½ cup (about ⅓ oz/10 g) arame or hijiki seaweed strips, optional
2 cups (16 fl oz/500 ml) cold water
1 tablespoon canola or safflower oil
1 teaspoon sesame oil
1 small onion, coarsely chopped
2 medium carrots, cut into thin julienne strips
1 cup (3½ oz/100 g) thinly sliced Chinese cabbage, firmly packed
½ cup (2½ oz/70 g) thinly sliced Chinese radish (loh bok)
6 cups (48 fl oz/1.5 liters) Vegetable or Chicken Stock (see page 52)
2½ oz (70 g) cellophane noodles
4 scallions (spring onions), sliced diagonally
1 cup (2 oz/60 g) mung bean sprouts
1 tablespoon reduced-sodium soy sauce

◆ If using, place the seaweed in a fine mesh sieve and rinse under cold running water. Place in a bowl, add the water and soak until doubled in size, about 10 minutes. Drain, reserving the liquid. Cut the seaweed into ¾ inch (2 cm) strips and set aside.
◆ Heat the canola and sesame oils in a large saucepan or wok over medium heat. Add the onion and sauté, stirring occasionally, until softened, about 5 minutes.
◆ Add the carrots, cabbage and radish and stir-fry over medium-high heat until the cabbage softens, about 2 minutes.
◆ Add the seaweed, reserved liquid, stock and noodles. Bring to a boil over high heat, stirring occasionally. Reduce the heat to medium-low, cover and simmer until the noodles are tender, about 8 minutes.
◆ Add the scallions, bean sprouts and soy sauce. Cover and simmer until warmed through, about 2 minutes.
◆ Serve hot in Chinese soup bowls.

ADZUKI TONG

Adzuki Bean Soup

TOTAL TIME: 2 HOURS

SERVES 6

Allow 1 to 1½ hours additional time if the Vegetable Stock is not already prepared.

Tofu, also known as bean curd, is often marinated to develop flavor.

½ cup (3½ oz/100 g) adzuki beans, washed and drained
⅓ cup (2½ oz/70 g) glutinous (short-grain) rice
6 cups (48 fl oz/1.5 liters) Vegetable Stock (see page 52)
½ cup (3 oz/90 g) diced firm tofu
1 tablespoon reduced-sodium tamari or soy sauce
2 scallions (spring onions), thinly sliced
1 tablespoon freshly squeezed lemon juice
1 tablespoon soybean paste (miso)
½ teaspoon Chinese five-spice powder
snipped chives, for garnish

◆ Place the adzuki beans and the rice in a large saucepan and add water just to cover. Bring to a boil and boil for 2 minutes. Remove from the heat, cover and let stand for 1 hour.
◆ Drain the beans and rice, then return them to the saucepan. Add the stock and bring to a boil over high heat. Reduce the heat and simmer until the beans and rice are tender, about 30 minutes. Remove the saucepan from the heat.

◆ Meanwhile, combine the tofu and tamari in a small bowl and marinate for about 15 minutes.
◆ Spoon half the bean and rice mixture into a blender or food processor. Process until puréed. Stir the purée into the mixture remaining in the saucepan, return to the heat and bring back to a boil.
◆ Add the tofu, scallions, lemon juice, miso and Chinese five-spice powder to the soup and simmer until warmed through, about 2 minutes.
◆ Serve hot in Chinese soup bowls, garnished with the chives.

NUTRITION NOTES

PER SERVING—Cellophane Noodle and Vegetable Soup: 76 calories/319 kilojoules; 2 g protein; 3.3 g fat, 39% of calories (0.4 g saturated, 4.7% of calories; 1.9 g monounsaturated, 22.5%; 1 g polyunsaturated, 11.8%); 10 g carbohydrate; 1.7 g dietary fiber; 187 mg sodium; 0.4 mg iron; 0 mg cholesterol.

PER SERVING—Adzuki Bean Soup: 120 calories/503 kilojoules; 6 g protein; 2.2 g fat, 16% of calories (0.4 g saturated, 2.9% of calories; 1 g monounsaturated, 7.3%; 0.8 g polyunsaturated, 5.8%); 20 g carbohydrate; 2.4 g dietary fiber; 258 mg sodium; 1.8 mg iron; 0 mg cholesterol.

CELLOPHANE NOODLES

The Chinese are known to have been eating noodles for well over 2000 years, and cellophane noodles are one of the many different types of noodles they enjoy. Shiny, thin, and translucent, their English name reflects their appearance. These traditional noodles are made from green mung beans, and are also known as mung bean vermicelli or bean threads. As with all Asian noodles, cellophane noodles are always cut into long strips as this is symbolic of longevity. Cellophane noodles are used in soups and stir-fry dishes and as an accompaniment to fish and meat dishes. Although they are dried, they can be added to soups without pre-soaking. Otherwise they should be soaked in hot water for ten minutes until soft, then drained, prior to further cooking. As they are bland, they will absorb the flavors of the other ingredients. They can also be deep-fried, straight from the packet, to make a crisp base for toppings or garnishes. Cellophane noodles are known as fun see in China, mién in Vietnam and woon sen in Thailand where they are also popular. They are available from Asian or speciality food stores and are normally sold tied in bundles and wrapped in cellophane. As with other dried noodles, they keep for a long time if stored in an airtight container in a dry place.

BOUILLON DE POULET, BOUILLON DE LÉGUMES

Chicken Stock and Vegetable Stock—France

*H*omemade stock is an invaluable ingredient in a creative kitchen. These nutritious stocks go well with all sorts of soups and casseroles—and homemade stocks require very little preparation time. One of the benefits of making your own stock is that you can control the salt content. Ready-made products, while quick and convenient, are often high in sodium.

BOUILLON DE POULET

Chicken Stock

TOTAL TIME: 2 TO 2½ HOURS
MAKES 4 TO 5 CUPS

This stock may be kept, covered, in the refrigerator for up to 3 days, or in the freezer for up to 3 months.

1 tablespoon canola or safflower oil
1 medium carrot, thickly sliced
1 stalk celery, thickly sliced
1 large onion, coarsely chopped
6 cups (48 fl oz/1.5 liters) water
1 small chicken, about 3 lb (1.5 kg), cut
   into 4 pieces, skin and excess fat
   removed
1 cup (2½ oz/75 g) mushroom stems,
   coarsely chopped, optional
¼ cup coarsely chopped parsley stalks
1 bay leaf
6 black peppercorns
2 whole cloves
¼ teaspoon freshly ground white pepper

BOUILLON DE LÉGUMES

Vegetable Stock

TOTAL TIME: 2 TO 2½ HOURS
MAKES 4 TO 5 CUPS

This stock may be kept, covered, in the refrigerator for up to 5 days, or in the freezer for up to 6 months.

1 tablespoon canola or safflower oil
2 medium carrots, thinly sliced
2 stalks celery, thinly sliced
1 cup (6 oz/185g) cubed turnip or
   butternut squash (butternut pumpkin)
1 large onion, coarsely chopped
6 cups (48 fl oz/1.5 liters) water
1 cup (2½ oz/75 g) coarsely chopped
   mushroom stems, optional
¼ cup coarsely chopped parsley stalks
1 bay leaf
6 black peppercorns
2 whole cloves
1 tablespoon yeast extract or miso
¼ teaspoon freshly ground white pepper

◆ Heat the oil in a large, heavy-bottomed, non-stick saucepan over medium heat. Add the carrot, celery, and onion (plus the turnip, for Vegetable Stock). Stir well, then reduce the heat to medium-low. Cover and cook gently, stirring often, until the onion is golden, about 10 minutes.
◆ Add the water (plus the chicken for Chicken Stock) mushroom stems, if using, the parsley stalks, bay leaf, peppercorns and cloves.
◆ Bring to a boil over high heat. Reduce the heat and simmer, partially covered, until a good flavor has developed, 1½ to 2 hours.
◆ For Vegetable Stock, add the yeast extract and stir until it has dissolved.
◆ Add the pepper, remove from the heat and cool slightly.
◆ Strain the stock through a cheesecloth-lined mesh sieve. Discard the solids.
◆ For Chicken Stock, skim off surface fat with a spoon and with strips of paper towels (as directed on page 49). If time allows, bring to room temperature and then chill the stock, covered, in the refrigerator for about 3 hours or overnight: the fat will solidify on the surface and can be removed easily with a spoon.
◆ Use the stock as required, or store as directed above. A good concentrated flavor can be developed in homemade stock by boiling it rapidly for 5 minutes, uncovered, in order to reduce its volume.

Chicken Stock (top) and Vegetable Stock

NUTRITION NOTES

PER CUP—Chicken Stock:
13 calories/53 kilojoules; 0.5 g protein; 1.2 g fat, 84% of calories (0.1 g saturated, 7% of calories; 0.8 g monounsaturated, 56%; 0.3 g polyunsaturated, 21%); 0.03 g carbohydrate; 0.02 g dietary fiber; 1 mg sodium; 0.2 mg iron; 0.8 mg cholesterol.

PER CUP—Vegetable Stock:
9 calories/39 kilojoules; 0.03 g protein; 1 g fat, 95% of calories (0.1 g saturated, 9.5% of calories; 0.6 g monounsaturated, 57%; 0.3 g polyunsaturated, 28.5%); 0.07 g carbohydrate; 0.04 g dietary fiber; 93 mg sodium; 0 mg iron; 0 mg cholesterol.

TOFU AND AVOCADO DIP

Australia

This is a healthy version of the popular but rich avocado dip. The addition of tofu reduces the fat content and retains the good avocado flavor. Both avocado and tofu are high in folate, which plays an important role in the production of red blood cells and the prevention of anemia. Serve with crisp raw vegetables such as broccoli and cauliflower florets and celery, carrots and zucchini cut into sticks, for dipping.

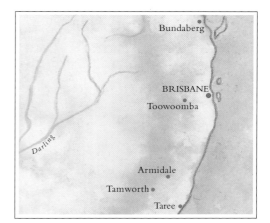

TOTAL TIME: 15 MINUTES

SERVES 6

Powdered kelp may be omitted if unavailable. The finished dip is coated with a thin drizzle of extra-virgin olive oil which prevents discoloring. This oil can be omitted if the dip is served immediately.

1 large avocado, coarsely chopped
1 cup (6 oz/185 g) firm or soft tofu,
    crumbled
2 teaspoons apple cider vinegar
2 teaspoons low-fat, plain yogurt
1 garlic clove, minced
1 teaspoon powdered kelp, optional
2 scallions (spring onions), thinly sliced
1 small, vine-ripened tomato, peeled,
    seeded and finely chopped
1 teaspoon extra-virgin olive oil
avocado slices, for garnish, optional
cherry tomatoes, for garnish, optional
basil sprigs, for garnish, optional

◆ Combine the avocado and tofu in a blender or food processor. Process until smooth, stopping and scraping down the sides as needed.
◆ Add the vinegar, yogurt, garlic and kelp, if using, to the avocado and tofu mixture. Blend until well combined.
◆ Transfer the mixture to a medium-sized bowl and fold in the scallions and tomato.
◆ Place the mixture in a serving bowl. Drizzle the oil over the top, then gently tilt the bowl so that the oil forms a thin layer on the surface of the dip.
◆ Add the garnishes, if using, and serve.

NUTRITION NOTES

PER SERVING: 71 calories/296 kilojoules; 3 g protein; 6 g fat, 76% of calories (1.3 g saturated, 16.5% of calories; 3.3 g monounsaturated, 41.8%; 1.4 g polyunsaturated, 17.7%); 1 g carbohydrate; 0.7 g dietary fiber; 5 mg sodium; 1 mg iron; 0 mg cholesterol.

MINESTRONE, ZUPPA DI PESCE

Vegetable Soup and Italian Fish Soup—Italy

There are many regional variations of Minestrone *in Italy. Here, we have combined navy beans with wholewheat pasta and a variety of fresh vegetables to provide a delicious, high-fiber, complete-protein feast. Meat was not always a standard part of the Italian diet. Fortunately, Italy's long coastline allowed them access to the riches of the sea. Fish dishes, like this fish soup, often provided needed protein. Serve it with crusty Italian bread or garlic croûtons.*

Vegetable Soup and Italian Fish Soup (top)

MINESTRONE

Vegetable Soup

TOTAL TIME: 3 TO 3½ HOURS

SERVES 8

Dried beans may be replaced with canned beans. Omit the soaking and reduce the stock's simmering time from 1½ hours to 30 minutes. Add the drained, canned beans with the tomatoes, cabbage, zucchini, green beans and pasta, then cook as directed.

---

1 cup (6½ oz/200 g) dried navy (haricot) beans or Great Northern beans
1 tablespoon plus 1 teaspoon virgin olive oil
1 large onion, finely chopped
2 garlic cloves, minced
8 cups (64 fl oz/2 liters) Vegetable Stock (see page 52)
2 medium carrots, thinly sliced
2 stalks celery, coarsely chopped
2 large, vine-ripened tomatoes, coarsely chopped
¼ small cabbage, cored and thinly sliced
1 medium zucchini, cut into ¼ inch (6 mm) dice
1 cup (about 4 oz/125 g) coarsely sliced green beans
½ cup wholewheat (wholemeal) pasta (macaroni or similar)
¼ cup finely chopped flat-leaf parsley
½ teaspoon freshly ground black pepper
¼ cup (1 oz/30 g) freshly grated Parmesan cheese, optional
¼ cup (1 oz/30 g) pine nuts, toasted
¼ cup basil leaves, for garnish

◆ Place the dried beans in a medium-sized saucepan, then add cold water just to cover. Bring to a boil, uncovered, over high heat. Boil for 2 minutes, remove from the heat, cover and set aside for 1 to 2 hours. Drain and rinse the beans.
◆ Heat the oil in a large, heavy-bottomed saucepan over medium heat. Add the onion and garlic and sauté, stirring occasionally, until softened, about 5 minutes.
◆ Add the drained beans, stock, carrots and celery. Cover and bring to a boil over medium-high heat. Reduce the heat to low and simmer until the beans are tender, about 1½ hours.
◆ Add the tomatoes, cabbage, zucchini, green beans and pasta. Increase the heat to medium and cook, covered until the pasta is tender, about 15 minutes. Stir in the parsley and pepper.
◆ Ladle the soup into warm bowls. Top each portion with some of the Parmesan cheese, if using, and the pine nuts, dividing equally. Garnish with the basil and serve immediately.

NAVY (HARICOT) BEANS

The navy bean (Phaseolus vulgaris) *is a small, oval, white bean, one of the many variants of haricot bean. Native to Central and South America the beans were an important part of the diet of the indigenous peoples of the area, including the Aztecs, before the Europeans arrived. The beans became staple foods for armies and navies, as they were easy to store and prepare. They were also the basis of Boston baked beans, the forerunner of the famous canned baked beans. The navy bean gets its name as a result of its ubiquitous appearance in meals served on US Naval ships at sea. Low in fat but high in nutritional value, these fairly bland beans make a good partner for other tastier ingredients in soups, casseroles and salads. They are the basis of the famous French dish* cassoulet. *Navy beans are available canned or dried. Because canned beans may have extra sodium added during processing it is best to cook with dried beans if sodium levels are a problem. If using dried beans they should be stored in a dry area out of the light and used within a year. The dried beans need lengthy soaking to soften them before cooking. Always discard the soaking water and use fresh water for cooking.*

ZUPPA DI PESCE

Italian Fish Soup

TOTAL TIME: 1½ HOURS

SERVES 8

Use a firm-textured, lean (white) fish, such as cod, snapper or porgy (bream) for this soup. Avoid oily fish in soup as their fat content is higher.

---

1 tablespoon plus 1 teaspoon virgin olive oil
1 medium onion, thinly sliced
2 garlic cloves, minced
2 lb (1 kg) vine-ripened tomatoes, peeled and coarsely chopped
3 lb (1.5 kg) mixed white fish, scaled and filleted, skin and bones reserved
4 cups (32 fl oz/1 liter) water
¼ cup chopped flat-leaf parsley leaves, stalks reserved
8 black peppercorns
½ cup (4 fl oz/125 ml) dry white wine
½ teaspoon freshly ground black pepper
¼ teaspoon salt

◆ Heat the oil in a large, heavy-bottomed saucepan over medium heat. Add the onion and garlic and sauté, stirring occasionally until softened, about 5 minutes.
◆ Add the chopped tomatoes, cover and cook over medium-low heat until soft, about 15 minutes.

◆ Meanwhile, make the fish stock. Place the fish skin and bones in a large saucepan. Add the water, parsley stalks and peppercorns. Cover and bring to a boil over high heat, then reduce the heat and simmer for 20 minutes. Strain the stock through a cheesecloth-lined sieve into a medium-sized bowl and reserve. Discard the solids.
◆ Cut the fish fillets into bite-sized pieces.
◆ Add the stock and fish pieces to the tomato mixture, cover and bring to a boil over medium heat. Reduce the heat and simmer until the fish is tender, 10 to 15 minutes.
◆ Stir in the chopped parsley, wine, pepper and salt. Bring back to a simmer, remove from the heat and ladle into warm soup bowls. Serve at once.

NUTRITION NOTES

PER SERVING—Italian Fish Soup:
227 calories/952 kilojoules; 29 g protein; 9.7 g fat, 38% of calories (3.1 g saturated, 12% of calories; 4.3 g monounsaturated, 17%; 2.3 g polyunsaturated, 9%); 3 g carbohydrate; 1.9 g dietary fiber; 196 mg sodium; 1.1 mg iron; 104 mg cholesterol.

PER SERVING—Vegetable Soup
(Analysis includes Parmesan cheese):
189 calories/794 kilojoules; 10 g protein; 8.1 g fat, 39% of calories (1.7 g saturated, 8.2% of calories; 3.8 g monounsaturated, 18.3%; 2.6 g polyunsaturated, 12.5%); 18 g carbohydrate; 9.1 g dietary fiber; 172 mg sodium; 2.9 mg iron; 4 mg cholesterol.

HUMMUS, BABA GANOUSH, FOULE

Chickpea Dip, Eggplant Dip and Fava Bean Dip—Lebanon

Hummus, *popular in the Middle East, is made from chickpeas, a legume rich in vegetable protein and dietary fiber.* Baba Ganoush *is a tasty, low-fat eggplant dip with a light texture.* Foule *combines the fava bean and lentil, both delicious and high in dietary fiber. Serve all three with vegetable crudités (small pieces of raw vegetables such as cauliflower florets and carrot, celery and cucumber sticks) and wedges of warm pita bread.*

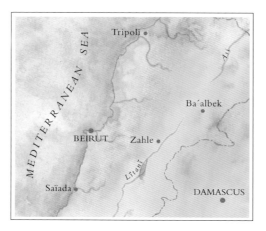

Chickpea Dip (bottom), Eggplant Dip (left) and Fava Bean Dip (top)

HUMMUS
Chickpea Dip

TOTAL TIME: 1¼ HOURS

SERVES 8

You may save time by using canned chick-peas, but dried chickpeas are cheaper.

¾ cup (6 oz / 185 g) dried chickpeas, soaked
    overnight in cold water
juice of 3 large lemons
½ cup (4 oz / 125 g) tahini
2 garlic cloves, minced
¼ teaspoon salt
2 teaspoons extra-virgin olive oil
pinch of paprika, for garnish

◆ Drain and rinse the soaked chickpeas. Place them in a large saucepan with cold water just to cover. Cover and bring to a boil over high heat. Reduce the heat and simmer until tender, about 1 hour. Drain, reserving ½ cup of the cooking liquid and a few whole chickpeas for garnish.
◆ Place half the chickpeas in a blender or food processor. Process to a crumbly texture. Add the remaining chickpeas and process again until finely ground, stopping and scraping down the sides as needed.
◆ Add the lemon juice, tahini, garlic and salt and purée until smooth, about 30 seconds. If the mixture is not a dipping consistency, add some of the reserved cooking liquid, one tablespoon at a time, until a "soft dip" texture is achieved.
◆ Pour the dip into a small serving bowl. Drizzle the olive oil on top and gently tilt the bowl so that the oil forms a thin layer on the surface of the dip. The oil prevents the dip from developing a dry surface crust. Sprinkle with paprika and garnish with the whole chickpeas. Serve the dip warm or cold.

BABA GANOUSH
Eggplant Dip

TOTAL TIME: 1 HOUR

SERVES 8

Tahini is available in health food stores and in some supermarkets.

1 lb (500 g) eggplant (aubergine)
2 tablespoons tahini
¼ cup (2 fl oz / 60 ml) freshly squeezed
    lemon juice
2 garlic cloves, minced
¼ teaspoon salt
½ teaspoon freshly ground black pepper
2 teaspoons extra-virgin olive oil

CHICKPEAS

The chickpea (Cicer arietinum) is grown throughout the Middle East, India and southern Europe. A nutty flavored legume, the chickpea is an excellent source of carbohydrate and protein. It is considered indispensable in Middle Eastern, North African and Indian cooking and is an important part of a vegetarian diet. Used in soups, stews, puréed and as a garnish, chickpeas are available dried, or precooked in cans. Dried chickpeas must be soaked for up to 12 hours before cooking.

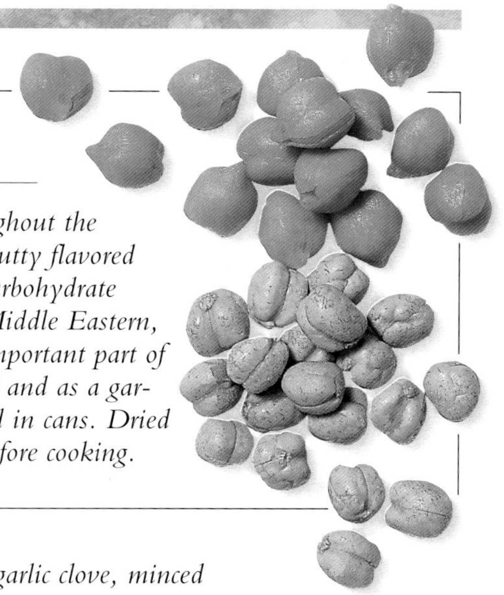

2 tablespoons thinly sliced scallions
    (spring onions)
2 tablespoons finely chopped parsley

◆ Preheat the broiler and adjust the oven rack so that the pan is 4 inches (10 cm) from the source of heat (or preheat the grill on High). Line the broiler pan with foil.
◆ Wash and dry the eggplant. Using a metal skewer, prick the eggplant in several places.
◆ Place the eggplant on the broiler pan and broil, turning frequently until the skin is charred on all sides, about 15 minutes. Using tongs, remove the eggplant from the broiler pan and wrap in a clean, wet kitchen towel. Let stand for 5 minutes until cool enough to handle.
◆ Remove the charred skin from the eggplant, then cut into quarters lengthwise, then crosswise into pieces. Place in a blender or food processor and blend until a thick pulpy texture is formed, about 1 minute.
◆ Add the tahini, lemon juice, garlic, salt and pepper, and purée until smooth, about 1 minute.
◆ Pour the dip into a small serving bowl. Drizzle the olive oil on top and gently tilt the bowl so that the oil forms a thin layer on the surface of the dip. Sprinkle the scallions and parsley on top. Cover and chill for at least 30 minutes before serving.

FOULE
Fava Bean Dip

TOTAL TIME: 1 HOUR

SERVES 4

If fresh fava beans are unavailable, substitute with frozen or dried beans. Soak the dried beans overnight in tepid water to loosen the skin, which can then be peeled off.

¼ cup (1½ oz / 45 g) red lentils, rinsed and
    drained
1 cup (5 oz / 155 g) shelled, peeled fava
    (broad) beans

1 garlic clove, minced
¼ teaspoon hot chili powder
¼ cup (2 fl oz / 60 ml) freshly squeezed
    lemon juice
1 tablespoon finely chopped flat-leaf parsley
2 tablespoons extra-virgin olive oil
pinch salt

◆ Bring a medium-sized saucepan of water to a boil. Add the lentils, reduce the heat to medium and cook, covered, until tender, about 15 minutes. Drain well and cool.
◆ Meanwhile, in another medium-sized saucepan, cook the fava beans in the same manner for 5 to 10 minutes, depending on the size of the beans. Drain well and cool.
◆ Combine the beans, lentils and garlic in a blender or food processor. Blend until smooth, stopping and scraping down the sides as needed.
◆ Add the chili powder, lemon juice, half the parsley, 1 tablespoon of the oil and the salt and blend again.
◆ Pour the dip into a small serving bowl. Drizzle the remaining oil on top and gently tilt the bowl so that the oil forms a thin layer on the surface of the dip.
◆ Sprinkle the remaining parsley on top, cover and chill in the refrigerator for at least 30 minutes before serving.

NUTRITION NOTES

PER SERVING—Chickpea Dip:
178 calories/749 kilojoules; 7 g protein; 12 g fat, 62% of calories (1.7 g saturated, 8.7% of calories; 5.2 g monounsaturated, 26.9%; 5.1 g polyunsaturated, 26.4%); 9 g carbohydrate; 6.2 g dietary fiber; 68 mg sodium; 2.5 mg iron; 0 mg cholesterol.

PER SERVING—Eggplant Dip:
31 calories/128 kilojoules; 1 g protein; 2.2 g fat, 63% of calories (0.4 g saturated, 12% of calories; 1.2 g monounsaturated, 34%; 0.6 g polyunsaturated, 17%); 2 g carbohydrate; 1.7 g dietary fiber; 53 mg sodium; 0.2 mg iron; 0 mg cholesterol.

PER SERVING—Fava Bean Dip:
119 calories/500 kilojoules; 5 g protein; 7.4 g fat, 57% of calories (1.2 g saturated, 9% of calories; 5.3 g monounsaturated, 41%; 0.9 g polyunsaturated, 7%); 8 g carbohydrate; 5 g dietary fiber; 110 mg sodium; 1.5 mg iron; 0 mg cholesterol.

CALDO DE ELOTE, SOPA DE PIMIENTO Y JITOMATE

Corn Chowder and Red Pepper and Tomato Soup—Mexico

Fresh corn is versatile and may be used in soups, casseroles and many other savory dishes. Corn Chowder uses a very simple method of producing a "cream" chowder quickly. Red Pepper and Tomato Soup combines these natives of the New World, both rich in vitamin C and fiber. They are broiled to enhance their flavor, producing a delicious low-calorie soup.

Corn Chowder (top) and Red Pepper and Tomato Soup

CALDO DE ELOTE
Corn Chowder

TOTAL TIME: 40 MINUTES

SERVES 4

Allow 2 to 2½ hours additional time if the Chicken Stock is not already prepared. Remove the kernels from ears of corn by stripping off the husks then standing the ears upright on a cutting board. Using a small, sharp knife, cut down the sides to dislodge the kernels.

3 large ears of corn, kernels removed
1 tablespoon margarine
1 small onion, chopped
2 tablespoons wholewheat (wholemeal) flour
¼ teaspoon ground cardamon
2 cups (16 fl oz/500 ml) skim milk
1 cup (8 fl oz/250 ml) Chicken Stock
    (see page 52)
1 tablespoon chopped oregano
¼ teaspoon freshly ground black pepper
¼ teaspoon salt
parsley or oregano sprigs or 2 tablespoons
    finely chopped cilantro (coriander), for
    garnish

◆ Place the corn kernels in a medium-sized saucepan and add cold water to cover. Bring to a boil, covered, over medium-high heat. Reduce the heat to medium and cook until the kernels are soft, about 5 minutes. Drain.
◆ Melt the margarine in a large, heavy-bottomed saucepan over medium heat. Add the onion and sauté, stirring occasionally, until softened, about 5 minutes.
◆ Reduce the heat to medium-low. Add the flour and cardamon and cook, stirring constantly, until blended, about 2 minutes.
◆ Pour in the skim milk and stock, add the chopped oregano, pepper and salt and bring to a boil, stirring constantly. Add the corn and simmer until heated through, about 5 minutes.
◆ Serve the chowder in a warm soup tureen or individual bowls, garnished with the parsley sprigs.

SOPA DE PIMIENTO Y JITOMATE
Red Pepper and Tomato Soup

TOTAL TIME: 1 HOUR

SERVES 6

Allow 1 to 1½ hours additional time if the Vegetable Stock is not already prepared. In summer, this soup may be made the day before, refrigerated and served chilled.

2 lb (1 kg) vine-ripened tomatoes
2 large red bell peppers (capsicums)
1 tablespoon plus 1 teaspoon virgin olive oil
1 large onion, finely chopped
3 cups (24 fl oz/750 ml) Vegetable Stock
    (see page 52)
pinch salt
½ cup (3 oz/100 g) low-fat, plain yogurt
oregano sprigs, for garnish

◆ Preheat the broiler and adjust the rack so that the pan is 3–5 inches from the source of heat (or preheat the grill on High). Line the broiler pan with foil.
◆ Using a small sharp knife, core the tomatoes and then score the skin around the circumference—this prevents the tomato from bursting. Cut the bell peppers in half lengthwise and remove the cores and seeds.
◆ Place the bell peppers, skin side up, and the tomatoes on the pan and broil until their skins darken and blister, about 5 minutes for tomatoes and 10 minutes for peppers. Place the tomatoes and pepper halves in a paper bag. Close tightly and set aside until cool enough to handle, 10 to 20 minutes. Peel off the charred skins with a knife.
◆ Place the tomatoes in a blender or food processor and purée.
◆ Heat the oil in a large, heavy-bottomed saucepan over medium heat. Add the onion and sauté, stirring occasionally, until softened, about 5 minutes.
◆ Add the tomato purée to the saucepan with the onion and bring to a boil. Reduce the heat and simmer for 10 minutes.
◆ Add the stock and bring to a boil over medium heat.
◆ Meanwhile, purée the peppers in the same manner as the tomatoes.
◆ Add the pepper purée to the tomato mixture and bring back to a boil. Stir in the salt, then remove the saucepan from the heat.
◆ Ladle the soup into bowls and top each portion with a small spoonful of yogurt and a sprig of oregano. Serve immediately.

NUTRITION NOTES

PER SERVING—Corn Chowder
(Analysis includes monounsaturated margarine):
145 calories/610 kilojoules; 7 g protein; 4 g fat, 25% of calories (0.6 g saturated, 4% of calories; 2.3 g monounsaturated, 14%; 1.1 g polyunsaturated, 7%); 20 g carbohydrate; 2.5 g dietary fiber; 176 mg sodium; 0.8 mg iron; 4 mg cholesterol.

PER SERVING—Red Pepper and Tomato Soup:
80 calories/335 kilojoules; 4 g protein; 3.9 g fat, 46% of calories (0.6 g saturated, 7.1% of calories; 2.8 g monounsaturated, 33%; 0.5 g polyunsaturated, 5.9%); 7 g carbohydrate; 2.8 g dietary fiber; 138 mg sodium; 0.7 mg iron; 1 mg cholesterol.

OREGANO

Sometimes referred to as wild marjoram, oregano (Origanum vulgare) belongs to the mint family. It can grow to a height of about 24 inches (60 cm) and has small, mid-green leaves and tiny white flowers. The oregano leaf has a stronger, more pungent flavor than marjoram, and harmonizes well with tomato-based dishes, pastas, pizzas and soups. The flowers can be used in the same way. US soldiers returning from World War II introduced oregano into the States where it has become one of the most popular herbs. There is also a Mexican variety of oregano which has a stronger flavor than the Mediterranean and complements the spiciness of that cuisine. Oregano is easily grown at home in the garden or in a pot and can be used fresh, or dried for later use. The dried leaves should be used sparingly as they have a more intense flavor than the fresh leaves. Fresh, dried and powdered oregano is available in most supermarkets. If purchased fresh, store in water in the refrigerator and use within a week; when dried, store in a cool, dark place and use within six months.

KURÍNY BULÍON S KLÉTSKAMI, BÓRSCHT

Chicken Soup with Matzo Dumplings and Beet Soup—Russia

Chicken Soup with Matzo Dumplings is rich in chicken—a good source of protein—and contains vegetables to provide fiber and vitamin C. The matzo meal dumplings provide tasty carbohydrate to give energy. This recipe for Beet Soup is a low-fat adaptation of a classic Russian dish. Originally just regarded as a sustaining peasant broth, this is now also valued for its nourishing protein, fiber and vitamin content. Serve with wholegrain or rye bread.

Chicken Soup with Matzo Dumplings and Beet Soup (top)

KURÍNY BULÍON S KLÉTSKAMI

Chicken Soup with Matzo Dumplings

TOTAL TIME: 1¾ HOURS

SERVES 6

Use poultry shears to cut the chicken into pieces, or ask your poultry supplier to do it for you.

MATZO DUMPLINGS

1½ cups (5 oz/155 g) matzo meal
3 large, free-range eggs, lightly beaten
⅓ cup (3 fl oz/90 ml) plus 1 tablespoon cold water
3 teaspoons canola or safflower oil
¼ cup finely chopped parsley
¼ teaspoon salt
¼ teaspoon freshly ground black pepper

1 small chicken, about 3 lb (1.5 kg), cut into 8 pieces, skin and excess fat removed
6 cups (48 fl oz/1.5 liters) water
2 large onions
4 medium carrots, thinly sliced
2 stalks celery, thinly sliced
¼ teaspoon salt
pinch paprika

◆ Combine all the ingredients for the matzo dumplings in a large bowl and mix well. Cover and let stand at room temperature for 1 hour.
◆ Meanwhile, place the chicken, water and one of the onions, quartered, in a large saucepan. Cover and bring to a boil over high heat. Reduce the heat and simmer until the chicken is tender and the juices run clear when pierced with a skewer in the thigh, about 45 minutes.
◆ Transfer the chicken to a plate. Strain the chicken stock into a large saucepan. Discard the onion. Remove any surface fat from the stock by floating strips of paper towel on the surface, then carefully removing them with tongs.
◆ Divide the dumpling mixture into 12 equal parts and roll each part into a ball. Bring a wide saucepan containing enough water to cover the dumplings to a boil. Slide the dumplings into the water gently and simmer for 30 minutes.
◆ Meanwhile, finely chop the remaining onion and add to the stock with the carrot and celery. Cover the saucepan and bring to a boil over medium-high heat, then reduce the heat to medium-low and cook until the vegetables are firm but tender, about 15 minutes.
◆ While the vegetables are cooking, remove the chicken meat from the bone and cut into ½ inch (1 cm) pieces. Discard any fat or gristle. Add the chicken meat, any accumulated juices on the plate, salt and paprika to the saucepan and bring back to a boil. Cook for 2 minutes.
◆ Using a slotted spoon, remove the dumplings from the water. Drain on a wire rack.
◆ Ladle the soup into 6 bowls, adding 2 dumplings to each bowl. Serve at once.

BEETS

The beet (Beta vulgaris), *also known as garden beet or beetroot, is a member of the beet family which includes the sugar beet. Although it was the leaves of the smaller, wild beet that were originally prized, today the cultivated beet is eaten for its thick root; the leaves, while very tasty when steamed, are often discarded. Small beets are delicious when grated raw and added to salads. However, beets are most commonly boiled or roasted whole and served hot or cold. They are excellent in soups. Cooked beets also feature cold in salads or appetizers. Beets are available fresh all year round from supermarkets and should be kept in the refrigerator for no longer than a week. They are also available ready cooked or pickled, in jars and cans.*

BÓRSCHT

Beet Soup

TOTAL TIME: 2 HOURS

SERVES 8

Cook the onion very slowly to caramelize the natural sugar content which adds color and flavor.

8 oz (250 g) lean stewing beef, trimmed of fat
1 tablespoon plus 1 teaspoon margarine or canola or safflower oil
1 large onion, finely chopped
8 cups (64 fl oz/2 liters) water
¼ small cabbage, cored and thinly sliced
1 small turnip, cut into ½ inch (1 cm) cubes
1 medium carrot, thinly sliced
1 bay leaf
2 medium, vine-ripened tomatoes, chopped
2 large raw beets (beetroot), grated
1 tablespoon finely chopped dill or parsley
¼ teaspoon salt
¼ teaspoon freshly ground black pepper
1 tablespoon apple cider vinegar or white wine vinegar
low-fat, plain yogurt, for garnish, optional
dill sprigs, for garnish, optional

◆ Chop the beef into ½ inch (1 cm) cubes.
◆ Melt the margarine in a large, heavy-bottomed saucepan over low heat. Add the onion and sauté, stirring occasionally, until soft, transparent and golden, about 15 minutes.
◆ Add the beef, water, cabbage, turnip, carrot and bay leaf. Cover and bring to a boil over medium-high heat. Reduce the heat to low and simmer until the meat is tender, about 1 hour.
◆ Add the tomatoes, beets, chopped dill, salt and pepper. Cover and bring to a boil over a medium-high heat. Reduce the heat to low and cook until the tomatoes and beets are tender, about 15 minutes.
◆ Stir in the vinegar and serve hot in individual warm bowls or in a soup tureen. Garnish with the yogurt and dill, if using.

NUTRITION NOTES

PER SERVING—Chicken Soup with Matzo Dumplings: 310 calories/1297 kilojoules; 31 g protein; 8.7 g fat, 30% of calories (2.5 g saturated, 8.6% of calories; 4.7 g monounsaturated, 16.2%; 1.5 g polyunsaturated, 5.2%); 24 g carbohydrate; 3.1 g dietary fiber; 287 mg sodium; 2.3 mg iron; 184 mg cholesterol.

PER SERVING—Beet Soup (Analysis uses monounsaturated margarine): 85 calories/357 kilojoules; 9 g protein; 3.2 g fat, 33% of calories (0.8 g saturated, 8.3% of calories; 1.8 g monounsaturated, 18.5%; 0.6 g polyunsaturated, 6.2%); 6 g carbohydrate; 3.1 g dietary fiber; 125 mg sodium; 1.4 mg iron; 19 mg cholesterol.

GEMENGEDE BOONTJIE SOP

Mixed Bean Soup—South Africa

South Africa is noted for both the quality and abundance of the fruit and vegetables grown there. Mixed Bean Soup is full of healthy vegetables and also includes fiber-rich black-eyed peas. These legumes, often associated with the American South, were taken there from Africa. This budget-stretching soup provides plenty of iron and vitamins B and C. It gives good value for money and tastes delicious, too!

TOTAL TIME: 3 HOURS

SERVES 6

Prepare the Vegetable Stock while the peas and beans are soaking. Reserve ¼ cup of the Swiss chard for sprinkling on top just before serving, if preferred.

½ cup (3 oz / 90 g) black-eyed peas (beans)
½ cup (3 oz / 90 g) pinto or borlotti beans
1 tablespoon plus 1 teaspoon canola or safflower oil
1 large onion, finely chopped
4 cups (32 fl oz / 1 liter) Vegetable Stock (see page 52)
2 large, vine-ripened tomatoes, chopped, about 2 cups
¼ cup (2 fl oz / 60 ml) tomato paste
1 teaspoon thyme leaves

1¼ cups thinly sliced Swiss chard (silverbeet) leaves, tightly packed
2 tablespoons pumpkin seeds, toasted

◆ Place the peas and beans in a large, heavy-bottomed saucepan, add cold water to cover and bring to a boil over medium heat. Cook for 2 minutes, then remove from the heat, cover and let stand for 1 hour.
◆ Drain the peas and beans and return them to the saucepan and add cold water to cover. Cover the saucepan and bring to a boil over high heat. Reduce the heat to medium-low and cook gently until tender, about 1 hour. Drain well.
◆ Place the peas and beans in a blender or food processor. Process to a coarse texture, then return them to the saucepan.
◆ Heat the oil in a large, heavy-bottomed saucepan over medium heat. Add the

onion and sauté, stirring occasionally, until softened, about 5 minutes.
◆ Add the stock, tomatoes, tomato paste, thyme, peas and beans to the saucepan. Bring to a boil over medium-high heat, stirring frequently. Reduce the heat to medium-low, cover and simmer, until the flavors are blended, about 20 minutes.
◆ Add the Swiss chard to the soup and simmer until tender, about 5 minutes.
◆ Serve the soup hot, sprinkled with the pumpkin seeds.

NUTRITION NOTES

PER SERVING: 158 calories / 663 kilojoules; 8 g protein; 4.5 g fat, 25% of calories (0.5 g saturated, 2.8% of calories; 2.6 g monounsaturated, 14.4%; 1.4 g polyunsaturated; 7.8%); 22 g carbohydrate; 4.9 g dietary fiber; 163 mg sodium; 2.6 mg iron; 0 mg cholesterol.

GAZPACHO

Chilled Tomato Soup—Spain

Gazpacho is the best known of the cold soups that are a speciality of Andalusia, in southern Spain. There are many local variations of this dish, many including bread crumbs or croûtons. They all showcase the excellent produce of this fertile region. Because the ingredients are not cooked, they retain their natural goodness. High in beta-carotene and vitamin C, which help the body fight disease and infection, Gazpacho is healthy and flavorful, too.

TOTAL TIME: 1½ TO 2½ HOURS

SERVES 8

If your blender or food processor is not large enough to purée the ingredients all together, divide into two batches and purée separately.

2 lb (1 kg) vine-ripened tomatoes, peeled and quartered
1 medium red onion, coarsely chopped
1 small green bell pepper (capsicum) seeded and coarsely chopped
1 small red bell pepper (capsicum) seeded and coarsely chopped
1 cucumber, about 8 inches (20 cm) long, peeled, seeded and coarsely chopped
1 garlic clove, minced
2 tablespoons snipped chives
1 tablespoon coarsely chopped parsley
juice of 1 lemon
1 tablespoon plus 1 teaspoon extra-virgin olive oil
1 tablespoon plus 1 teaspoon white wine vinegar
cucumber slices, for garnish, optional
basil sprigs, for garnish, optional

◆ Combine the tomatoes, onion, green and red bell peppers and chopped cucumber in a blender or food processor. Add the garlic, half the chives and the parsley and blend to a coarse purée.
◆ Pour the purée into a soup tureen. Stir in the lemon juice, oil and vinegar. Cover and chill in the refrigerator for 1 to 2 hours.
◆ Sprinkle the remaining chives on top and garnish with the cucumber slices and basil, if using. Serve in chilled soup bowls.

NUTRITION NOTES

PER SERVING: 51 calories/215 kilojoules; 2 g protein; 2.5 g fat, 49% of calories (0.4 g saturated, 8% of calories; 1.8 g monounsaturated, 35%; 0.3 g polyunsaturated, 6%); 4 g carbohydrate; 2.4 g dietary fiber; 14 mg sodium; 0.7 mg iron; 0 mg cholesterol.

TOM YAM GOONG

Hot and Sour Shrimp Soup—Thailand

Soup is an essential part of a meal in Thailand, although it is not necessarily eaten as a first course—all the dishes are served together. This is a fragrant, spicy-hot and sour, light-textured soup that refreshes appetites in hot weather. As a bonus, it is good for a low-fat diet! Tom Yam Goong has several variations in different regions of Thailand, and all include chili, fish sauce, lemongrass and lime—the flavors that give this Thai soup its name.

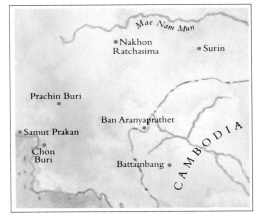

TOTAL TIME: 1 HOUR

SERVES 4

Allow 1 to 1½ hours additional time if the Vegetable Stock is not already prepared. Use a nonreactive saucepan because the lime juice is very acidic. Dried shiitake mushrooms and Asian fish sauce are available in Asian food stores.

6 raw jumbo shrimp (green king prawns),
    about 1 lb (500 g)
2 cups (16 fl oz/500 ml) water
½ cup (1 oz/30 g) dried shiitake or
    Chinese mushrooms
2 cups (16 fl oz/500 ml) Vegetable Stock
    (see page 52)
¼ cup (2 fl oz/60 ml) freshly squeezed
    lime juice
2 tablespoons Asian fish sauce
1 tablespoon Asian chili sauce
½ teaspoon light brown sugar
4 scallions (spring onions), thinly sliced
    diagonally
2 garlic cloves, minced
1 red chili pepper, seeded and finely chopped
1 tablespoon thinly sliced lemongrass
1 teaspoon finely chopped cilantro
    (coriander) root
1 teaspoon finely chopped fresh ginger
1 tablespoon cilantro (coriander) leaves
2 kaffir lime or lemon leaves, cut into thin
    strips

◆ Shell and devein the shrimp and slice in half lengthwise. Place the shrimp in a bowl, cover and refrigerate. Retain the shrimp shells.
◆ Place the shells in a small saucepan. Add the water, cover and bring to a boil over medium-high heat, then reduce the heat to low and simmer for 15 minutes. Strain the stock and set aside. Discard the shells.
◆ Meanwhile, place the mushrooms in a small bowl, add boiling water to cover and soak for 15 minutes to soften. Drain and thinly slice.

◆ Place the Vegetable Stock in a non-reactive saucepan and pour in the shrimp stock. Add the lime juice, fish sauce, chili sauce, sugar, scallions, garlic, chili, lemongrass, cilantro root, ginger and mushrooms. Cover and bring to a boil over medium-high heat. Reduce the heat to low and simmer until the flavors are well blended, about 5 minutes.
◆ Add the shrimp, cilantro leaves and lime leaves to the soup. Simmer, uncovered, just until the prawns turn pink-orange, 3 to 5 minutes. Remove from the heat.
◆ Serve immediately in warm soup bowls.

NUTRITION NOTES

PER SERVING: 90 calories/376 kilojoules; 12 g protein; 2.3 g fat, 23% of calories (0.6 g saturated, 6% of calories; 0.9 g monounsaturated, 9%; 0.8 g polyunsaturated, 8%); 5 g carbohydrate; 3.7 g dietary fiber; 332 mg sodium; 0.8 mg iron; 42 mg cholesterol.

COLD TOMATO AND AVOCADO SOUP

The United States

The flavors of Mexico have had a strong influence on the cuisine of the United States. Avocados, first cultivated by the Aztecs, are now an important crop in California and Florida. Raw vegetables contain antioxidants, such as beta-carotene, vitamins C and E, which help prevent damage to cell tissue. Uncooked soups make good use of these vegetables and are high in fiber. Serve this soup as soon as possible. The color loses its brightness if allowed to stand.

TOTAL TIME: 15 MINUTES

SERVES 6

Kelp is available at most health food stores. It tends to give this soup a dark color and it tastes delicious! There is no substitute for kelp, so if it is not obtainable, you will have to omit it.

2 large, vine-ripened tomatoes, quartered
1 large avocado, sliced
4 scallions (spring onions), sliced
2 stalks celery, thinly sliced
½ cup (4 fl oz/125 ml) water
2 teaspoons powdered kelp
juice of 1 lemon
½ cup (1 oz/30 g) basil leaves, loosely
   packed
1 teaspoon honey
cherry tomato slices, for garnish
basil sprigs, for garnish

◆ Combine the vine-ripened tomatoes, avocado, scallions, celery, water, powdered kelp, lemon juice, basil leaves and honey in a blender or food processor. Blend until smooth, stopping and scraping down the sides as needed.

◆ Pour the mixture into chilled shallow bowls and garnish with the cherry tomato slices and basil sprigs. Serve immediately.

NUTRITION NOTES

PER SERVING: 75 calories/314 kilojoules; 2 g protein; 5.8 g fat, 72% of calories (1.3 g saturated, 16.1% of calories; 3.6 g monounsaturated, 44.7%; 0.9 g polyunsaturated, 11.2%); 4 g carbohydrate; 2.1 g dietary fiber; 23 mg sodium; 0.8 mg iron; 0 mg cholesterol.

PUMPKIN AND CAULIFLOWER SOUP AND CHILLED LETTUCE SOUP

The United States

Pumpkin and Cauliflower Soup is high in fiber, low in cholesterol and easy to digest. Serve it with crusty bread or homemade croûtons. Chilled Lettuce Soup is a light-textured refreshing soup which is very low in calories. Serve in summer, when appetites are jaded, and garnish each bowl with a teaspoon of low-fat, plain yogurt for added appeal. The soup is delicious served warm, too.

Pumpkin and Cauliflower Soup (top) and Chilled Lettuce Soup

PUMPKIN AND CAULIFLOWER SOUP

TOTAL TIME: 55 MINUTES

SERVES 8

Allow 1 to 1½ hours additional time if the Vegetable Stock is not already prepared. For variation, try substituting broccoli for cauliflower and puréed carrots in place of squash. Keep the proportions the same.

3 cups (24 fl oz/750 ml) Vegetable Stock (see page 52)
2 cups cauliflower florets
1 large, vine-ripened tomato, coarsely chopped
1 medium onion, finely chopped
1 bay leaf
2 cups puréed cooked butternut squash (butternut pumpkin)
¼ teaspoon ground ginger
¼ teaspoon freshly ground white pepper
¼ teaspoon salt
1 cup (8 fl oz/250 ml) skim milk or soy drink
⅓ cup (2 oz/60 g) low-fat, plain yogurt, for serving
1 tablespoon finely chopped parsley, for garnish
croûtons, for garnish, optional

◆ Combine the stock, cauliflower, tomato, onion and bay leaf in a large saucepan. Cover and bring to a boil over medium-high heat. Reduce the heat and simmer until the vegetables are tender, about 10 minutes.
◆ Remove the saucepan from the heat and allow the mixture to cool slightly. Remove the bay leaf and discard, then transfer the mixture to a blender or food processor. Blend until smooth, stopping and scraping down the sides as needed. Clean out the saucepan and pour in the purée.
◆ Stir in the squash, ginger, pepper and salt. Bring to a boil over medium heat, stirring constantly. Stir in the milk, bring back to a boil and remove from the heat.
◆ Ladle the soup into warm bowls. Add 2 teaspoons of the yogurt to the center of each portion and garnish with the parsley and croûtons, if using. Serve at once.

CHILLED LETTUCE SOUP

TOTAL TIME: 1 HOUR 50 MINUTES

SERVES 8

Allow 2 to 2½ hours additional time if the stock is not already prepared. This soup may be prepared a day ahead and chilled overnight in the refrigerator.

PARSLEY

Parsley is a biennial plant, native to the Mediterranean, that has been widely used for centuries. It was popular with the Ancient Greeks and Romans who used it in cooking and for medicinal purposes. Parsley was taken to America in the seventeenth century by British colonists. Today parsley is one of the most widely grown and used herbs. Rich in vitamins A, B and especially C, parsley is one of the main components of a bouquet garni and enhances other flavors. An attractive garnish, it complements just about every savory dish. The flavor is more concentrated in the stalks than in the leaves, so use this portion of the plant for a stronger taste. Parsley is also added to marinades, stocks, soups, sauces and vinaigrettes. The most popular varieties include the curly-leaf parsley (Petroselinum crispum) used for garnishes and salads, and the stronger-flavored flat-leaf (or Italian) parsley (P. sativum), which is good for cooking. Parsley is easily grown in a garden or in a pot on a sunny window ledge. Fresh parsley is best stored in the refrigerator, with its stalks in water, or wrapped in plastic and stored in the crisper. Parsley is also available dried from supermarkets.

2 large iceberg lettuce, thinly sliced
2 tablespoons virgin olive oil
2 small white onions, finely chopped
2 tablespoons all-purpose (plain) flour
8 cups (32 fl oz/2 litres) Chicken or Vegetable Stock (see page 52)
2 tablespoons tarragon leaves
¼ teaspoon ground nutmeg
¼ teaspoon freshly ground white pepper
¼ teaspoon salt
¾ cup (5 oz/50 g) low-fat, plain yogurt
¼ cup (2 fl oz/60 ml) light sour cream
½ cup julienne of peeled seeded cucumber, for garnish, optional
1 small carrot, cut into thin julienne strips, for garnish, optional
tarragon sprigs, for garnish

◆ Heat the oil in a very large, heavy-bottomed saucepan over medium heat. Add the onions and sauté, stirring occasionally, until softened, about 5 minutes.
◆ Add the lettuce to the saucepan and stir until soft, about 5 minutes.
◆ Add the flour and stir for 1 minute. Add half the stock, increase the heat to medium-high and bring to a boil, stirring constantly. Stir in the tarragon, nutmeg, pepper and salt. Cover, reduce the heat and simmer until the flavors are blended, about 15 minutes, then remove from the heat and set aside to cool until lukewarm.
◆ Working in batches if necessary, add the lettuce mixture to a blender or food processor. Process until puréed and then transfer to a large bowl.
◆ Add the remaining stock, the yogurt and the sour cream. Mix well. Cover and chill in the refrigerator for at least 1 hour or overnight if desired.
◆ Ladle the soup into chilled soup bowls. Garnish each portion with some cucumber and carrot julienne strips, if using, and tarragon sprigs. Serve immediately.

NUTRITION NOTES

PER SERVING—Lettuce Soup:
87 calories/367 kilojoules; 3 g protein; 6.4 g fat, 66% of calories (1.7 g saturated, 17.5% of calories; 3.9 g monounsaturated, 40.2%; 0.8 g polyunsaturated, 8.3%); 4 g carbohydrate; 1.3 g dietary fiber; 86 mg sodium; 0.7 mg iron; 7 mg cholesterol.

PER SERVING—Pumpkin and Cauliflower Soup:
50 calories/209 kilojoules; 4 g protein; 0.6 g fat, 13% of calories (0.2 g saturated, 4.3% of calories; 0.3 g monounsaturated, 6.5%; 0.1 g polyunsaturated, 2.2%); 7 g carbohydrate; 1.4 g dietary fiber; 116 mg sodium; 0.5 mg iron; 1.5 mg cholesterol.

SALADS & DRESSINGS

A simple salad is defined as a dish of various salad greens, raw or cooked vegetables, fresh herbs and sometimes fruit. Meat, fish, eggs, cheese, legumes, nuts or seeds are added to make a main course. Most salads are tossed with a dressing that binds and seasons the components. The tradition of eating raw leaves and vegetables for health is a long one: two thousand years ago the Greeks were prescribing them for a variety of conditions. But their appeal was not only medicinal—fresh leaves were dressed with a vinegar dressing and enjoyed as part of a meal.

Salads are versatile. They add color and tangy flavor to bland meals and introduce crispness to otherwise soft-textured lunches and dinners. Salads are almost always an

important source of nutrients including dietary fiber, vitamins and minerals. Use only the freshest of ingredients, so that the flavors are at their best.

Salads have more variety than ever these days! Just when you think you have tasted every new salad green imaginable, a new one arrives in the market place. Thanks to the demands of modern restaurateurs and chefs, the efforts of horticulturists and growers and the marketing skills of entrepreneurs, the consumer is the beneficiary of a delicious array of interesting lettuces and greens. Exotic greens, once only available in their land of origin, are nowadays being grown all over the world as local growers expand their range of products. And the availability of refrigerated transport has made it possible for a huge variety of superb salad ingredients to be easily taken across the world, if necessary to cheat the seasons. Planes loaded with lettuces and other salad greens fly daily. This availability of fresh produce allows chefs freedom to prepare all sorts of exotic salads all year long.

Left: There are many varieties of olives, differing in flavor and size; this display is in Seville, Spain. Below: Visiting the market is a daily event for many Indian women; this market is in Rajasthan.

A garden salad is the glory of lunch and dinner tables in France! Fresh greens are simply tossed with a classic dressing and served as a perfect accompaniment to roast meats, baked chicken or broiled/grilled fish. Traditionally served after the main course in France, green salads are regarded by the French as excellent for refreshing the palate and enhancing the flavor of main courses. Many other countries have adopted this tasty and healthy custom.

On the world stage, salads are much more than a simple mixture of greens. The infinite variety of fascinating fresh produce is a source of unlimited inspiration to creative chefs and cooks. Alfalfa Sprout Salad, from China; Avocado Salad, from Australia; and Greek Salad all make delightful nutritious accompaniments to main courses.

Certain salads are often grouped together and enjoyed as a popular part of a buffet or smorgasbord table. New Potato Salad, from Switzerland; New Age Coleslaw, from the United States; and *Caponata*, from Italy are good examples. Certain salads made from ingredients with firm textures are hearty enough to travel well. Red Cabbage and Radicchio Salad, from Mexico; *Tabbouleh*, from Lebanon; and Carrot, Apple and Raisin Salad, from the United

Above: *The lettuce, commonly associated with salads, in fact is a much more versatile vegetable; picking lettuces in Salinas Valley, California.* Right: *Vegetables are one of the main components of a healthy diet; this cheerful display is at the market in St Paul de Vence, France.*

States are ideal at barbecues, picnics and dining alfresco.

Meat, dairy and vegetable protein foods can turn an ordinary salad into a delicious, well-balanced main course. Examples of recipes containing chicken, seafood, eggs, cheese, beans, nuts or seeds that make great main meal salads are Pasta and Chicken Pesto Salad, from Italy; Curried Rice and Chicken Salad, from the United States; Goat Cheese Salad, from France; Shrimp and Mango Salad, from Thailand; Marinated Fish Salad, from Indonesia; and Bean Salad, from Japan.

The preparation of salad dressings deserves careful attention when following a low-fat diet. The original French dressing, or vinaigrette, is based on a proportion of 3 parts oil to 1 part vinegar. This proportion has been changed radically, without loss of flavor, in the development of healthy recipes for this book! The oil can be largely replaced with fresh and natural fruit juices, such as orange, lemon, lime, grape or apple juice, which give a much lower-fat dressing. Try fresh-tasting Citrus

Dressing, from the United States; and spicy Thai Dressing. Creamy dressings are made with low-fat yogurt, low-fat cottage cheese or soft-textured silken tofu rather than cream for a lighter and healthier salad. Tofu Dressing, from Switzerland; Curry Dressing and Tahini Dressing, from the United

States are good examples. Low-fat versions of traditional dressings, like Trim French Dressing and Trim Pesto Dressing, are also included. Many of these dressings may be prepared in larger quantities and stored in the refrigerator until needed. Keep covered in nonreactive containers for best results.

AVOCADO SALAD

Australia

In Australia, as in the United States, the most popular avocados are the dark-skinned Haas and the smaller, green-skinned Fuerte varieties. These much-loved fruits do not have to be banned from a healthy diet—just used sparingly. Here, the avocado is complemented with crisp, low-calorie fruits and vegetables and French dressing with a reduced amount of olive oil. This salad is a good accompaniment to broiled fish or poached chicken breasts.

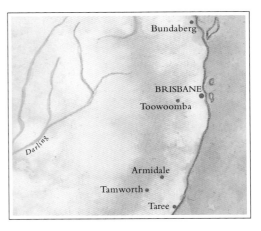

TOTAL TIME: 20 MINUTES

SERVES 4

Use a sharp serrated knife to remove the peel and white pith from the citrus fruit. To remove neat sections of orange and grapefruit, cut on either side of each membrane.

---

1 small-medium Boston (butter) or green oakleaf lettuce
1 medium fennel bulb, cored and thinly sliced
1 medium pink grapefruit, sectioned
1 medium navel orange, sectioned
12½ oz (400 g) canned hearts of palm, drained and thinly sliced
1 large avocado, halved and thinly sliced
Trim French Dressing (see page 75)

◆ Tear the lettuce leaves into a manageable size and place in a large salad bowl. Arrange the fennel, grapefruit, orange, hearts of palm and avocado slices on top.

◆ Pour the dressing over and gently toss until all the salad is coated.
◆ Serve immediately.

NUTRITION NOTES

PER SERVING: 207 calories/870 kilojoules; 4 g protein; 16 g fat, 72% of calories (3.5 g saturated, 15.8% of calories; 10.3 g monounsaturated, 46.3%; 2.2 g polyunsaturated, 9.9%); 11 g carbohydrate; 7.2 g dietary fiber; 149 mg sodium; 1.7 mg iron; 0 mg cholesterol.

ALFALFA SAH LOT

Alfalfa Sprout Salad—China

Alfalfa, also known as lucerne, is one of the plants first cultivated by humans. Surprisingly, it contains more protein per ounce than beef. It is claimed that it was first grown by the Arabs for horse feed and that this was the secret of their horses' remarkable strength. Alfalfa "sprouts" from the alfalfa seed or grain, whereas mung beans "sprout" from the mung bean. Both are widely used in China, where vegetable-based dishes are more common than meat-based.

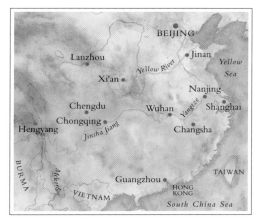

TOTAL TIME: 15 MINUTES

SERVES 4

If you do not have a steamer, a metal colander can be placed in a large saucepan with boiling water and covered with a lid or foil. Make sure the water does not touch the colander itself. Dried seaweed, sesame oil and tamari are available in most health food stores. If baby squash are not available, use zucchini instead.

4 oz (125 g) yellow baby squash, trimmed
¼ cup dried hijiki or okame seaweed threads
2 cups baby spinach (English spinach) leaves
1 cup alfalfa sprouts
½ cup mung bean sprouts
4 scallions (spring onions), sliced diagonally
¼ cup thinly sliced, seeded red bell pepper (capsicum)
2 tablespoons cashews, toasted and coarsely chopped
1 tablespoon poppy seeds

DRESSING

3 tablespoons freshly squeezed lemon juice
1 tablespoon sesame oil
1 tablespoon reduced-sodium tamari or reduced-sodium soy sauce
1 garlic clove, minced

◆ Bring water to a boil in a medium-sized steamer. Add the squash, cover and steam over medium-high heat until firm but tender, about 5 minutes. Remove the squash from the steamer and plunge into a bowl of iced water for about 20 seconds. Drain, then cover and refrigerate for 5 minutes. (Refreshing with ice retains the vegetable's lovely bright yellow color.) Cut the squash into wedges.
◆ Place the seaweed in a small bowl and add enough warm water to cover. Set aside to soften for 10 minutes. Drain.
◆ Meanwhile, to make the dressing, combine the lemon juice, sesame oil, tamari and garlic in a glass jar with a plastic screw-top lid and shake well to combine. Chill in the refrigerator until needed.
◆ In a salad bowl, combine the spinach leaves, squash, alfalfa sprouts, mung bean sprouts, scallions, seaweed and bell pepper.
◆ Add the dressing and toss lightly until combined. Sprinkle the cashews and poppy seeds over the top. Serve immediately.

NUTRITION NOTES

PER SERVING: 86 calories/359 kilojoules; 4 g protein; 6.1 g fat, 65% of calories (0.9 g saturated, 9.6% of calories; 2.1 g monounsaturated, 22.4%; 3.1 g polyunsaturated, 33%); 4 g carbohydrate; 2.9 g dietary fiber; 168 mg sodium; 1 mg iron; 0 mg cholesterol.

SALADE VERTE AVEC VINAIGRETTE LÉGÈRE, SALADE AU FROMAGE DE CHÈVRE

Garden Salad with Trim French Dressing and Goat Cheese Salad—France

Goat Cheese Salad is just right as part of a special occasion menu, or to serve with crusty French bread as a light meal. The French often serve salad to refresh the palate. Thanks to an immense variety of lettuces, greens and vegetables, salads such as this Garden Salad are popular everywhere.

Garden Salad with Trim French Dressing (top) and Goat Cheese Salad

SALADE VERTE
Garden Salad

TOTAL TIME: 15 MINUTES

SERVES 4

It is very important to thoroughly wash and dry salad greens. This is necessary to ensure crispness and to prevent the delicious flavor of a dressing from being watered down.

1 small crisp lettuce, such as Boston
   (butter), green leaf or romaine (cos)
1 cup arugula (rocket) or mesclun salad greens
1 cup watercress sprigs or snow pea
   (mangetout) sprouts, trimmed
1 stalk celery, sliced
¼ cup sliced cucumber
1 medium Belgian endive (witloof) or
   fennel bulb, thinly sliced, optional
½ cup sliced, canned artichoke hearts,
   optional
½ avocado, sliced, optional
2 tablespoons Trim French Dressing
   (see recipe below)

◆ Tear the lettuce leaves into large pieces and place in a large salad bowl.
◆ Add the arugula, watercress sprigs, celery and cucumber.
◆ Add the endive, artichoke hearts and avocado, if using.
◆ Pour the dressing over the salad and toss lightly until every leaf glistens with dressing.
◆ Serve the salad immediately.

VINAIGRETTE LÉGÈRE
Trim French Dressing

TOTAL TIME: 10 MINUTES

MAKES ½ CUP

Most dressings contain vinegar or lemon juice. For best results, make and store dressings in a glass jar with a plastic screw-top lid or similar nonreactive container.

¼ cup (2 fl oz/60 ml) extra-virgin olive oil
¼ cup (2 fl oz/60 ml) tarragon-flavored
   white wine vinegar
2 teaspoons dry mustard
2 teaspoons superfine (caster) sugar
1 teaspoon freshly ground black pepper
1 teaspoon salt
4 garlic cloves, minced
¼ cup finely chopped herbs like basil,
   thyme, rosemary or parsley, optional

◆ To make the dressing, combine all the ingredients in a glass jar with a plastic screw-top lid and shake until the oil is well combined with the other ingredients.
◆ Use at once, or store, covered, in the refrigerator for up to 3 months.

SALADE AU FROMAGE DE CHÈVRE
Goat Cheese Salad

TOTAL TIME: 25 MINUTES

SERVES 4

Mesclun salad is a mixture of young salad greens and herbs. It is often available at farmers' markets and specialty food stores. If unavailable, substitute a combination of Boston and oakleaf lettuce leaves mixed with baby spinach leaves. The dressing can be made in larger quantities and kept in the refrigerator for up to 3 months.

DRESSING

2 teaspoons walnut oil
2 teaspoons basil- or tarragon-flavored
   white wine vinegar
1 tablespoon plus 1 teaspoon unsweetened
   grape or apple juice
½ teaspoon wholegrain mustard
pinch superfine (caster) sugar
¼ teaspoon freshly ground black pepper

3 cups mesclun salad greens
1 cup arugula (rocket)
2 medium green-skinned pears
juice of 1 lemon
¼ cup (about 1 oz/30 g) walnut or
   pecan halves

EDIBLE FLOWERS

Flower buds or blooms of many species are often used to enhance color, flavor and aroma. Larger blossoms, such as those of the squash family, are often stuffed. Petals add flavor and color to salads and some cooked dishes. Flowers often used for such purposes include roses, carnations, lilacs, nasturtiums, chrysanthemums, marigolds, pansies and violets. However, not all flowers are appropriate for such use. Since some plants may have been sprayed with pesticides, it is wise to pick edible flowers from your own garden or buy them from specialty food stores or larger supermarkets. Store the flowers in an airtight container in the crisper section of the refrigerator, and use within a week.

3 oz (90 g) soft chèvre (goat cheese), cubed
   or crumbled
¼ cup edible flower petals, optional

◆ Combine the walnut oil, vinegar, juice, mustard, sugar and pepper in a glass jar with a plastic screw-top lid. Cover securely and shake until well mixed. Chill until needed.
◆ Combine the mesclun greens and arugula in a large salad bowl, and toss gently.
◆ Cut the pears in half lengthwise and remove the cores. Cut the flesh into halves again, then slice into thin wedges.
◆ Drizzle or brush the pear wedges with lemon juice on both sides to prevent them from turning brown.
◆ Add the pears and walnuts to the bowl and top with the chèvre. Pour the dressing over, toss gently and serve at once, garnished with the flower petals, if using.

NUTRITION NOTES

PER SERVING—Garden Salad:
49 calories/203 kilojoules; 1 g protein; 3.8 g fat, 73% of calories (0.6 g saturated, 11.5% of calories; 2.7 g monounsaturated, 51.9%; 0.5 g polyunsaturated, 9.6%); 2 g carbohydrate; 2.1 g dietary fiber; 138 mg sodium; 1.2 mg iron; 0 mg cholesterol.

PER TABLESPOON—Trim French Dressing:
72 calories/301 kilojoules; 0.3 g protein; 7.3 g fat, 92% of calories (1.1 g saturated, 13.9% of calories; 5.4 g monounsaturated, 68%; 0.8 g polyunsaturated, 10.1%); 1 g carbohydrate; 0.3 g dietary fiber; 195 mg sodium; 0.1 mg iron; 0 mg cholesterol.

PER SERVING—Goat Cheese Salad:
253 calories/1061 kilojoules; 9 g protein; 18 g fat, 64% of calories (6.9 g saturated, 24.5% of calories; 4.8 g monounsaturated, 17.1%; 6.3 g polyunsaturated, 22.4%); 14 g carbohydrate; 4.6 g dietary fiber; 187 mg sodium; 1.2 mg iron; 25 mg cholesterol.

HORIÁTIKI SALÁTA

Greek Salad—Greece

In Greece this is often called "country salad," as it is served in most rural and island tavernas. There are many variations, but salad greens, feta cheese and olives are always included. Here, pistachio nuts and fresh figs add color and texture. Usually a side dish, it can also be enjoyed as a light lunch or supper. The feta cheese and pistachio nuts provide plenty of protein. Serve with warm crusty bread or boiled new potatoes in their skins.

TOTAL TIME: 25 TO 30 MINUTES

SERVES 4

This dressing can be prepared up to 3 months in advance and stored in the refrigerator until required.

OIL AND LEMON DRESSING

2 tablespoons extra-virgin olive oil
1 tablespoon freshly squeezed lemon juice
1 tablespoon finely chopped oregano
¼ teaspoon freshly ground black pepper

1 small romaine (cos) lettuce
1 cup baby spinach (English spinach) leaves
    or sorrel leaves
2 medium, vine-ripened tomatoes, cut into
    wedges
½ cup sliced or cubed cucumber
4 kalamata olives, pitted and halved
4 oz (125 g) feta cheese, cut into ¾ inch
    (2 cm) cubes
4 medium fresh figs, quartered
1 tablespoon pistachio nuts, coarsely chopped
½ cup thinly sliced green bell pepper
    (capsicum), optional
1 small red onion, thinly sliced, optional

◆ To make the dressing, combine the oil, lemon juice, oregano and pepper in a glass jar with a plastic screw-top lid. Shake well to combine, then chill.
◆ Tear the lettuce leaves into small pieces in a large salad bowl. Add the spinach, tomatoes, cucumber, olives, feta , figs, pistachio nuts, and bell pepper and onion, if using.
◆ Pour the dressing over the salad and toss gently just before serving.

NUTRITION NOTES

PER SERVING: 208 calories/869 kilojoules; 8 g protein; 17 g fat, 71% of calories (6.7 g saturated, 27.9% of calories; 8.3 g monounsaturated, 34.7%; 2 g polyunsaturated, 8.4%); 7 g carbohydrate; 3.2 g dietary fiber; 465 mg sodium; 1.1 mg iron; 22 mg cholesterol.

IKAN BUMBU SAYUR

Marinated Fish Salad—Indonesia

The waters surrounding Indonesia's many islands are rich in seafood. The technique of "cooking" fish with lime juice is popular in many of the world's tropical and subtropical areas. In Indonesia, where coconut trees thrive, a delicious coconut-milk dressing enhances the "cooked" fish. Fish is an easy-to-digest protein that is complemented here with refreshing high-fiber salad ingredients. Serve with a rice salad.

TOTAL TIME: 8¾ HOURS

SERVES 4

In this recipe, the fish is "cooked" by marinating it with lime juice for 8 hours or overnight, in the refrigerator.

1 lb (500 g) fish fillets, such as porgy
   (bream), snapper or similar coarse-
   textured fish, skin removed
¼ teaspoon salt
¾ cup (6 fl oz/175 ml) freshly squeezed
   lime juice
⅓ cup (3 fl oz/90 ml) unsweetened
   coconut milk
⅓ cup (3 fl oz/90 ml) unsweetened
   pineapple juice
½ cucumber, about 4 oz (125 g)
1 small onion, thinly sliced

1 medium carrot, coarsely grated
1 cup (4 oz/125 g) papaya (pawpaw) cut
   into ½ inch (1 cm) cubes
lettuce leaves, for serving
lime wedges, for serving

◆ Cut the fish into ¾ inch (2 cm) pieces and place in a shallow glass dish. Sprinkle with the salt and pour in the lime juice. Gently stir to coat the fish with lime juice.

◆ Cover with plastic wrap and marinate in the refrigerator for 8 hours, or overnight, until all the fish flesh has turned opaque.

◆ Drain and discard the lime juice and transfer the fish to a large bowl. Mix the coconut milk with the pineapple juice in a small bowl, then pour over the fish pieces.

◆ Cut the cucumber in half lengthwise and use a small spoon to scoop out the seeds.

Cut the flesh into ¼ inch (6 mm) cubes.

◆ Add the onion, carrot and cucumber to the fish mixture and gently fold with a rubber spatula. Carefully place the papaya on the top of the salad to avoid crushing. Cover and chill for a further 30 minutes.

◆ To serve, place the lettuce leaves in a large serving bowl or on individual plates and spoon the fish salad on top. Garnish with the lime wedges and serve immediately.

NUTRITION NOTES

PER SERVING: 230 calories/964 kilojoules; 26 g protein; 9.5 g fat, 37% of calories (5.1 g saturated, 19.9% of calories; 2.5 g monounsaturated, 9.7%; 1.9 g polyunsaturated, 7.4%); 9 g carbohydrate; 2.9 g dietary fiber; 228 mg sodium; 1.1 mg iron; 92 mg cholesterol.

CAPONATA,
INSALATA DI PASTA E POLLO AL PESTO

Cooked Vegetable Salad and Pasta and
Chicken Pesto Salad—Italy

*P*asta is a healthy, versatile food: a good source of energy, high in fiber, niacin and thiamin. Pasta and Chicken Pesto Salad is a delicious way to serve pasta in hot weather. A variety of Mediterranean vegetables are used to make Caponata, *which is rich in vitamins and minerals and low in fat.*

Pasta and Chicken Pesto Salad (top) and Cooked Vegetable Salad

INSALATA DI PASTA E POLLO AL PESTO

Pasta and Chicken Pesto Salad

TOTAL TIME: 40 MINUTES

SERVES 4

To save time, buy cooked chicken for the salad. Remove the skin and any visible fat before chopping it.

8 sundried tomatoes
8 oz (250 g) fusilli pasta
8 oz (250 g) asparagus, cut into 1½ inch (4 cm) pieces
2 cups (8 oz/250 g) chopped, cooked skinless chicken breast
1 cup (8 oz/250 g) quartered cherry tomatoes
basil leaves, for garnish

TRIM PESTO DRESSING

2 cups basil leaves
2 garlic cloves, minced
¼ teaspoon coarse (rock) salt
1 tablespoon pine nuts
1 tablespoon plus 1 teaspoon extra-virgin olive oil
¼ cup (1 oz/30g) freshly grated Parmesan cheese
3 tablespoons lukewarm water

◆ Place the sundried tomatoes in a small bowl and add boiling water to cover. Set aside until plump, about 30 minutes. Drain, then gently squeeze out excess water and pat dry on paper towels. Cut the tomatoes into long, thin strips.

◆ Meanwhile, bring a large saucepan of water to a boil over high heat. Add the pasta, stir well and boil rapidly, uncovered, until tender, about 10 minutes.

◆ While the pasta is cooking, bring water to a boil in a large steamer. Add the asparagus, cover and steam over medium-high heat until firm but tender, about 5 minutes. Remove the asparagus from the steamer and plunge into a bowl of iced water for about 20 seconds. Drain, then cover and refrigerate for 5 minutes.

◆ To make the dressing, combine the basil, garlic, salt and pine nuts in a blender or food processor. Mix to a coarse paste. Add the oil, Parmesan cheese and water to the mixture. Process until smooth, stopping and scraping down the sides as needed.

◆ Drain the pasta and place in a large bowl. Add the pesto dressing and toss well. Set aside for 30 minutes to cool and for the pesto flavor to be absorbed.

◆ Add the chicken, sundried tomatoes, asparagus and cherry tomatoes. Stir gently.

◆ Transfer the mixture to a large serving bowl. Garnish with the basil leaves and serve immediately.

CAPONATA

Cooked Vegetable Salad

TOTAL TIME: 1 HOUR 10 MINUTES

SERVES 8

To eliminate bitterness, eggplants are often salted and left to drain. If you select a good quality specimen—not too young, not too ripe—the salting process can be eliminated. This can be prepared up to 3 days in advance, and stored in the refrigerator. If prepared well in advance, let the salad stand at room temperature for 1 hour before serving for maximum flavor.

2 tablespoons virgin olive oil
1 large onion, finely chopped
1 cup celery, sliced
1 medium red bell pepper (capsicum), seeded and cut in ¾ inch (2 cm) squares
1 medium, green sweet pepper (banana pepper), seeded and cut in ¾ inch (2 cm) squares
1 large eggplant (aubergine), about 1 lb (500 g)
1 tablespoon capers, drained
2 large, vine-ripened tomatoes, coarsely chopped
2 tablespoons balsamic or red wine vinegar
1 tablespoon no-added-sodium tomato paste
4 canned anchovy fillets, soaked in milk for 10 minutes, drained and coarsely chopped
8 black or green olives, for garnish, optional
lemon wedges, for serving

◆ Heat the oil in a large, non-stick frying pan over medium heat. Add the onion and sauté, stirring frequently, until golden, about 5 minutes.

◆ Add the celery, bell pepper and sweet pepper and cook for 2 minutes to develop flavor. Cover and cook until firm but tender, about 3 minutes longer.

◆ Meanwhile, with a vegetable peeler, peel a ¾ inch (2 cm) strip of skin from the eggplant, peeling lengthwise. Leave a strip width of skin, then peel another strip off, working around it, until you have a "striped" eggplant. Cut across the striped eggplant into ¾ inch (2 cm) thick slices, and cut each slice into 8–12 wedges.

◆ Add the eggplant to the frying pan, cover and cook, stirring often, until the eggplant is almost tender, about 8 minutes.

◆ Add the capers, tomatoes, vinegar, tomato paste and anchovies and bring to a boil, stirring constantly. Reduce the heat to medium-low and simmer slowly, uncovered, until the mixture has a thick, chunky texture, about 10 minutes.

◆ Transfer the mixture to a serving bowl and cool. Cover and chill in the refrigerator for at least 30 minutes before serving.

◆ Garnish with the olives, if using, and serve with the lemon wedges.

CAPERS

The caper bush (Capparis spinosa) *has grown wild in the Mediterranean region since Ancient Greek times. The Ancient Greeks and the Romans apparently used to eat both the flowers and buds of the plant, much in the same way that edible flowers are used today. However, nowadays it is the unopened buds of the caper that are pickled in brine or vinegar and used as a condiment, in salads and sauces (particularly with fish), as a garnish for appetizers and in pizza toppings. Capers vary in size from tiny (delicate and sought after) to fingernail size, and are sold either pickled or salted. Rinse before use as they can be extremely salty. Available in bottles from larger supermarkets or specialty stores, capers should be stored in the refrigerator where they will keep for up to 6 months.*

NUTRITION NOTES

PER SERVING—Pasta and Chicken Pesto Salad: 466 calories/1951 kilojoules; 31 g protein; 15 g fat, 29% of calories (4.3 g saturated, 8.3% of calories; 7.6 g monounsaturated, 14.7%; 3.1 g polyunsaturated, 6%); 50 g carbohydrate; 5.1 g dietary fiber; 288 mg sodium; 3.9 mg iron; 87 mg cholesterol.

PER SERVING—Cooked Vegetable Salad: 64 calories/269 kilojoules; 2 g protein; 4 g fat, 57% of calories (0.6 g saturated, 8.6% of calories; 2.9 g monounsaturated, 41.3%; 0.5 g polyunsaturated, 7.1%); 4 g carbohydrate; 2.7 g dietary fiber; 118 mg sodium; 0.5 mg iron; 1 mg cholesterol.

JIYAPPAN MAME SALADA

Bean Salad—Japan

*T*he cultivation of the soy (or soya) bean has spread from China to Japan where it is widely used for a large variety of products like tofu (or bean curd, often used as a meat substitute in Asian cooking) and soy sauce. The soy bean is a valuable source of protein and a good source of fiber. Like the adzuki bean, soy beans are delicious in salads. If the crisp, juicy Asian pear is difficult to obtain, use any green-skinned ripe but firm pear instead.

TOTAL TIME: 3½ TO 4½ HOURS

SERVES 4

If time is limited, use 1 cup of canned soy beans (rinsed and drained) in place of the combined soy beans and adzuki beans. Rice wine vinegar, sesame oil, tamari and wasabi paste are all available from Asian food stores.

½ cup (2½ oz/75 g) adzuki beans
½ cup (2½ oz/75 g) soy beans
1 cup (4 oz/125 g) firmly packed green
beans cut into 1½ inch (3 cm) lengths

4 scallions (spring onions), thinly sliced
diagonally
1 tablespoon chopped pickled ginger or
preserved ginger
2 medium Asian (nashi) pears, cut into thin
wedges
juice of 1 lemon
1 cup snow pea (mangetout) sprouts

DRESSING

1 tablespoon rice wine vinegar
1 teaspoon sesame oil
1 teaspoon reduced-sodium tamari or
reduced-sodium soy sauce
1 garlic clove, minced
½ teaspoon syrup from preserved ginger or
½ teaspoon light brown sugar
½ teaspoon wasabi paste (Japanese
horseradish)

◆ Place the adzuki beans and soy beans in separate medium-sized saucepans and add water to cover. Bring each to a boil over high heat and boil for 2 minutes. Remove both from the heat, cover and let stand for 1 hour.
◆ Drain the beans, return them to separate rinsed saucepans and add water to cover. Bring to a boil over high heat. Reduce the heat to medium and simmer, covered, until tender, about 30 minutes for the adzuki beans and 2 to 3 hours for the soy beans.

(Alternatively, cook the drained soy beans in a pressure cooker for about 1 hour.)
◆ Drain the cooked beans and set aside.
◆ Bring water to a boil in a medium-sized steamer. Add the green beans, cover and steam over medium-high heat until firm but tender, about 5 minutes. Remove the beans from the steamer and plunge into a bowl of iced water for about 20 seconds. Drain, then cover and refrigerate for 5 minutes.
◆ Place the adzuki beans, soy beans, green beans, scallions and ginger in a medium-sized salad bowl.
◆ Brush the Asian pear with the lemon juice to prevent discoloring. Add the Asian pear and sprouts to the salad bowl.
◆ To make the dressing, combine the vinegar, sesame oil, tamari, garlic, ginger syrup and wasabi paste in a glass jar with a plastic screw-top lid and shake well to combine.
◆ Just before serving, pour the dressing over the bean salad and toss lightly until well combined.

NUTRITION NOTES

PER SERVING: 189 calories/791 kilojoules; 12 g protein; 5.6 g fat, 27% of calories (1 g saturated, 4.8% of calories; 1 g monounsaturated, 4.8%; 3.6 g polyunsaturated, 17.4%); 23 g carbohydrate; 9.7 g dietary fiber; 55 mg sodium; 4 mg iron; 0 mg cholesterol.

ADZUKI BEANS

The adzuki bean (Phaseolus angularis) is a small, oval-shaped, reddish brown bean with a sweetish nutty flavor. Native to China, adzuki beans are also widely grown throughout Japan and are associated with the cuisines of both countries. Over the last 2000 years the red bean has become a symbol of good luck in both Japan and China. Adzuki beans are an excellent source of protein, dietary fiber, and iron while being low in fat and cholesterol. Because meat is not a large part of the Japanese diet, the protein contained in beans plays an important nutritional role. Adzuki beans may be served on their own, with rice, in salads or added to soups and casseroles. They can also be sprouted and added to salads. A favorite way to prepare the beans in Asia is to cook them whole with some sugar and serve as a sweet garnish, or make them into a sweet paste which is then used in desserts and confections. Adzuki beans are also ground into a flour. As with other dried beans, adzuki beans need to be soaked before they are cooked. Available from Asian and health food stores and in some supermarkets they will keep very well if stored in a cool, dry place.

TABBOULEH

Bulghur and Parsley Salad—Lebanon

Sometimes regarded as Lebanon's national salad, this healthy high-fiber dish uses wheat which is washed, steamed and hulled, then dried and crushed to produce bulghur. Parsley, mint, tomatoes and lemon juice are the other main ingredients. Serve as part of a Middle Eastern meal or on a buffet table. Tabbouleh can also be served as a first course, to be scooped up with lettuce or pita bread. Add to a sandwich to provide valuable fiber.

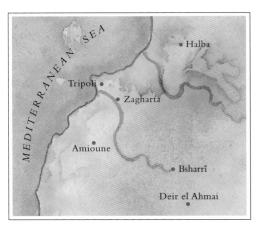

TOTAL TIME: 1 HOUR 15 MINUTES

SERVES 8

For a delicious variation, add a spoonful of chopped pomegranate to the salad.

⅔ cup (4 oz/125 g) bulghur
4 thinly sliced scallions (spring onions)
2 cups coarsely chopped flat-leaf parsley
¼ cup shredded mint
½ cup (4 oz/125 g) cherry tomatoes, quartered

DRESSING

2 tablespoons plus 2 teaspoons extra-virgin olive oil
¼ cup (2 fl oz/60 ml) freshly squeezed lemon juice
¼ teaspoon freshly ground black pepper
¼ teaspoon salt

◆ Place the bulghur in a small bowl. Add water to cover and leave to soak until tender, about 30 minutes.
◆ Drain the bulghur through a cheesecloth-lined sieve. Gather up the cheesecloth around the bulghur and squeeze to extract as much water as possible.
◆ Transfer the bulghur to a medium-sized bowl and add the scallions, parsley, mint and tomatoes. Mix well.
◆ To make the dressing, combine the olive oil, lemon juice, pepper and salt in a glass jar with a plastic screw-top lid and shake well to combine.
◆ Pour the dressing over the salad and toss gently until evenly coated. Cover and chill in the refrigerator for 30 minutes.
◆ Transfer to a bowl before serving.

NUTRITION NOTES

PER SERVING: 93 calories/391 kilojoules; 2 g protein; 5.1 g fat, 49% of calories (0.8 g saturated, 7.7% of calories; 3.6 g monounsaturated, 34.6%; 0.7 g polyunsaturated, 6.7%); 10 g carbohydrate; 3.4 g dietary fiber; 61 mg sodium; 1.2 mg iron; 0 mg cholesterol.

ENSALADA DE REPOLLO ROJO Y RADICCHIO

Red Cabbage and Radicchio Salad—Mexico

Radicchio is a variety of chicory, and while often served cooked, it is more commonly served as a salad "green"—even though its leaves range from light pink to dark burgundy. This salad is bursting with healthy fiber, has a light tangy dressing and adds color to most menus. Fruit and vegetables such as these are an important part of Mexican cuisine.

TOTAL TIME: 20 MINUTES

SERVES 8

Cabbage and radicchio can be stored in the refrigerator for up to one week. Place them, unwashed, in a plastic bag with a paper towel to absorb moisture.

DRESSING

3 tablespoons freshly squeezed lemon juice
3 tablespoons red wine vinegar
2 tablespoons extra-virgin olive oil
2 garlic cloves, minced
½ teaspoon chili powder

*½ medium red cabbage, trimmed and very
    thinly sliced*
8 large radishes, thinly sliced
*8 scallions (spring onions), thinly sliced
    diagonally*
1 stalk celery, thinly sliced
*1 cup (8 oz/250 g) halved small cherry
    tomatoes*
¼ cup finely chopped flat-leaf parsley
1 small radicchio

◆ Combine the lemon juice, vinegar, oil, garlic and chili powder in a glass jar with a plastic screw-top lid and shake well. Chill in the refrigerator until ready to use.
◆ Combine the cabbage, radishes, scallions and celery in a large bowl. Toss gently until well combined.
◆ Just before serving, add the tomatoes, parsley and dressing. Gently toss until the cabbage is well coated.
◆ Line a large salad bowl with the radicchio leaves. Pile the cabbage mixture into the center and serve immediately.

NUTRITION NOTES

PER SERVING: 67 calories/278 kilojoules; 3 g protein; 4 g fat, 55% of calories (0.7 g saturated, 9.6% of calories; 2.8 g monounsaturated, 38.5%; 0.5 g polyunsaturated, 6.9%); 4 g carbohydrate; 5.2 g dietary fiber; 30 mg sodium; 1.4 mg iron; 0 mg cholesterol.

SALAT AUS NEUEN KARTOFFELN, SALATSAUCE AUS TOFU

New Potato Salad and Tofu Dressing—Switzerland

This potato salad has been made low-fat by replacing the traditional mayonnaise with Tofu Dressing. Serve with broiled or barbecued fish and a green salad for a delicious yet healthy casual meal. The Tofu Dressing is a healthy low-fat substitute for traditional mayonnaise and it can be used with other salads, and in sandwiches. Use silken tofu if possible—it is the smoothest.

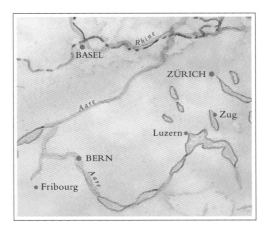

TOFU

Tofu is also known as bean curd, a name that decribes it well because it is made from puréed soy (or soya) beans that are curdled to produce an easily digested and nutritious food. It originated in China about 2000 years ago and was taken to Japan 800 years later by Buddhist monks. Tofu is an important and inexpensive source of protein in Asian cookery and is used in a multitude of ways; stuffed, diced, shredded and puréed. Because of its protein content, tofu is also valued by vegetarians. Tofu comes in three different textures; silken tofu (bottom) is very smooth, slippery and shiny; soft tofu (center) is a lot firmer but will still crumble fairly easily; firm or hard tofu (top) is well pressed to remove as much moisture as possible and slices more easily than either silken or soft tofu. Available in Asian food stores and health food stores, tofu is usually sold in blocks surrounded by liquid and will keep for 3 to 4 days in the refrigerator. Tofu is sometimes available in powdered form.

NUTRITION NOTES

PER SERVING—New Potato Salad:
132 calories/554 kilojoules; 8 g protein; 4 g fat, 28% of calories (0.7 g saturated, 4.9% of calories; 1.3 g monounsaturated, 9.1%; 2 g polyunsaturated, 14%); 16 g carbohydrate; 2.9 g dietary fiber; 80 mg sodium; 2.1 mg iron; 0 mg cholesterol.

PER ¼ CUP—Tofu Dressing:
53 calories/222 kilojoules; 4 g protein; 3.3 g fat, 59% of calories (0.5 g saturated, 8.9% of calories; 1 g monounsaturated, 17.9%; 1.8 g polyunsaturated, 32.2%); 1 g carbohydrate; 0.4 g dietary fiber; 49 mg sodium; 1.3 mg iron; 0 mg cholesterol.

SALAT AUS NEUEN KARTOFFELN
New Potato Salad

TOTAL TIME: 35 MINUTES
SERVES 8

Pink peppercorns are available from specialty food stores. They can be ground with a small mortar and pestle or in a peppermill.

12 small new potatoes
¼ cup (2 fl oz/60 ml) buttermilk
1 quantity Tofu Dressing (see recipe below)
8 thinly sliced scallions (spring onions)
½ cup sliced dill pickle (pickled cucumber)
2 cups finely chopped celery
¼ cup finely chopped dill
2 teaspoons sesame seeds, toasted
1 teaspoon freshly ground pink or black peppercorns

◆ Place the potatoes in a large saucepan and add enough cold water to cover. Bring to a boil over medium-high heat, cover and cook until tender but firm, about 15 minutes. Drain and cool slightly.
◆ Cut each potato into 4 wedges while warm. Place in a bowl, add the buttermilk and gently fold in with a rubber spatula until the wedges are evenly coated. Set aside to cool and let flavors develop.
◆ Combine the spring onions, dill pickle, celery and dill in a large bowl and gently stir to mix.
◆ Add the potatoes, buttermilk and Tofu Dressing. Gently fold in using a rubber spatula, until all the ingredients are evenly coated and well combined.
◆ Transfer the potato salad to a large serving bowl and sprinkle the sesame seeds and pepper on top. Serve at room temperature for best results.

SALATSAUCE AUS TOFU
Tofu Dressing

TOTAL TIME: 10 MINUTES
MAKES 2 CUPS

Miso is available from Asian food stores and health food stores. This dressing can be made in advance and stored in the refrigerator for up to 5 days. Stir thoroughly just before using.

1⅓ cups (12 oz/375 g) silken tofu
⅓ cup (3 fl oz/90 ml) freshly squeezed lemon juice
⅓ cup (3 fl oz/90 ml) lukewarm water
2 garlic cloves, minced
2 teaspoons miso
1 teaspoon wholegrain Dijon mustard
2 tablespoons sesame seeds, toasted

◆ Combine the tofu, lemon juice, water, garlic, miso and mustard in a blender or food processor. Process until smooth, stopping and scraping down the sides as needed.
◆ Add the sesame seeds and quickly process for a few seconds to coarsely blend in.
◆ Cover and store in the refrigerator if not using at once.

YUM MA MAUNG, NAM JIM

Shrimp and Mango Salad and Thai Dressing—Thailand

This salad combines seafood and tropical fruit with a fragrant light dressing. It is a luscious culinary experience that will leave you asking for more. Traditional Thai flavoring ingredients add an exotic touch to the dressing. The dressing not only tastes good, it is healthier and lower in fat than traditional mayonnaise or tartar sauce. Serve with warm bread to tear into bite-sized pieces and mop up the tangy dressing.

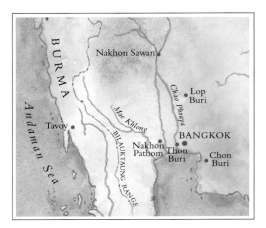

YUM MA MAUNG

Shrimp and Mango Salad

TOTAL TIME: 30 MINUTES

SERVES 4

To hasten the ripening process of mangos, place in a paper bag and store at room temperature. Mangos are ripe when the fruit yields slightly to the touch.

1 lb (500 g) jumbo shrimp
   (king prawns), heads removed
½ cup small snow peas
   (mangetout)
1 large mango
2 cups snow pea (mangetout) sprouts
1 quantity Thai Dressing (see
   recipe below)

◆ Peel and devein the shrimp. If they are thick, slice them in half lengthwise to better absorb the dressing.

◆ Bring water to a boil in a small steamer. Add the snow peas, cover and steam over medium-high heat until firm but tender, about 5 minutes. Remove the snow peas from the steamer and plunge into a bowl of iced water for about 20 seconds. Drain, then cover and refrigerate for 5 minutes. (Refreshing in ice preserves the fresh color and crisp texture of the vegetable.)

◆ Cut a thick slice from both flat sides of the mango. Score the flesh of each slice into cubes, being careful not to cut the skin. Turn inside-out by pushing the center of the slice up from the skin side and separate the cubes. Slice the cubes neatly away from the skin. Repeat the process with the narrow sides of the mango.

◆ Place the shrimp, snow peas, mango cubes and snow pea sprouts in a medium-sized salad bowl. Pour over the dressing and gently toss until the salad glistens with the dressing.

◆ Serve the salad at once.

NAM JIM

Thai Dressing

TOTAL TIME: 10 MINUTES

MAKES ⅓ CUP

Lemongrass, fish sauce, palm sugar, coriander and fresh red chilis are available in Asian food stores and in some supermarkets.

¼ cup coarsely chopped cilantro (coriander)
¼ cup (2 fl oz / 60 ml) freshly squeezed
   lime juice
2 teaspoons fish sauce
2 teaspoons thinly sliced lemongrass
2 teaspoons grated lime zest
2 teaspoons palm or light brown sugar
1 teaspoon finely chopped cilantro
   (coriander) root
1 teaspoon finely chopped fresh ginger
1 small red chili, seeded and finely
   chopped
1 garlic clove, minced
1 tablespoon canola oil or sunflower
   seed oil

◆ Combine all the ingredients in a glass jar with a plastic screw-top lid and shake well to combine.

◆ Store in the refrigerator until required. This dressing will store well for up to 6 weeks in the refrigerator.

LEMONGRASS

Lemongrass (Cymbopogon citratus) is an aromatic herb that grows in most tropical regions of the world. It grows in large clumps with thin, sharp-edged leaves and has a bulbous base similar to a leek or scallion. The base is cut up and used in curries and soups. Its subtle flavor complements the hot spices used in Asian cooking. The lower, more tender part of the stalk is pounded to release its strong lemon flavor. This is then used to give a dish the sharp freshness that is so characteristic of Thai and other Asian cuisines. Also known as citronella, lemongrass— in particular its oil—is used as an insect repellent.

Lemongrass can be bought in jars, dried or in powdered form. Lemongrass stalks are generally sold fresh in bunches from Asian food stores, and may be kept in the refrigerator for up to 2 weeks, or in a container of water in a cool area of the kitchen—change the water every day. Lemongrass can also be successfully frozen.

NEW AGE COLESLAW WITH TAHINI DRESSING

The United States

This popular high-fiber salad is most appealing when tossed with a delicious Tahini Dressing, which is lower in fat than mayonnaise-based dressings. Use it to dress other salads, and to spread on sandwiches. The salad vegetables in this coleslaw are given an extra fiber boost with the addition of seeds. Serve with rye or pumpernickel bread for a light meal.

NEW AGE COLESLAW

TOTAL TIME: 20 MINUTES

SERVES 4

To save time, cut the cabbage into wedges and then slice in a food processor fitted with the shredder attachment.

3 cups thinly sliced, tightly packed green cabbage
1 cup coarsely grated carrot
4 fresh dates, cut into thin strips
4 thinly sliced scallions (spring onions)
2 tablespoons golden raisins (sultanas)
2 tablespoons sunflower seeds
¼ teaspoon caraway seeds or fennel seeds
1 quantity Tahini Dressing (see recipe below)

◆ Combine the cabbage, carrot, dates, scallions, golden raisins, sunflower and caraway seeds in a large bowl and toss gently.
◆ Pour the Tahini Dressing over the salad and gently toss to coat. Cover with plastic wrap and chill for about 30 minutes before serving.
◆ Transfer the coleslaw to a serving bowl and serve at once.

TAHINI DRESSING

TOTAL TIME: 10 MINUTES

MAKES ½ CUP

Tahini Dressing can be made up in double quantity and stored, covered, in the refrigerator for up to 5 days. It can be used as a tasty substitute for margarine or butter.

2 tablespoons tahini
2 tablespoons low-fat, plain yogurt
1 tablespoon honey
1 tablespoon freshly squeezed lemon juice
1 tablespoon wholegrain mustard
1 teaspoon reduced-sodium tamari or reduced-sodium soy sauce
1 garlic clove, minced

◆ Combine the tahini, yogurt, honey, lemon juice, mustard, tamari and garlic in a glass jar with a plastic screw-top lid and shake well to combine.
◆ Use immediately or store as directed. Stir or shake well before using.

NUTRITION NOTES

PER SERVING—New Age Coleslaw:
152 calories/636 kilojoules; 5 g protein; 7.6 g fat, 44% of calories (1 g saturated, 5.8% of calories; 2.5 g monounsaturated, 14.5%; 4.1 g polyunsaturated, 23.7%); 17 g carbohydrate; 6.5 g dietary fiber; 139 mg sodium; 1.6 mg iron; 0.2 mg cholesterol.

PER ¼ CUP—Tahini Dressing:
144 calories/603 kilojoules; 5 g protein; 9.3 g fat, 59% of calories (1.3 g saturated, 8% of calories; 3.6 g monounsaturated, 23%; 4.4 g polyunsaturated, 28%); 10 g carbohydrate; 2.6 g dietary fiber; 213 mg sodium; 1 mg iron; 1 mg cholesterol.

CARROT, APPLE AND RAISIN SALAD AND CITRUS DRESSING

The United States

This salad is not only colorful; it's also very nutritious. Fresh, raw carrots are a good source of fiber and an excellent source of beta-carotene, which our bodies convert to vitamin A. Serve the salad with broiled chicken, or with cottage cheese for a light and delicious vegetarian meal. Try the Citrus Dressing with other salads, too.

CARROT, APPLE AND RAISIN SALAD

TOTAL TIME: 25 MINUTES

SERVES 4

Carrot ribbons require a little extra time and patience to prepare, but they look more elegant than grated carrot. A sharp, stainless steel vegetable peeler helps to make this preparation easier.

6 young carrots, about 1 lb (500 g)
1 medium red apple, thinly sliced into
    wedges
juice of 1 lemon
4 scallions (spring onions), thinly sliced
    diagonally
¼ cup (1½ oz/45 g) golden raisins
    (sultanas)
¼ cup finely chopped flat-leaf parsley
1 quantity Citrus Dressing (see recipe
    below)
8 romaine (cos) lettuce leaves

◆ Using a sharp vegetable peeler, cut each carrot lengthwise into long thin ribbons. Set aside.
◆ Place the apple wedges in a small bowl, pour over the lemon juice and stir or toss to coat.
◆ Combine the carrot ribbons, apple, scallions, golden raisins and flat-leaf parsley in a medium-sized bowl.
◆ Pour the Citrus Dressing over the carrot mixture and gently toss to mix.
◆ Tear the lettuce leaves into small pieces, place in a shallow serving bowl and arrange the carrot mixture on top.
◆ Serve the salad at once.

CITRUS DRESSING

TOTAL TIME: 10 MINUTES

MAKES ⅔ CUP

Macadamia nut oil and olive oil both help lower blood cholesterol, and either will give a delicious rich flavor to the dressing.

juice of 1 orange
1 tablespoon macadamia nut oil or extra-
    virgin olive oil
1 tablespoon apple cider vinegar
1 teaspoon finely chopped fresh ginger
1 teaspoon wholegrain mustard
1 garlic clove, minced

◆ Combine the orange juice, oil, vinegar, ginger, mustard and garlic in a glass jar with a plastic screw-top lid and shake well to combine.
◆ Store in the refrigerator until required.

CURRIED RICE AND CHICKEN SALAD

The United States

Rice, one of the most important grains in the world, is high in dietary fiber. It helps maintain a healthy digestive system and is a good source of B-complex vitamins. Multi-grain rice, used in this healthy salad, is a mixture of brown rice and wild rice. Despite its name, wild rice is actually the seed of a native American grass. Serve this dish as a main course accompanied by a green salad for a well-balanced meal.

TOTAL TIME: 1 HOUR

SERVES 4

Use a mixture of red, green and yellow peppers for a colorful variation.

2 cups (16 fl oz/500 ml) water
1 cup (6 oz/185 g) multi-grain rice (see Glossary)
1 lb (500 g) boneless, skinless, chicken breasts
½ cup (4 fl oz/125 ml) dry white wine
2 teaspoons wholegrain mustard
¼ teaspoon salt
½ cup red bell pepper (capsicum) cut into ¼ in (6 mm) dice
2 tablespoons slivered almonds, toasted

1 cup green seedless grapes, halved lengthwise
watercress sprigs or snow pea (mangetout) sprouts, for garnish

CURRY DRESSING

¾ cup (5 oz/155 g) low-fat, plain yogurt
¼ cup (2 fl oz/60 ml) freshly squeezed orange juice
2 tablespoons mango chutney, fruit finely diced
2 teaspoons medium-hot curry paste or curry powder
½ teaspoon honey

◆ Bring the water to a boil in a medium-sized, heavy-bottomed saucepan. Add the rice and stir well. Cover the saucepan, reduce the heat to medium-low and simmer until tender, 30 to 35 minutes. Remove the lid and stir with a fork. Transfer the rice to a mixing bowl and set aside to cool.

◆ Place the chicken pieces between 2 sheets of waxed (greaseproof) paper. Beat with a mallet or the handle of a large knife until flattened to an even thickness, about ½ inch (1 cm). Cut the chicken into long, finger-width strips.

◆ Place the chicken in a large, non-stick frying pan. Add the wine, mustard and salt. Cover and bring to a boil over medium heat.

◆ Reduce the heat to medium-low and poach the chicken until tender, about 5 minutes. Remove from the heat and set aside to cool in the cooking liquid.

◆ While the rice and chicken are cooling, combine the dressing ingredients in a small bowl and mix well. Cover with plastic wrap and chill in the refrigerator until needed.

◆ Add the bell pepper, almonds and half the grapes to the rice. Stir gently until evenly combined.

◆ Add the dressing and half of the chicken strips. Fold in with a rubber spatula until well mixed.

◆ Arrange the rice mixture on a serving platter. Using a slotted spoon, remove the remaining chicken strips from the pan and arrange on top of the rice. Spoon half the cooking liquid over the salad and sprinkle the remaining grapes on top.

◆ Cover the salad with plastic wrap and chill for no longer than 30 minutes.

◆ Garnish with the watercress sprigs and serve immediately.

ALMONDS

The almond (Prunus dulcis) is a member of the peach family and its kernels are among the world's most enjoyed nuts. Probably originating in central Asia, almonds have been found on Crete among Bronze Age relics. There are also references to almonds in the Bible. Today half of the world's supply is grown in California. There are two main types of almond: sweet, which is the familiar nut used for snacking and in cooking, and bitter (used mainly for its non-drying oil), which contains prussic acid and should never be eaten raw. Almonds are used whole, chopped, slivered or ground, blanched or toasted. Toasting can intensify the taste of the nut and toasted almonds are often used in salads or as a garnish where they add texture and flavor. Almond paste is made from finely ground blanched almonds and is used to decorate cakes. Almonds are high in monounsaturated oil, and a good source of fiber and vitamin E. The nuts are available from supermarkets and good food stores and should be kept in an airtight container either in the refrigerator or in a cool, dark place and used within 6 months.

NUTRITION NOTES

PER SERVING: 442 calories/1850 kilojoules; 38 g protein; 6.5 g fat, 13% of calories (1.4 g saturated, 2.8% of calories; 3.7 g monounsaturated, 7.4%; 1.4 g polyunsaturated, 2.8%); 53 g carbohydrate; 2.6 g dietary fiber; 316 mg sodium; 1.7 mg iron; 63 mg cholesterol.

SIDES & SNACKS

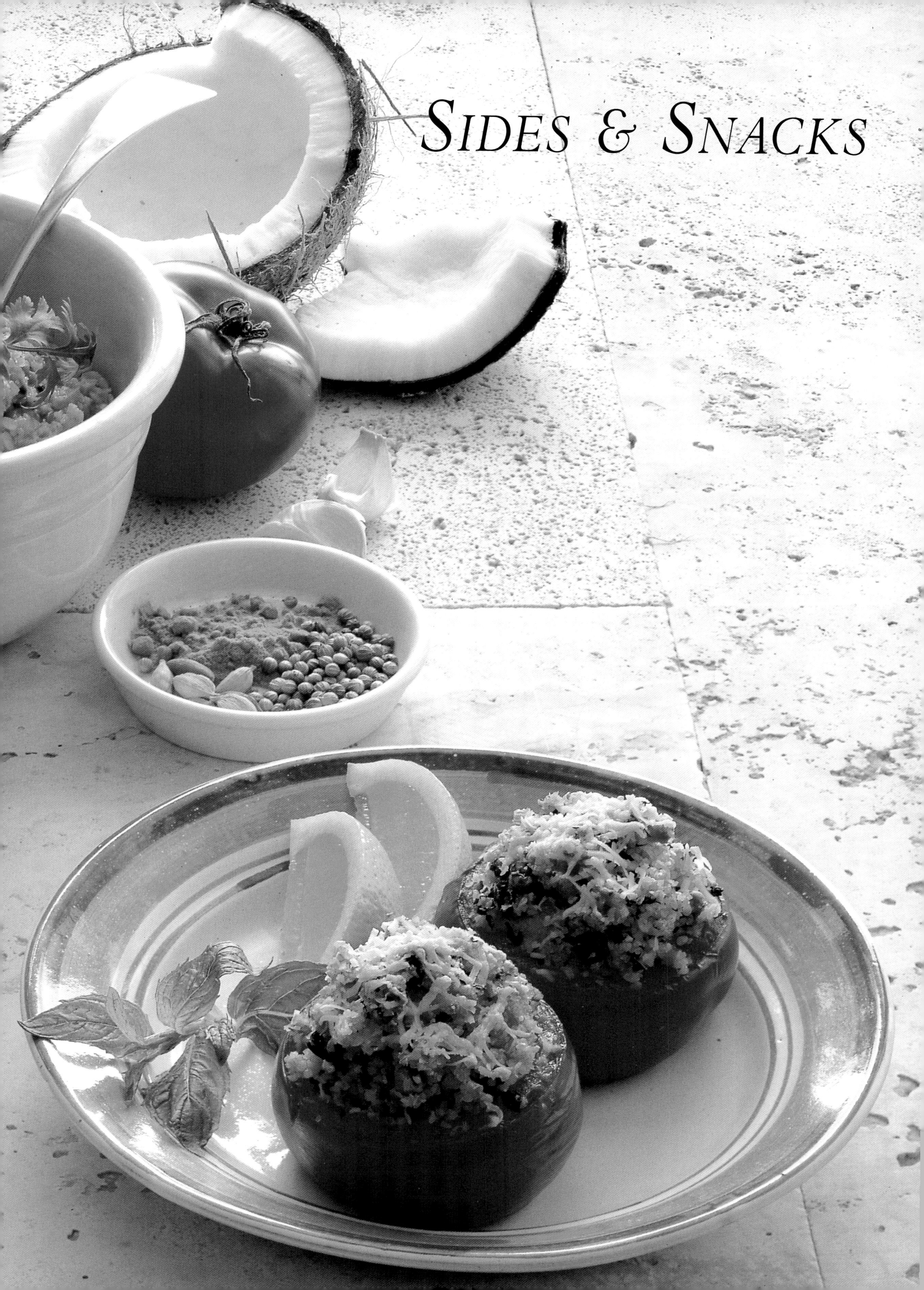

A snack is a casual or hurried mini-meal. As lifestyles become busier and mealtimes more flexible, the snack has come into its own. The sports enthusiast enjoys a snack after morning training; the student grabs a snack after a late class; the worker compensates for working through lunchtime with an afternoon snack; and the teenager seems to need a continual supply of snacks just to survive until the next meal. The important factor in the definition of a snack is that it is indeed a mini-meal and so it should be nutritionally well-balanced. A good snack should provide protein, carbohydrate, vitamins and minerals, and satisfy hunger.

Your health is precious! Surely it is worth some time spent preparing healthy snacks. The highly profitable snack food

and fast food industries can be improved upon quite easily at home, both nutritionally and financially. Tasty snacks can be quick, easy and relatively cheap. Choose ingredients such as reduced-fat cheese, lean, low-sodium ham or fish canned in springwater and arrange them on toasted bagels, foccacia or bruschetta. Then top with a colorful selection of salad ingredients and a few pickled vegetables.

In hot weather, the easiest and simplest snacks consist of fresh fruit and raw vegetable sticks, with or without healthy low-fat dips. In cold weather, try wholewheat toasted sandwiches or your favorite bread topped with healthy ingredients. These can be accompanied by a bowl of steaming high-fiber soup.

Tasty snacks such as these provide an attractive powerhouse of nourishing food high in fiber and low in fat. Follow our recipes here for more healthy alternatives.

"Sides" is a relatively new word in the vocabulary of cooking and eating. It refers to a dish that complements and enhances the main part of the meal. The term comes from the accompanying dishes that are sometimes displayed on a sideboard or side table in formal dining rooms. The side dish gives the cook an opportunity to add nutritional balance to the main course.

While a selection of simply prepared fresh vegetables will always be a popular

complement to the main course, there are many other options available. Try new combinations of vegetables and other ingredients, or choose a cereal like quinoa, rice or bulghur, flavored with a variety of herbs and spices.

The following recipes will inspire you to prepare healthy and delicious snacks and side dishes from around the world.

Try the tasty Tempeh and Tomato Roll, from Indonesia; or the satisfying Lean Beef Club Sandwich, from the United States. These are quick-to-fix snacks which serve two and can be halved easily to make one portion or doubled to serve four.

There are also some excellent ideas for healthy family snacks—the delicious Egg and Sprouts Lavash, from Lebanon, is an unusual and refreshing, hot-weather snack; alternatively, try the light and easy Squash Frittata, from Italy; or choose the Mediterranean-style Bulghur-Stuffed Tomatoes, from Greece.

For more sustaining family snacks, try the spicy Curried Vegetables on Chapatis, from India; or the satisfying Stuffed Baked Potatoes, from Britain—both bursting with wholesome fiber-rich ingredients.

Left: *Chinese vegetables are often stir-fried so that the flavor and crunchy texture are retained.* Below: *An open-air market in Da Lat showcases the raw ingredients of Vietnamese cuisine.*

For in-between meal snacking, there is the traditional *Falafel* from Lebanon—baked, not fried! These versatile chickpea balls are also ideal to serve with healthy dips (see page 56) to offer nourishment while satisfying hunger.

Sandwiches make great snacks, with fillings limited only by your imagination. A healthy Wholegrain Roll, from the United States is the perfect base for salad, lean meat, cheese or low-fat spreads in any combination.

For more interesting side dishes that add nutritional balance to a main course of simply prepared meat, chicken or fish, try the tender, crisp Stir-Fried Vegetables, from China; Eggplant with Spicy Yogurt, from Russia; Black-Eyed Peas and Vegetable Bredie, from South Africa; Brussels Sprouts and Cauliflower in Cashew Apple Sauce, from the United States; or Cornbread with Vegetable Sauce, from Mexico. These are all high-fiber, low-fat dishes with their own light tasty sauce supplied as an added attraction. There is no need to make a fatty, high-salt sauce to moisten the meal.

This chapter also features some traditional healthy Indian side dishes including Lemon Saffron Rice, Spicy Dahl and Spicy Sweet Potato with Peas. These are flavorful high-fiber, low-fat dishes that are perfect to serve with your next curry.

Finally, there is a selection of side dishes featuring wholegrain cereals that have passed the test of time. Brown Rice Pilaf, from Greece; Bulghur Risotto, from Russia; and Savory Quinoa, from Mexico, are all high in fiber and delicious.

All of the recipes in Sides and Snacks are satisfying and good for you—enjoy them.

Above: *Freshly roasted sweet potatoes make a hot treat for visitors to the Todaiji Temple near Nara, Japan.*

Top: *Traditional methods for harvesting rice are still used in many parts of southern and central China, where rice is part of every meal.*

STUFFED BAKED POTATOES

Britain

Savory-filled or stuffed baked potatoes in their "jackets" are healthy and appetizing. As a snack, they can be economical and are a popular choice for today's lifestyle. Potatoes are rich in vitamin C and provide fiber and carbohydrate. Two choices of filling are given here—one needs only to be quickly mixed together and the other requires only a minimum of cooking. Try your own combinations for variety.

TOTAL TIME: 1½ HOURS

SERVES 4

Choose wide, flat, oval potatoes for stuffing. Look for reduced-sodium, reduced-fat ham in the cold cuts (or delicatessen) section of the supermarket.

4 large baking potatoes, preferably Idaho
    (or Pontiac or Desiree), about 7 oz
    (220 g) each
olive oil cooking spray

FILLING 1

1 cup (8 oz/250 g) reduced-sodium,
    low-fat cottage cheese
½ cup (2 oz/60 g) grated reduced-fat
    Cheddar cheese
½ cup (3 oz/90 g) low-fat, plain yogurt
2 large, vine-ripened tomatoes, cut into
    ¼ inch (6 mm) dice
2 tablespoons snipped chives or finely
    chopped parsley

FILLING 2

1 tablespoon margarine or butter
1 cup (2½ oz/75 g) coarsely chopped
    mushrooms
2 oz (60 g) reduced-sodium, reduced-fat
    ham, chopped
½ cup (4 fl oz/125 ml) buttermilk
¼ cup sliced scallions (spring onions)
1 tablespoon thyme leaves
2 teaspoons wholegrain mustard

◆ Preheat the oven to 400°F (200°C).
◆ Remove the eyes from the potatoes with a small sharp knife. Scrub the potatoes and dry them well with a kitchen towel. Prick their skins in several places with a metal skewer.
◆ Arrange the potatoes on a shelf in the oven so that they are not touching and bake until tender, about 45 minutes.
◆ While the potatoes are cooking prepare your choice of filling.

◆ _Filling 1:_ Combine the cottage cheese, Cheddar cheese, yogurt, tomatoes and chives in a medium-sized bowl. Mix well.
◆ _Filling 2:_ Melt the margarine in a medium-sized, heavy-bottomed frying pan over medium heat. Add the mushrooms and sauté, stirring frequently, until tender, about 5 minutes. Transfer the mushrooms to a small bowl and set aside to cool for 2 to 3 minutes. Combine the mushrooms, ham, buttermilk, scallions, thyme and mustard in a small bowl. Mix well.
◆ Remove the potatoes from the oven and set aside until cool enough to handle.
◆ Cut a slice, about ½ inch (1 cm), off the top of each potato. Scoop the cooked flesh out with a teaspoon. Place in a potato ricer and purée (or transfer to a bowl and mash coarsely with a fork or potato masher).
◆ Lightly spray the potato shells inside and outside with the cooking spray.
◆ Place the potato shells on a baking tray and bake until warmed through, about 10 minutes.

◆ Meanwhile, combine the chosen filling and the potato purée in a medium-sized bowl and stir well until combined.
◆ Spoon the mixture into the potato shells, dividing equally.
◆ Return the filled potatoes to the oven and bake until hot and the filling is golden brown on top, about 15 minutes.
◆ Serve immediately for a snack.

NUTRITION NOTES

PER SERVING—USING FILLING 1:
261 calories/1096 kilojoules; 20 g protein; 6.4 g fat, 22% of calories (3.1 g saturated, 11% of calories; 2.4 g monounsaturated, 8%; 0.9 g polyunsaturated, 3%); 30 g carbohydrate; 4.3 g dietary fiber; 274 mg sodium; 1.4 mg iron; 20 mg cholesterol.

PER SERVING—USING FILLING 2
(Analysis uses monounsaturated margarine): 241 calories/1013 kilojoules; 13 g protein; 8 g fat, 30% of calories (1.4 g saturated, 5% of calories; 4.8 g monounsaturated, 18%; 1.8 g polyunsaturated, 7%); 28 g carbohydrate; 4.1 g dietary fiber; 418 mg sodium; 1.2 mg iron; 13 mg cholesterol.

CHAO JUP CHOY

Stir-Fried Vegetables—China

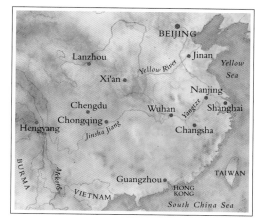

Stir-frying vegetables helps to retain nutrients, gives a lovely fresh color and ensures a pleasant, crisp texture. You can substitute other vegetables in this recipe: sweet potatoes in place of the carrots, sugar snap peas or asparagus in place of the snow peas; and broccoli florets or spinach instead of the Chinese greens, for example. Serve stir-fried vegetables as a side dish with broiled fish or lean beef.

TOTAL TIME: 30 MINUTES

SERVES 4

Allow 2 to 2½ hours additional time if the Vegetable Stock is not already prepared. Thorough preparation is one of the secrets to successful stir-frying. Be sure to have all the vegetables prepared before you even reach for the wok! A Chinese chan is a special wooden spatula.

1 tablespoon cornstarch (cornflour)
2 tablespoons mirin or dry sherry
1 tablespoon hoisin sauce or oyster sauce
1 tablespoon reduced-sodium soy sauce
  or tamari
¾ cup (6 fl oz/185 ml) Vegetable Stock
  (page 52)
1 tablespoon peanut or canola oil
2 medium onions, each cut into 12 wedges
2 garlic cloves, minced
¾ inch (2 cm) piece fresh ginger, finely chopped
1 cup (about 5 oz/155 g) carrots, thinly
  sliced diagonally
1 medium red bell pepper (capsicum),
  seeded and thinly sliced
1 stalk celery, thinly sliced diagonally
1 cup shredded Chinese greens (Chinese
  cabbage, bok choy or similar), firmly packed
1 cup snow peas (mangetout) or green
  beans, trimmed
4 scallions (spring onions), sliced in ¾ inch
  (2 cm) pieces
1 cup mung bean sprouts
herbs, for garnish, optional

◆ In a small bowl, blend the cornstarch with the mirin, hoisin sauce and soy sauce until smooth. Add the stock and mix well.
◆ Heat the oil in a non-stick wok, or large, non-stick frying pan over medium–high heat. Add the onion, garlic and ginger and stir-fry, using a wooden spoon or a Chinese chan, for 1 minute.
◆ Add the carrots, bell pepper and celery and stir-fry for 2 minutes.
◆ Add the Chinese greens, snow peas and scallions and stir-fry for 1 minute.

◆ Add the stock mixture and bring to a boil, stirring constantly. Reduce the heat to low and simmer until the vegetables are firm but tender, about 1 minute.
◆ Stir in the bean sprouts and cook until heated through, about 10 seconds.
◆ Garnish with your choice of herbs, if using, and serve at once.

NUTRITION NOTES

PER SERVING: 108 calories/455 kilojoules; 4 g protein; 4.4 g fat, 35% of calories (0.5 g saturated, 4% of calories; 2.4 g monounsaturated, 19.1%; 1.5 g polyunsaturated, 11.9%); 12 g carbohydrate; 5.5 g dietary fiber; 255 mg sodium; 1.3 mg iron; 0 mg cholesterol.

DOMÁTES YEMISTÉS, PILÁFI ME SKOÚRO RÍZI

Bulghur-Stuffed Tomatoes and Brown Rice Pilaf—Greece

Tasty Bulghur-Stuffed Tomatoes make a great sustaining snack for people on the run. The complex carbohydrate stuffing can be used to fill other vegetables, like bell peppers, eggplant, zucchini and large flat mushroom caps. Serve as a snack or as a side dish with broiled fish or grilled chicken. Brown Rice Pilaf is high in dietary fiber and B-complex vitamins. Serve with lamb dishes.

Bulghur-Stuffed Tomatoes and Brown Rice Pilaf (top)

DOMÁTES YEMISTÉS

Bulghur-Stuffed Tomatoes

TOTAL TIME: 1 HOUR

SERVES 4

Garlic lovers may like to use garlic-flavored olive oil, available in most specialty food stores and some supermarkets.

¾ cup (4 oz / 125 g) fine-grade bulghur
4 large, vine-ripened tomatoes
1 tablespoon virgin olive oil
4 scallions (spring onions), thinly sliced
1 garlic clove, minced
½ cup (2 oz / 60 g) freshly grated, fat-reduced Cheddar or mozzarella cheese
½ cup (2½ oz / 75 g) green peas
¼ cup shredded mint
juice of 1 lemon
¼ teaspoon freshly ground black pepper
¼ cup (1 oz / 30 g) freshly grated Parmesan cheese
mint sprigs, for garnish
lemon wedges, for garnish

◆ Preheat the oven to 325°F (160°C).
◆ Place the bulghur in a medium-sized bowl and add cold water to cover. Set aside to soak until soft, about 15 minutes. Drain through a cheesecloth-lined sieve. Gather up the ends of the cheesecloth around the bulghur and squeeze out as much water as possible. Transfer to a large bowl.
◆ Cut a slice ½ inch (1 cm) from the smooth end of the tomatoes, opposite the stalk end. (The stuffed tomatoes stand upright better on the stalk end.) Using a small teaspoon, scoop out the seeds and juices. (Reserve these juices for use later in a soup, sauce or casserole.) Scoop out the soft flesh into a small bowl and set aside.
◆ Stand the tomatoes cut side down on a plate to drain while preparing the filling.
◆ Chop the reserved tomato flesh into ¼ inch (6 mm) pieces and add to the bowl.
◆ Heat the oil in a small, non-stick frying pan over medium heat. Add the scallions and garlic and sauté, stirring constantly, until softened, about 1 minute. Add to the bulghur mixture.
◆ Add the Cheddar cheese, peas, mint, lemon juice and pepper to the bulghur mixture. Mix well.
◆ Place the tomatoes, stem-side down, in a baking dish. Spoon the bulghur mixture into the tomato cases, dividing equally. Sprinkle with the Parmesan cheese.
◆ Bake the tomatoes until just tender, 20 to 25 minutes.
◆ Serve immediately, garnished with the mint sprigs and lemon wedges.

PILÁFI ME SKOÚRO RÍZI

Brown Rice Pilaf

TOTAL TIME: 1 HOUR

SERVES 4

Use a food processor to chop the vegetables in this and similar recipes. It saves time and is very efficient.

1 cup (6½ oz / 200 g) brown rice
1 tablespoon virgin olive oil
1 cup (2½ oz / 75 g) finely chopped mushroom caps
1 large onion, finely chopped
1 zucchini or 2 okra, thinly sliced, about 3 oz (90 g)
¼ cup (1½ oz / 45 g) currants
grated zest and juice of 1 lemon
¼ cup chopped oregano or marjoram
1 tablespoon shelled pistachio nuts, coarsely chopped
1 tablespoon sesame seeds, toasted
sprigs of oregano, for garnish

◆ Bring a large saucepan of water to a boil over high heat. Stir in the rice and cook, uncovered, until tender, about 35 minutes. Drain and rinse under hot running water to separate the grains. Set aside.

◆ Heat the oil in a large, heavy-bottomed frying pan over medium-high heat. Add the mushrooms and onion. Cook, stirring occasionally, until the onion is softened, about 5 minutes.
◆ Reduce the heat to medium and add the zucchini, currants, lemon zest and juice. Stir well, cover and cook until the zucchini is tender, about 4 minutes.
◆ Add the rice, chopped oregano, pistachios and sesame seeds. Stir until the rice is heated through, about 5 minutes.
◆ Transfer the pilaf to a warm serving bowl, garnish with the oregano sprigs and serve immediately.

NUTRITION NOTES

PER SERVING—Bulghur-Stuffed Tomatoes:
256 calories / 1075 kilojoules; 14 g protein; 11 g fat, 38% of calories (4.9 g saturated, 17% of calories; 4.9 g monounsaturated, 17%; 1.2 g polyunsaturated, 4%); 25 g carbohydrate; 9.5 g dietary fiber; 233 mg sodium; 2.6 mg iron; 18 mg cholesterol.

PER SERVING—Brown Rice Pilaf:
296 calories / 1242 kilojoules; 7 g protein; 7.7 g fat, 24% of calories (1.2 g saturated, 4% of calories; 4.5 g monounsaturated, 14%; 2 g polyunsaturated, 6%); 49 g carbohydrate; 5.2 g dietary fiber; 14 mg sodium; 1.5 mg iron; 0 mg cholesterol.

PISTACHIO NUTS

The pistachio nut (Pistacia vera) is small and pale green with a thin, reddish skin which is enclosed in a smooth, brittle, cream- or red-colored shell. The fruit of a tree native to the Middle East and Asia, the pistachio nut has long been prized for its unique flavor and color. The nut is now widely grown in the countries of the Mediterranean region, India, eastern Asia, Mexico and on the west coast of the United States. The delicate, sweet taste of pistachio nuts complements savory dishes well, in particular those using white meats. Pistachio nuts can be salted and served as a snack, or used plain in salads and cooked dishes. To use in cooking, break the shell open and take the kernel out. The kernel can be used whole or ground or chopped. The subtle shade of green has made the nut popular for use in pastry, cookies, cakes, desserts and especially in ice creams and confectionery. They are often included in manufactured pâtés and sausages to give a richer flavor. Pistachio nuts are high in monounsaturated oil, calcium, iron and vitamin A. They are available all year, shelled or unshelled, raw or roasted. When purchasing unshelled pistachios select ones that are partially open—this indicates that the nut is ripe. It also makes the pistachio nut easier to extract. Store the nuts in an airtight container.

Masala Aloo Mattur, Nimbu Kesar Chaval

Spicy Sweet Potato with Peas and Lemon Saffron Rice—India

*T*he cultivation of rice originated in India during Neolithic times and now it is the staple food of the region. It is low in fat and is a good source of carbohydrate. Lemon Saffron Rice combines this cherished grain with a wondrous blend of spices. Serve with fish, meat and vegetables. Spicy Sweet Potato with Peas is a colorful dish that can be served with broiled fish or chicken.

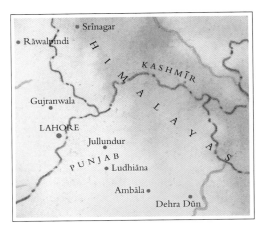

Spicy Sweet Potato with Peas and Lemon Saffron Rice (top)

MASALA ALOO MATTUR

Spicy Sweet Potato with Peas

TOTAL TIME: 50 MINUTES

SERVES 6

This sweet potato dish is subtly spiced and flavored with orange juice. Crisp snow peas and sugar snap peas add color and texture.

2 teaspoons ground cumin
1 teaspoon ground coriander
1 teaspoon ground turmeric
1 tablespoon plus 1 teaspoon canola or safflower oil
2 garlic cloves, minced
3 medium (orange) sweet potatoes, about 1 lb (500 g), peeled and sliced ¼ inch (6 mm) thick
½ cup (4 fl oz / 125 ml) freshly squeezed orange juice
4 oz (125 g) snow peas (mangetout), trimmed
4 oz (125 g) sugar snap peas, trimmed
2 tablespoons sunflower seeds, toasted

◆ Mix the cumin, coriander and turmeric together in a small bowl.
◆ Heat 2 teaspoons of the oil in a large, non-stick frying pan over medium heat. Add half the spice mixture and half the garlic and cook, stirring constantly, until the flavors are blended, about 1 minute.
◆ Add half the sweet potatoes and sauté, turning occasionally, until tender, 8 to 10 minutes. Using a slotted spoon, transfer the cooked sweet potatoes to a plate.
◆ Heat the remaining oil in the frying pan and cook the remaining spices, garlic and sweet potatoes in the same manner.
◆ Return the first batch of sweet potatoes to the cooked potatoes in the frying pan. Add the orange juice, then cover, reduce the heat and simmer until all the potatoes are heated through, about 5 minutes.
◆ Add the snow peas and sugar snap peas and increase the heat to medium. Cook, covered, until the vegetables are firm but tender, about 6 minutes.
◆ Transfer the mixture to a warm serving platter. Sprinkle the sunflower seeds on top and serve immediately.

NIMBU KESAR CHAVAL

Lemon Saffron Rice

TOTAL TIME : 50 MINUTES

SERVES 4

Cook the rice in a cast iron, ceramic-lined Dutch oven to help prevent it from sticking.

SAFFRON

Saffron comes from the stigmas of the light purple, autumn-flowering crocus (Crocus sativus) *that originally grew wild in Asia Minor and the countries of the Mediterranean region. The flower, which produces 3 stigmas, is hand picked and then the stigmas (saffron threads) dried. About 25,000 blooms are needed to make 1 pound (500 g) of saffron threads which makes it the world's most expensive spice. However, only a small amount is needed to add an intense aroma and deep orange color to a dish. In ancient times saffron was sought after for its medicinal properties, and was also used as a fabric dye, particularly in India. Today, the cost of saffron means that the spice is used mainly for cooking. Although saffron is used in the cuisine of many countries, people associate it with that of India, where this crocus is cultivated in huge fields. It is most often used to enhance rice with its aromatic flavor and beautiful color, and is used as an essential ingredient in traditional dishes like* bouillabaisse *and* paella. *It is also used in sauces and baked foods. Saffron threads impart a better flavor than powdered saffron. For the best flavor crush the saffron threads and soak in warm water for 10 to 15 minutes just before using. Save the soaking liquid for use in soups, stews and sauces. Both the threads and the powder should be stored in airtight containers and used within 6 months of purchase.*

1½ cups (10 oz / 300 g) basmati rice or long-grain rice
1 teaspoon saffron threads
2½ cups (20 fl oz / 625 ml) plus 2 tablespoons boiling water
1 tablespoon canola or safflower oil
1 large onion, finely chopped
1 cinnamon stick
¼ teaspoon ground cinnamon
4 whole cloves
2 whole star anise
finely grated zest of 1 lemon
¼ cup (2 fl oz / 60 ml) freshly squeezed lemon juice
2 tablespoons slivered almonds, toasted, optional
2 tablespoons shredded coconut, toasted, optional
cilantro (coriander) sprigs, for garnish
lemon wedges, for garnish

◆ Wash the rice under cold running water until the water runs clear. Drain well.
◆ Place the saffron in a small bowl, add 2 tablespoons of the boiling water and set aside to let the threads dissolve, at least 10 minutes.
◆ Meanwhile, heat the oil in a large, heavy-bottomed saucepan over medium-high heat. Add the onion, cinnamon stick, ground cinnamon, cloves and star anise. Cook, stirring frequently, until the onion is soft and golden, about 8 minutes.

◆ Using a slotted spoon, transfer half of the onion mixture from the saucepan to a small bowl, cover and keep warm.
◆ Add the rice to the saucepan and stir constantly until it is pale golden in color, about 5 minutes.
◆ Add the saffron with its liquid and the remaining boiling water to the rice mixture. Bring to a boil, reduce the heat to low, cover and cook until the rice is tender and has absorbed the liquid, about 20 minutes.
◆ Discard the cinnamon stick, cloves and star anise. Add the lemon zest and lemon juice to the rice and gently mix with a fork.
◆ Place the rice mixture in a warm serving bowl, sprinkle with the reserved onion, the almonds and coconut shreds, if using. Garnish with the cilantro sprigs and lemon wedges and serve at once.

NUTRITION NOTES

PER SERVING—Spicy Sweet Potato with Peas:
135 calories / 569 kilojoules; 4 g protein; 5.1 g fat, 34% of calories (0.6 g saturated, 4% of calories; 2.4 g monounsaturated, 16%; 2.1 g polyunsaturated, 14%); 18 g carbohydrate; 3.8 g dietary fiber; 12 mg sodium; 1.3 mg iron; 0 mg cholesterol.

PER SERVING—Lemon Saffron Rice:
304 calories / 1277 kilojoules; 5 g protein; 4 g fat, 12% of calories (0.4 g saturated, 1.2% of calories; 2.4 g monounsaturated, 7.2%; 1.2 g polyunsaturated, 3.6%); 61 g carbohydrate; 2.2 g dietary fiber; 9 mg sodium; 0.7 mg iron; 0 mg cholesterol.

SUBZI CHAPATI, MASALAKI DAHL

Curried Vegetables on Chapatis and Spicy Dahl—India

Vegetables in contrasting colors and textures can be combined to make a curry appealing to both the eye and the palate. The Curried Vegetables here are an excellent choice for cooking in advance as they mature in flavor when allowed to stand overnight. Lentils are richer in protein than all other legumes except soy beans. Red lentils are called for in this recipe for Spicy Dahl but any variety can be used. Serve with rice and almost any curry dish.

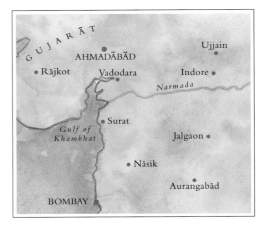

Curried Vegetables on Chapatis (top) and Spicy Dahl

SUBZI CHAPATI
Curried Vegetables on Chapatis

TOTAL TIME: 1 HOUR 10 MINUTES
SERVES 6

Allow 2 to 2½ hours additional time if the Vegetable Stock is not already prepared. Homemade Chapatis can be prepared while the vegetables are simmering. Use an electric coffee grinder, spice grinder or food processor to prepare the masala. To cut down on fat, chill the canned coconut milk and allow the thick solids to rise to the top. Remove the thick solids and use the thin liquid underneath for a healthier dish. Three tablespoons of good-quality, prepared curry paste can be substituted for the masala, if desired.

MASALA

1 tablespoon poppy seeds
1 teaspoon cardamom seeds
6 whole cloves
2 tablespoons raw cashew nuts, coarsely chopped
1 tablespoon water
1 small green chili, seeded and finely chopped
1 teaspoon finely chopped fresh ginger
1 garlic clove, crushed

1 tablespoon canola or safflower oil
1 medium onion, coarsely chopped
1 medium carrot, sliced
1 cup diced butternut squash (butternut pumpkin) in ¾ inch (2 cm) pieces
1 medium potato cut into ¾ inch (2 cm) cubes
1 large, vine-ripened tomato, coarsely chopped
¼ cup (2 fl oz/60 ml) unsweetened coconut milk
¾ cup (6 fl oz/185 ml) Vegetable Stock (see page 52)
1 cup (4 oz/125 g) green peas or sliced green beans
¼ cup (1½ oz/45 g) low-fat, plain yogurt
12 warm Homemade Chapatis (see page 31), for serving

◆ To make the masala, place the poppy seeds, cardamom seeds and cloves in an electric coffee grinder or spice grinder and grind until the spices are coarsely ground, about 2 minutes. Combine the cashews, water, chili, ginger and garlic in a blender or food processor. Add the ground spices and mix until a smooth paste is formed, stopping and scraping down the sides as needed.
◆ Heat the oil in a large, heavy-bottomed saucepan over medium heat. Add the onion and sauté, stirring occasionally, until softened, about 5 minutes.
◆ Add the masala mixture and stir for 1 minute to release the flavor of the spices.
◆ Add the carrot, butternut squash, potato, tomato, coconut milk and stock to the pan. Bring to a boil, stirring occasionally. Reduce the heat to medium-low, cover and simmer until the vegetables are almost tender, about 25 minutes.
◆ Add the peas and simmer until tender, about 10 minutes longer.
◆ Reduce the heat to low and stir in the yogurt. Gently heat through without boiling. (The yogurt will curdle if the mixture boils.)
◆ Serve the curried vegetables over the warm chapatis.

MASALAKI DAHL
Spicy Dahl

TOTAL TIME: 35 MINUTES
SERVES 4

If you are on a low-fat diet, follow the directions at the start of the preceding recipe. Alternatively, the coconut milk may be replaced with chicken or vegetable stock.

1 cup (6½ oz/200 g) red lentils
3 cups (24 fl oz/750 ml) water
1 tablespoon plus 1 teaspoon canola or sunflower-seed oil
1 teaspoon mustard seeds
1 teaspoon ground cardamom
1 teaspoon ground coriander
1 teaspoon ground cumin
½ teaspoon ground turmeric
1 medium onion, finely chopped
1 garlic clove, minced
pinch salt
¼ cup (2 fl oz/60 ml) unsweetened coconut milk
juice of 1 lemon
¼ cup shredded mint
mint sprigs, for garnish
lemon wedges, for serving

◆ Rinse the lentils in cold water and drain. Bring the water to a boil in a medium-sized saucepan. Add the lentils, stir well with a wooden spoon, cover and cook over medium heat until tender, about 10 minutes. Drain and set aside.
◆ Heat the oil in a large frying pan over medium heat. Add the mustard seeds and cook until they start to "pop" or burst, about 2 minutes.
◆ Add the cardamom, coriander, cumin and turmeric and stir constantly until the flavors are blended, about 1 minute.
◆ Add the onion and garlic. Cook, stirring frequently, until the onion is softened, about 5 minutes.
◆ Add the lentils, salt, coconut milk, lemon juice and shredded mint to the pan. Bring to a boil, stirring constantly, until heated through. Remove from the heat.
◆ Transfer the mixture to a warm serving bowl, garnish with the mint sprigs and serve with the lemon wedges.

NUTRITION NOTES

PER SERVING—Curried Vegetables on Chapatis: 378 calories/1588 kilojoules; 13 g protein; 15 g fat, 37% of calories (3.5 g saturated, 8.6% of calories; 7.9 g monounsaturated, 19.5%; 3.6 g polyunsaturated, 8.9%); 46 g carbohydrate; 11 g dietary fiber; 64 mg sodium; 3.6 mg iron; 0.5 mg cholesterol.

PER SERVING—Spicy Dahl: 209 calories/878 kilojoules; 13 g protein; 8.2 g fat, 36% of calories (2.7 g saturated, 11.9% of calories; 3.4 g monounsaturated, 14.9%; 2.1g polyunsaturated, 9.2%); 20 g carbohydrate; 7.9 g dietary fiber; 104 mg sodium; 4.3 mg iron; 0 mg cholesterol.

CARDAMOM

Native to India, cardamom (Elettaria cardamomum) is a highly aromatic plant with a pungent, sweet, spicy flavor. The cardamom pods—either green or bleached white—are small, thin-skinned capsules that contain up to 20 red-brown to black seeds. Used to flavor curries, sweetmeats and coffee in its native India, cardamom is not often used in North America or Europe. In Arab countries, cardamom seeds, either on their own or mixed with other spices such as cloves, are offered as a digestive to chew on after a meal. Cardamom can be bought either in the pod, as seeds or ground and is available from large supermarkets or Asian food stores. The pod is preferable because the seeds tend to lose their essential oils when they are ground.

PASTEL TEMPEH DANTOMAT

Tempeh and Tomato Roll—Indonesia

Tempeh *is a soy bean mixture compressed into cakes and fermented. It is a popular source of protein in Indonesia and other Asian countries. When marinated in a spicy mixture and then lightly cooked, it takes on the flavor of the marinade.* Tempeh *is a delicious and nutritionally well-balanced food. Here it is combined with lettuce and tomato on a bread roll—a healthier version of the popular bacon, lettuce and tomato sandwich.*

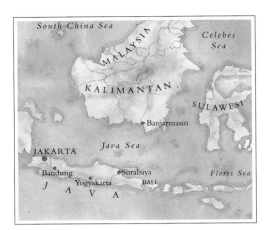

TOTAL TIME: 15 MINUTES

SERVES 2

Keep Tofu Dressing or Tahini Dressing on hand for these kinds of healthy snacks.

1 tablespoon peanut or canola oil
2 garlic cloves, minced
4 oz (125 g) tempeh, crumbled
1 teaspoon ground coriander
1 tablespoon reduced-sodium soy sauce
2 round wholegrain (wholemeal) rolls, 4–5 inches (10–12 cm) in diameter
2 tablespoons Tofu Dressing (see page 85) or Tahini Dressing (see page 88)

2 small lettuce leaves
1 medium, vine-ripened tomato, sliced
1 small carrot, coarsely grated, about 1 cup

◆ Heat the oil in a small, non-stick frying pan over medium heat. Add the garlic and cook, stirring constantly, until softened, about 5 minutes.
◆ Add the tempeh and coriander and cook, stirring occasionally, until heated through, about 2 minutes
◆ Remove the pan from the heat, add the soy sauce, stir gently and set aside to cool.
◆ Split the rolls in half and spread with equal amounts of the dressing.

◆ Place a lettuce leaf on the bottom half of each roll and cover with the tomato slices. Top with the tempeh mixture and grated carrot. Cover with the remaining half of each roll and serve immediately.

NUTRITION NOTES

PER SERVING: 405 calories/1701 kilojoules; 19 g protein; 13 g fat, 29% of calories (1.9 g saturated, 4.2% of calories; 5.9 g monounsaturated, 13.2%; 5.2 g polyunsaturated, 11.6%); 53 g carbohydrate; 10 g dietary fiber; 1069 mg sodium; 6.1 mg iron; 0 mg cholesterol.

FRITTATA DI ZUCCHINI

Squash Frittata—Italy

Although technically the Italians regard a frittata as a main course dish, it can be light enough to serve as a snack. Low in fat, this typical Italian dish makes a healthy light snack that can be served hot or cold. A simple green salad will make the snack a light meal. Frittatas make good use of seasonal vegetables. Try substituting other vegetables as they come into season: the result will be just as good.

TOTAL TIME: 1 HOUR 10 MINUTES

SERVES 6

Italians use an ovenproof frying pan for this classic dish. The frittata is first cooked over direct heat, then finished in the oven or under a broiler. This recipe eliminates cooking over direct heat and is done entirely in the oven. A quiche dish will give the best results. If baby squash are not available, use zucchini or yellow summer squash instead.

olive oil cooking spray
2 green baby squash, about 4 oz (125 g), sliced ¼ inch (5 mm) thick
2 yellow baby squash, about 4 oz (125 g), sliced ¼ inch (5 mm) thick
1 small leek, thinly sliced, about 1 cup
½ cup (about 1 oz/30 g) coarsely chopped mushrooms
1 garlic clove, quartered
2 tablespoons wholewheat (wholemeal) flour
3 large, free-range eggs
1 large egg white
½ cup (4 oz/125 g) reduced-sodium, low-fat cottage cheese
½ cup (about 3 fl oz/90 g) low-fat, plain yogurt
¼ cup (1 oz/30 g) crumbled feta cheese
2 tablespoons finely chopped flat-leaf parsley
¼ teaspoon freshly ground white pepper
1 teaspoon poppy seeds
1 tablespoon plus 1 teaspoon freshly grated Parmesan cheese

◆ Preheat the oven to 350°F (180°C). Spray a round, shallow ovenproof dish, 9 inches (23 cm) in diameter, with olive oil cooking spray.
◆ Bring water to a boil in a medium-sized steamer. Add the squash, leek, mushrooms and garlic, cover and steam over medium-high heat until the vegetables are firm but tender, about 5 minutes.
◆ Remove the vegetables from the steamer and sprinkle with the flour. Set aside.

◆ Combine the eggs and egg white in a medium-sized bowl and beat well with a fork until the mixture runs smoothly through the tines.
◆ Add the cottage cheese, yogurt, feta cheese, parsley and pepper to the egg mixture. Mix until blended.
◆ Place the vegetables in the ovenproof dish and carefully pour the egg mixture over. Sprinkle with the poppy seeds and Parmesan cheese.
◆ Bake in the oven until the frittata is firm and golden brown, 25 to 30 minutes.
◆ Cut into wedges and serve at once, or set aside to cool.

NUTRITION NOTES

PER SERVING: 123 calories/516 kilojoules; 12 g protein; 5.8 g fat, 42% of calories (2.8 g saturated, 20.3% of calories; 2.2 g monounsaturated, 15.9%; 0.8 g polyunsaturated, 5.8%); 5 g carbohydrate; 2 g dietary fiber; 216 mg sodium; 0.9 mg iron; 114 mg cholesterol.

BYED LOUBEY SAJAN, FALAFEL

Egg and Sprouts Lavash and Chickpea Croquettes—Lebanon

Lavash is a flat, soft bread perfect for wrapping around fillings. Here, the filling is made from crisp sprouts, fiber-rich Tabbouleh and eggs. Eggs are a versatile and economical source of protein, to be enjoyed in moderation. Most nutritionists advise that up to four eggs a week can be part of a normal diet if cholesterol is not a problem. Tiny Chickpea Croquettes are great for picnics and parties. The Lebanese often use them as a sandwich filling.

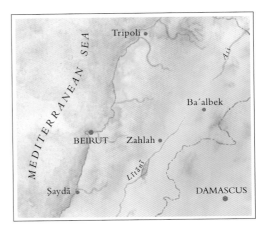

Egg and Sprouts Lavash (top) and Chickpea Croquettes

BYED LOUBEY SAJAN

Egg and Sprouts Lavash

TOTAL TIME: 20 MINUTES

SERVES 4

Low-fat, low-sugar prepared mayonnaise, or a mayonnaise diluted with 50 percent low-fat, plain yogurt, can be used instead of the Tofu or Tahini Dressing. Vinegar added to the cooking water stops the egg white from seeping out of a cracked egg.

2 large, free-range eggs
1 cup Tabbouleh (see page 82)
½ cup green bell pepper (capsicum) cut into ¼ inch (6 mm) dice
½ cup (3 oz/90 g) vine-ripened tomato cut into ¼ inch (6 mm) dice
4 sheets lavash or other soft, flatbread, each sheet 10 x 6 inches (25 x 15 cm)
⅓ cup Tofu Dressing (see page 85) or Tahini Dressing (see page 88)
1¼ cups alfalfa sprouts
½ cup mung bean sprouts

◆ Bring a small nonreactive saucepan of water to a boil over high heat. Add a few drops of vinegar and gently lower the eggs into the pan. Reduce the heat to medium when the water returns to a boil, and cook the eggs for 10 minutes.
◆ Remove the eggs from the water with a slotted spoon and place in a bowl of cold water. Set aside until cool enough to handle. Remove the eggs from the water and gently tap each shell to crack and release the sulphur (this prevents the egg white turning yellow around the yolk). Return the eggs to fresh cold water and cool for about 5 minutes. Remove the shells from the eggs.
◆ Coarsely chop the eggs and transfer to a medium-sized bowl.
◆ Add the Tabbouleh, bell pepper and tomato to the eggs and mix well.
◆ Spread the dressing over the lavash sheets. (Leave ½ inch/1 cm of a shorter end uncovered.) Top with equal amounts of the

ALFALFA SPROUTS

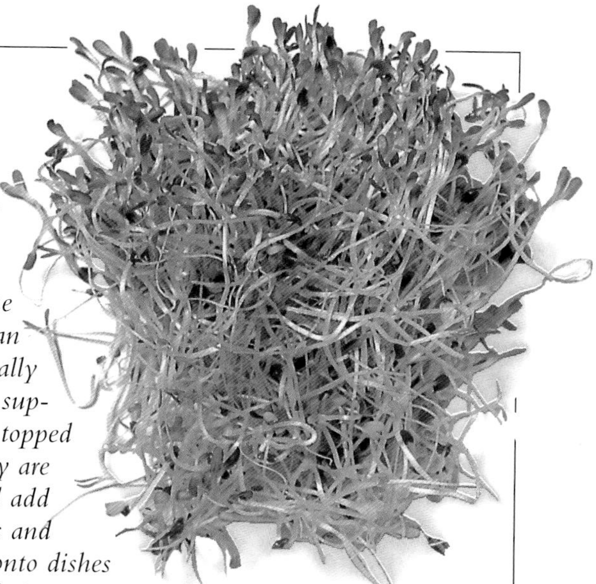

Alfalfa sprouts (also known as lucerne sprouts) are the seed sprouts of Medicago sativa. Any grain or legume seed can be sprouted, and the practice of storing seeds as a ready source of protein goes back some 5000 years to when the Chinese first began sprouting mung beans. Alfalfa was originally sprouted by the Arabs to use as a protein supplement for their horses. The thin stalks, topped by tiny green leaves, are eaten raw. They are low in calories but high in vitamin C and add interesting texture and color to sandwiches and salads. Alfalfa sprouts are also sprinkled onto dishes to provide contrast. While readily available in supermarkets and farmer's markets, you can sprout seeds at home. Keep the sprouts in the crisper section of the refrigerator and use within a week.

egg mixture, 1 cup of the alfalfa sprouts and the mung bean sprouts.
◆ Starting with the covered short end of a lavash, roll it up firmly and neatly to enclose the filling. Slice in half. Repeat with the remaining lavash.
◆ Transfer the rolls to serving plates, garnish with the remaining alfalfa sprouts and serve immediately.

FALAFEL

Chickpea Croquettes

TOTAL TIME: 2½ HOURS

SERVES 8

Canned chickpeas may be used here, if desired. Processing or blending the chickpeas in stages gives a finer, smoother purée. Bulghur is found in health food stores and in most supermarkets.

1¾ cups (10 oz/310 g) cooked chickpeas (see page 57)
1 cup (4 oz/125 g) fine-grade bulghur
½ cup (2 oz/60 g) coarsely shredded pita bread
⅓ cup (3 fl oz/90 ml) freshly squeezed lemon juice
3 garlic cloves, minced
2 teaspoons ground coriander
1 teaspoon finely chopped, seeded red chili
1 teaspoon ground cumin
½ teaspoon salt
¼ teaspoon freshly ground black pepper
olive oil cooking spray

◆ Place ¾ cup of the bulghur in a medium-sized bowl and add cold water to cover. Set aside to soak until soft, about 15 minutes.

Drain through a cheesecloth-lined sieve. Gather the ends of the cheesecloth around the bulghur and squeeze out as much water as possible. Transfer to a large bowl and set aside.
◆ Meanwhile, place the pita bread in a small bowl, add cold water to cover and set aside to soak until softened, about 15 minutes. Drain through a fine mesh sieve then squeeze out the water with your fingertips.
◆ Combine half of each of the chickpeas and lemon juice with the garlic, coriander, chili, cumin, salt and pepper in a blender or food processor. Process until smooth, stopping and scraping down the sides as needed.
◆ Add the remaining chickpeas and lemon juice and process until smooth, stopping and scrapping down the sides as needed.
◆ Add the soaked bulghur and pita bread and process until evenly combined.
◆ Sprinkle the remaining bulghur on a large piece of waxed (greaseproof) paper.
◆ With clean, cold hands, take a rounded tablespoon of the mixture, and roll into a ball 1 inch (2.5 cm) in diameter. Place the ball on the sprinkled bulghur and roll around gently until coated. Repeat this process until all the mixture is used. (Makes about 32 balls.)
◆ Transfer the balls to a clean piece of waxed (greaseproof) paper and set aside to dry at room temperature for 1 hour.
◆ Preheat the oven to 350°F (180°C).
◆ Spray 2 baking trays with the olive oil cooking spray. Place the balls on the trays and then spray them lightly with the olive oil spray.
◆ Bake until light golden brown, about 30 minutes.
◆ Serve the chickpea balls warm or cold.

CONDIMENTADO QUINOA, PAN DE MAIZ CON SALSA DE VERDURAS

Savory Quinoa and Cornbread with Vegetable Sauce—Mexico

Quinoa contains more protein than any other edible grain. This recipe for Savory Quinoa combines the ancient grain with colorful fiber-rich vegetables. Corn comes from the maize plant, a healthy and versatile grain native to South America. Cornbread with Vegetable Sauce is a good dish for feeding a crowd. It complements roast chicken, and can also be served as a snack.

Savory Quinoa (top) and Cornbread with Vegetable Sauce

CONDIMENTADO QUINOA

Savory Quinoa

TOTAL TIME: 45 MINUTES

SERVES 4

Allow 2 to 2½ hours additional time if the Vegetable Stock is not already prepared. Rinse quinoa before using. Even prewashed varieties can contain a bitter coating that sometimes remains after packaging. Buy a curry paste of medium intensity from an Asian food store—if paste is unavaliable, curry powder may be used instead. Chili powder may be used to add extra flavor.

1 tablespoon canola or safflower oil
1 medium onion, thinly sliced
1 garlic clove, minced
1 small red chili, seeded and thinly sliced
1 tablespoon plus 1 teaspoon curry paste or curry powder
2 cups (about 8 oz / 250 g) butternut squash (butternut pumpkin) cut into ¾ inch (2 cm) cubes,
1 medium red bell pepper (capsicum), seeded and thinly sliced
2 large, vine-ripened tomatoes, cut into wedges
1 medium banana, sliced

¼ cup no-added-salt tomato paste
1 tablespoon golden raisins (sultanas)
½ cup (4 fl oz / 125 ml) Vegetable Stock (see page 52) or water
1 cup (6 oz / 185 g) quinoa
2 cups (16 fl oz / 500 ml) water
juice of 2 limes or 1 lemon
cilantro (coriander) sprigs, for garnish, optional

◆ Heat the oil in a large, non-stick frying pan over medium heat. Add the onion and garlic and sauté, stirring occasionally, until the onion is soft, about 5 minutes.

- Add the chili and curry paste, stirring constantly, until the chili is softened, about 1 minute.
- Add the squash and pepper, reduce the heat to medium-low, cover and cook until tender, about 10 minutes.
- Add the tomatoes, banana, tomato paste, raisins and stock. Bring to a boil over medium heat, uncovered, and cook until the tomatoes are soft, about 5 minutes.
- Meanwhile, place the quinoa in a fine mesh sieve and rinse under cold running water, then drain. Transfer to a medium-sized saucepan, add the water and bring to a boil over high heat. Reduce the heat to medium-low, cover and simmer until the quinoa is soft and translucent and the liquid has been absorbed, 10 to 15 minutes.
- Stir in the lime juice.
- Transfer to a warm serving platter and spoon the squash mixture over the top.
- Serve immediately garnished with the cilantro sprigs, if using.

PAN DE MAIZ CON SALSA DE VERDURAS

Cornbread with Vegetable Sauce

TOTAL TIME: 1¼ HOURS

SERVES 8

Allow 2 to 2½ hours additional time if the Vegetable Stock is not already prepared. Yogurt adds richness without fat.

olive oil cooking spray
1½ cups (9 oz/275 g) yellow or white cornmeal
2 teaspoons baking powder
1¾ cups (14 oz/440 g) canned cream-style (creamed) corn
1 cup (6½ oz/200 g) low-fat, plain yogurt
½ cup sliced scallions (spring onions)
¼ cup (2 fl oz/60 ml) canola or safflower oil
2 large egg whites
1 large, free-range egg, lightly beaten
¾ cup (3 oz/90 g) freshly grated, reduced-fat Cheddar cheese
¼ cup (1 oz/30 g) freshly grated Parmesan cheese
8 chili "flowers," for garnish (see page 138)

SAUCE

1 small red bell pepper (capsicum), seeded and halved lengthwise
1 small green bell pepper (capsicum), seeded and halved lengthwise
1 tablespoon plus 1 teaspoon margarine or butter
1 small red onion, thinly sliced
2 garlic cloves, minced

QUINOA

Quinoa (Chenopodium quinoa), pronounced keen-wa, is a grain with a high protein content which the Incas called "the mother grain." It is believed to be a complete protein because of its balance of essential amino acids. Although it was grown by the Incas for thousands of years, quinoa has only recently been "rediscovered" and is now cultivated in both North and South America. There are nearly two thousand varieties of quinoa but only a few are sold commercially. The small ivory-colored pellets are easy to cook; they swell to four times their volume and become translucent. The flavor is delicate and has been compared to couscous. Although quinoa is lighter, its use is similar to that of rice—as a side dish, in salads, soups, desserts and stuffings. The grains should be thoroughly washed before cooking to remove their bitter coating. Quinoa is available in health food stores and some larger supermarkets. Store in a cool, dry place out of direct sunlight.

4 oz (125 g) mushroom caps, sliced
½ cup (4 fl oz/125 ml) evaporated skim milk
½ cup (4 fl oz/125 ml) Vegetable Stock (see page 52)
4 drops Tabasco sauce
2 tablespoons finely chopped parsley

- Preheat the oven to 325°F (160°C). Spray a 9 inch (23 cm) square cake pan with the olive oil cooking spray.
- Combine the cornmeal and baking powder in a medium-sized bowl. Make a well in the center.
- In a separate bowl, combine the corn, yogurt, scallions, oil, egg whites and egg and mix well.
- Mix the cheeses together in a small bowl.
- Pour the egg and corn mixture into the well of the dry ingredients and mix together quickly to blend.
- Spoon half the cornmeal mixture into the prepared cake pan and spread to level. Sprinkle with three-quarters of the mixed cheeses. Cover with the remaining cornmeal mixture, then sprinkle with the remaining cheese.
- Bake until a skewer inserted into the center comes out clean, about 45 minutes. Transfer to a wire rack and cool for 5 minutes. Remove the cornbread from the pan and keep warm.
- While the cornbread is baking, prepare the sauce. Preheat the broiler and adjust the rack so that the pan is 3–5 inches from the source of heat (or preheat the grill on High). Line the broiler rack with foil.

- Place the pepper halves, skin-side up, on the broiler rack. Broil until the skins are charred and blistered, about 5 minutes.
- Place the peppers in a paper bag until cool enough to handle, about 5 minutes. Remove the charred skin with a small knife and cut the flesh into thin slices.
- Melt the margarine in a medium-sized, frying pan over medium heat. Add the onion and garlic and sauté, stirring frequently, until softened, about 5 minutes.
- Add the peppers and mushrooms and cook, stirring frequently, until the mushrooms are soft, about 2 minutes. Reduce the heat and stir in the evaporated milk. Add the stock, Tabasco sauce and parsley and heat, stirring constantly. Do not boil.
- Cut the cornbread into 8 long narrow slices. Serve on individual plates and top with the vegetable sauce. Garnish each serving with a chili "flower."

NUTRITION NOTES

PER SERVING—Savory Quinoa:
303 calories/1273 kilojoules; 10 g protein; 7.4 g fat, 22% of calories (1.7 g saturated, 5.1% of calories; 3.4 g monounsaturated, 10.1%; 2.3 g polyunsaturated, 6.8%); 48 g carbohydrate; 8.1 g dietary fiber; 45 mg sodium; 1.3 mg iron; 0 mg cholesterol.

PER SERVING—Cornbread with Vegetable Sauce (Analysis uses monounsaturated margarine): 331 calories/1391 kilojoules; 14 g protein; 15 g fat, 42% of calories (3.9 g saturated, 10.9% of calories; 7.7 g monounsaturated, 21.6%; 3.4 g polyunsaturated, 9.5%); 34 g carbohydrate; 3.8 g dietary fiber; 467 mg sodium; 1.1 mg iron; 42 mg cholesterol.

REESOTTO VOLGII,
BAKLAZHÁN C OSTRYM KEFIROM

Bulghur Risotto and Eggplant with Spicy Yogurt—Russia

Bulghur Risotto is a delicious high-fiber side dish or snack. A source of protein and B vitamins, it is high in complex carbohydrate. Eggplant with Spicy Yogurt combines this lovely soft-textured vegetable-fruit with yogurt, an important source of protein and calcium. Use yogurt that contains an acidophilus culture, an indication that this is a "true" yogurt. This aids the digestion.

Bulghur Risotto (right) and Eggplant with Spicy Yogurt

NUTRITION NOTES

PER SERVING—Bulghur Risotto:
260 calories/1092 kilojoules; 13 g protein; 4.3 g
fat, 15% of calories (0.7 g saturated, 2.4% of
calories; 1.8 g monounsaturated, 6.3%; 1.8 g
polyunsaturated, 6.3%); 41 g carbohydrate; 12 g
dietary fiber; 153 mg sodium; 2.1 mg iron;
4 mg cholesterol.

PER SERVING—Eggplant with Spicy Yogurt:
98 calories/410 kilojoules; 6 g protein; 4.2 g fat,
40% of calories (0.8 g saturated, 7.6% of calories;
2.9 g monounsaturated, 27.6%; 0.5 g polyunsaturated, 4.8%); 9 g carbohydrate; 3.9 g dietary fiber;
181 mg sodium; 0.7 mg iron; 3 mg cholesterol.

SWISS CHARD (SILVERBEET)

*Swiss chard, also known as silverbeet, is a member
of the beet family (genus* Beta*) with dark green,
glossy leaves and silvery stalks. Its high iron content makes it a valuable part of a vegetarian diet.
First mentioned in Roman writings in the third
century* BC*, it is the oldest type of beet known. Like
spinach, Swiss chard can be cooked in a variety of
ways—steamed, poached or stir-fried. It can be stored
in the crisper section of the refrigerator for 3 to 4 days.*

REESOTTO VOLGII

Bulghur Risotto

TOTAL TIME: 55 MINUTES

SERVES 6

Allow 2 to 2½ hours additional time if the
Vegetable Stock is not already prepared.
Vegetables are steamed on top of the
bulghur in this recipe, which helps conserve
their nutrients.

2 cups (11 oz/345 g) bulghur
1 tablespoon canola or safflower oil
1 large onion, finely chopped
2 garlic cloves, minced
4 cups (32 fl oz/1 liter) boiling Vegetable
    Stock (see page 52)
1 cup (5 oz/155 g) diced rutabaga (swede)
1 cup (3 oz/90 g) broccoli florets
1 cup (5 oz/155 g) green peas
1 cup thinly sliced Swiss chard (silverbeet)
    or kale, tightly packed
1 cup (6½ oz/200 g) low-fat, plain
    yogurt, for serving

◆ Place the bulghur in a medium-sized
bowl and add cold water to cover. Soak
until soft, about 15 minutes, then drain well.
◆ Heat the oil in a large, heavy-bottomed
saucepan over medium-high heat. Add the
onion and garlic and sauté, stirring occasionally, until the onion is softened, about
5 minutes.
◆ Add the bulghur and stir constantly until
coated with oil, about 1 minute.
◆ Add the boiling stock and stir well. Reduce the heat to medium-low. Layer the
rutabaga, broccoli, peas and Swiss chard on
top of the bulghur mixture. Press the layered vegetables down gently with the back
of a wooden spoon so that the rutabaga is
covered by stock. Cover and simmer until
the bulghur and the vegetables are tender,
about 20 minutes. Carefully stir the vegetables into the bulghur.
◆ Transfer to a warm serving dish and serve
immediately. Serve the yogurt on the side.

BAKLAZHÁN C OSTRYM KEFIROM

Eggplant with Spicy Yogurt

TOTAL TIME: 50 MINUTES

SERVES 4

A good quality non-stick frying pan is a
great asset when cooking vegetables in a
small amount of oil.

1 tablespoon virgin olive oil
1 medium onion, thinly sliced
1 garlic clove, minced
1 teaspoon ground coriander
1 teaspoon ground cumin
1 teaspoon ground turmeric
¼ teaspoon chili powder
1 lb (500 g) eggplant (aubergine),
    cut into ¾ inch (2 cm) cubes
⅓ cup (3 fl oz/90 ml) water
1 large, vine-ripened tomato, chopped
¼ teaspoon salt
1 cup (6½ fl oz/200 g) low-fat, plain
    yogurt
herbs, for garnish

◆ Heat the oil in a large, non-stick frying
pan over medium heat. Add the onion and
garlic and cook, stirring frequently, until
the onion is soft, about 5 minutes.
◆ Add the coriander, cumin, turmeric and
chili powder and stir constantly to blend
the flavors, about 1 minute.
◆ Add the eggplant and water, stir well,
cover and reduce the heat to medium-low.
Cook until tender, about 20 minutes.
◆ Add the tomato and salt, cover and cook
until the tomato is softened, about 5
minutes.
◆ Reduce the heat to low, add the yogurt
and heat through, stirring constantly, about
2 minutes. Do not boil.
◆ Garnish with herbs and serve at once.

SWARTOOG ERTJIES EN GROENTE BREDIE

Black-Eyed Peas and Vegetable Bredie—South Africa

A colorful medley of Dutch, Indian and African cuisines, a "bredie" is a popular stew in South Africa. When served as a main course it may also include meat. Black-eyed peas have long been popular in African cooking and are equally popular in the southern United States. A rich source of vegetable protein, they complement rice and broiled fish or chicken.

TOTAL TIME: 2 HOURS 10 MINUTES

SERVES 8

Allow 2 to 2½ hours additional time if the Vegetable Stock is not already prepared. To vary this recipe, replace the Swiss chard with okra. Trim the okra, cut in half lengthwise and add to the bredie when adding the apricots, fennel and pumpkin seeds.

1 cup (6 oz/185 g) black-eyed peas
   (black-eyed beans)
1 tablespoon plus 1 teaspoon virgin olive oil
1 medium leek or large onion, chopped
1 garlic clove, minced
1 teaspoon finely chopped fresh ginger
1 teaspoon ground cardamom
½ teaspoon fennel seeds
¼ teaspoon ground nutmeg
8 oz (250 g) potatoes, cut into 1 inch
   (2 cm) pieces
2 large, vine-ripened tomatoes, coarsely
   chopped
1 medium green bell pepper (capsicum),
   cut into 1 inch (2 cm) squares
1¼ cups (10 fl oz/300 ml) Vegetable Stock
   (see page 52)
¼ cup (2 fl oz/60 ml) no-added-salt
   tomato paste
2 cups shredded Swiss chard (silverbeet)
   leaves, tightly packed
½ cup chopped (2½ oz/75 g) dried apricots
   or pitted prunes
¼ cup chopped fennel
¼ cup (1 oz/30 g) pumpkin seeds, toasted

◆ Place the black-eyed peas in a large heavy-bottomed saucepan and add water to cover. Bring to a boil over high heat and boil for 2 minutes. Remove from the heat and set aside for 1 hour.
◆ Drain the peas and return to the saucepan and add fresh water to cover. Bring to a boil over high heat, reduce the heat to medium-low, and simmer, covered, until tender, 40 to 45 minutes. Drain and set aside.
◆ Meanwhile, heat the oil in a large, heavy-bottomed saucepan over medium-high heat. Add the leek, garlic and ginger and sauté, stirring occasionally, until softened, about 5 minutes.
◆ Add the cardamom, fennel seeds and nutmeg to the onions and cook to develop the flavor of the spices, stirring constantly, for 2 minutes.
◆ Add the potatoes, tomatoes, bell pepper, stock and tomato paste. Bring to a boil and stir well. Reduce the heat, cover and simmer until the vegetables are tender, 20 to 25 minutes.
◆ Stir in the Swiss chard, black-eyed peas, apricots, fennel and pumpkin seeds. Cover and cook until tender, about 5 minutes.
◆ Transfer to a warm serving bowl and serve at once.

NUTRITION NOTES

PER SERVING: 181 calories/762 kilojoules; 9 g protein; 5.1 g fat, 25% of calories (0.8 g saturated, 3.9% of calories; 2.4 g monounsaturated, 11.8%; 1.9 g polyunsaturated, 9.3%); 25 g carbohydrate; 6.7 g dietary fiber; 91 mg sodium; 3.3 mg iron; 0 mg cholesterol.

BRUSSELS SPROUTS AND CAULIFLOWER IN CASHEW APPLE SAUCE

The United States

This dish of green- and cream-colored vegetables is served with an unusual but surprisingly delicious nut-fruit sauce. Brussels sprouts and cauliflower belong to the same family as cabbage, all vegetables bursting with dietary fiber, vitamin C and iron. Serve it as a side dish with broiled fish or steamed chicken or as a healthy vegetarian snack.

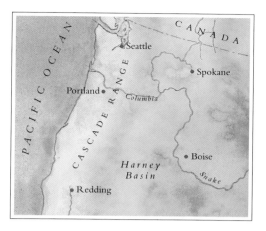

TOTAL TIME: 40 MINUTES

SERVES 4

To keep steamed vegetables warm, remove the steamer from the heat and set aside, covered, until ready to use.

2 cups (8 oz/250 g) Brussels sprouts, trimmed
2 cups (5 oz/155 g) cauliflower florets
2 stalks celery, sliced ½ inch (1 cm) thick
¾ cup (6 fl oz/175 ml) water
⅓ cup (2 oz/60 g) raw cashews
2 tart green apples, preferably Granny Smith, coarsely grated
1 tablespoon margarine
1 tablespoon wholewheat (wholemeal) flour
¼ teaspoon ground nutmeg
¼ teaspoon ground cinnamon
pinch of salt
¼ teaspoon freshly ground black pepper
1 tablespoon pumpkin seeds, toasted, for garnish

◆ Cut a cross into the stalk end of each Brussels sprout. This will allow heat to penetrate during cooking.
◆ Bring a medium-sized steamer of water to a boil over high heat. Place the Brussels sprouts, cauliflower and celery in the steamer, cover and steam over medium-high heat until tender, about 15 minutes. Remove from the heat and keep warm.
◆ Combine the water and cashews in a blender or food processor. Process for 30 seconds, stop and scrape down sides, process for 30 seconds longer, stop and scrape down again. Add the grated apple and process until well combined, about 30 seconds.
◆ Melt the margarine in a medium-sized, non-stick saucepan over medium heat. Stir in the flour and cook, stirring constantly, until gritty and granular, about 1 minute. Add the apple mixture and bring to a boil, stirring constantly. Stir in the nutmeg, cinnamon, salt and pepper. Simmer to blend the flavors, about 1 minute longer.
◆ Transfer the vegetables to a warm serving bowl and coat with the sauce. Sprinkle the pumpkin seeds on top and serve at once.

NUTRITION NOTES

PER SERVING (Analysis uses monounsaturated margarine): 179 calories/751 kilojoules; 6 g protein; 11 g fat, 53% of calories (2 g saturated, 9.6% of calories; 6.8 g monounsaturated, 32.8%; 2.2 g polyunsaturated, 10.6%); 15 g carbohydrate; 6.2 g dietary fiber; 180 mg sodium; 1.9 mg iron; 0 mg cholesterol.

LEAN BEEF CLUB SANDWICH AND WHOLEGRAIN BREAD ROLLS

The United States

A club sandwich is a good example of a well-balanced snack. There is complex carbohydrate in the wholegrain bread; protein, iron and vitamin B in the beef; vitamins, minerals and fiber in the lettuce and tomato. Try this delicious, healthy version of an old favorite. These high-fiber Wholegrain Bread Rolls are satisfying and fun to make. They are a perfect partner for homemade soup.

Lean Beef Club Sandwich and Wholegrain Bread Rolls (top)

NUTRITION NOTES

PER SERVING—Lean Beef Club Sandwich:
252 calories/1058 kilojoules; 21 g protein; 7 g fat,
25% of calories (2.4 g saturated, 9% of calories;
3.1 g monounsaturated, 11%; 1.5 g polyunsatu-
rated, 5%); 26 g carbohydrate; 6.1 g dietary fiber;
418 mg sodium; 4.2 mg iron; 43 mg cholesterol.

PER SERVING—Wholegrain Bread Rolls:
123 calories/514 kilojoules; 5 g protein; 2 g fat,
15% of calories (0.4 g saturated, 3% of calories;
1 g monounsaturated, 7.5%; 0.6 g polyunsatu-
rated, 4.5%); 21 g carbohydrate; 2.4 g dietary
fiber; 93 mg sodium; 1 mg iron; 0.2 mg cholesterol.

LEAN BEEF CLUB SANDWICH

TOTAL TIME: 15 TO 20 MINUTES

SERVES 2

Buy good quality lean beef, such as tenderloin or fillet.

olive oil cooking spray
1 slice of beef fillet (about 4 oz/125 g),
    cut 1 inch (2.5 cm) thick
½ teaspoon virgin olive oil
freshly ground black pepper
4 slices wholewheat (wholemeal) bread,
    sliced about ¼ inch (6 mm) thick
1 teaspoon wholegrain mustard
1 teaspoon prepared horseradish (sauce)
1 teaspoon balsamic vinegar, optional
small crisp lettuce leaves
1 medium, vine-ripened tomato, sliced
½ cup (1 oz/30 g) alfalfa bean sprouts

◆ Preheat the broiler and adjust the rack so that the pan is about 3–5 inches from the source of the heat (or preheat the grill on High). Spray a broiler pan lightly with olive oil cooking spray.
◆ Brush the beef with a little of the olive oil and place on the broiler pan. Season with the pepper.
◆ Broil the beef for 2 minutes, turn and brush with more oil. Broil for 3 minutes longer for rare beef, 5 minutes longer for medium, 7 minutes longer for well-done.
◆ Cut the beef in half to make 2 thin slices.
◆ Place 2 slices of the bread on a clean board. Combine the mustard and the horseradish in a very small bowl. Spread the mustard mixture over the 2 slices of bread, dividing equally.
◆ Place a slice of beef on each slice of bread and sprinkle with the vinegar, if using.
◆ Arrange the lettuce leaves over the beef, cover with the tomato slices and sprinkle the alfalfa sprouts on top. Place the remaining slices of bread on top and secure with ornamental toothpicks.
◆ Serve immediately.

WHOLEGRAIN BREAD ROLLS

TOTAL TIME: 2½ TO 2¾ HOURS

MAKES 24

When cooking with yeast, it is important to work in a warm, draft-free kitchen so that the yeast has the right conditions to be active in the mixture.

1 cup (6 oz/185 g) cornmeal
¾ cup (about 1 oz/30 g) unprocessed bran
1 cup (8 fl oz/250 ml) boiling water
1 teaspoon honey
3 cups (12 oz/375 g) all-purpose (plain) flour
1 cup (5 oz/155 g) wholewheat
    (wholemeal) flour
1 teaspoon salt
2 envelopes, ¼ oz (7 g) each, active dried yeast
½ cup (2½ oz/75 g) pumpkin seeds, toasted
1 cup (6½ oz/200 g) low-fat, plain yogurt
1 tablespoon plus 1 teaspoon virgin olive oil
olive oil cooking spray
extra lukewarm water, as needed
sesame seeds, for sprinkling

◆ Combine the cornmeal and bran in a large bowl. Using a wooden spoon, stir in the boiling water and honey and set aside to cool slightly, about 5 minutes.
◆ Meanwhile, in another bowl, combine the all-purpose flour, wholewheat flour, salt, yeast and pumpkin seeds. Add to the cooled cornmeal mixture with the yogurt and oil. Pour in enough extra lukewarm water to make a soft dough and mix well.
◆ Turn the dough out onto a cool, lightly floured surface and knead until smooth and satiny. Lightly coat a warm bowl with the olive oil cooking spray. Form the dough into a ball and place in the bowl, turning the ball to coat its surface with oil.
◆ Cover the bowl with a damp cloth and set aside in a warm place until the dough has doubled in bulk, 45 to 60 minutes.
◆ Preheat the oven to 425°F (220°C). Coat 2 baking trays with the cooking spray.
◆ Punch the dough down, turn out onto a lightly floured surface and divide into 24 pieces. Cover and set aside for 10 minutes.
◆ Knead each piece and shape into a roll. Transfer the rolls to the baking trays.
◆ Cover with a damp cloth and set aside in a warm, draft-free place, to proof (prove) until almost doubled in size, about 30 minutes. Test by lightly pressing the dough with your finger—the impression should stay.
◆ Lightly brush the rolls with lukewarm water and sprinkle sesame seeds on top.
◆ Bake until the rolls sound hollow when tapped lightly with your knuckle, 15 to 20 minutes. Cool on a wire rack.

HORSERADISH

Horseradish, a member of the mustard family, is a perennial plant that is best grown as an annual. While its leaves are occasionally harvested for salads, it is grown commercially for its white, pungent root. The horseradish (Armoracia rusticana) originates in southeastern Europe, and is one of the bitter herbs of the Jewish Passover ceremonies. Thinly sliced or grated, horseradish is used as a condiment or added to sauces. It is also mixed with vinegar and cream or mayonnaise, which lessens its very hot, biting, taste, and served as a relish, traditionally as an accompaniment to beef. It is less pungent when dried and needs to be reconstituted before it can be served. Use as soon as possible after grating because its natural essences will be lost quickly through evaporation. Horseradish is high in vitamin C and has certain antibiotic properties that help to keep the intestine healthy. It is also a stimulant to the appetite. Prepared horseradish is available in bottles from supermarkets. Fresh horseradish is available in some supermarkets and should be kept in the refrigerator, wrapped in plastic.

MAIN MEALS

The main course of a meal is the principal dish, the most important in size or extent, on a given menu. This is the course most cooks focus on when preparing a meal. The preparation of such an important feature of a menu requires time, care and patience.

Because it is the most important meal of the day, there is a need to stimulate the senses with the main course. Other meals are often rushed, even missed completely, in a busy lifestyle, but most people look forward to their main meal. It is a pleasure to walk into a kitchen that exudes a wonderful aroma. It is a joy to look at an attractively presented meal. Both of these factors are important in a healthy diet. Because a positive reaction from the senses of smell and sight stimulates the gastric juices. This stimulus is a necessary chemical reaction for complete digestion and correct absorption of our food. In simple words, this is how we enjoy the smell and flavor of our food and how it does us good!

This chapter is a virtual treasure of nutritious, healthy recipes from around the world. As you will appreciate when you taste some of these main courses, you don't have to suffer or deny yourself when living on healthy food. Quite the reverse! You will enjoy your food and find a new source of energy and inner vitality. Many of these recipes will give pleasure to the whole family while others are ideal for entertaining. Lots of the dishes are surprisingly easy to prepare.

We visit the countries of Asia and the Mediterranean to enjoy the benefits of their healthy diets (discussed on page 19). Both diets are based on high-fiber, low-fat dishes with an abundance of grains flavored with vegetables and legumes. Notice that there is a preference for monounsaturated oil, made from peanuts in Asia and from olives in the Mediterranean—these are

Left: *Typical of the Asian food pyramid, the Vietnamese diet includes lots of healthy fresh vegetables and fish.*
Below: *Lush pastures, Tasmania, Australia. New lean cuts of meat are proving popular with health-conscious consumers.*

healthy choices to adopt. Spicy Noodles with Shrimp, from Indonesia, and Whole-wheat Pizza with Garden Vegetables, from Italy, demonstrate these principles. These regional diets have passed the test of time and have provided us with conclusive research material proving the advantages of a healthy diet. Universal favorites include Beef and Broccoli Stir-Fry or Chicken Stir-Fry accompanied by rice, from China; Millet Patties or Couscous with Chicken, from Morocco; and Red Lentil Lasagne, from Italy.

There are also many delicious recipes from the light and fresh modern cuisines of Australia and the United States. Barbecued Garlic Shrimp, Chicken and Apricots and Roast Fillet of Lamb with Vegetable Purées typify the healthy trends in today's Australian cuisine. Cioppino, Broiled Tuna with Fresh Tomato Salsa and Chicken Creole are light and healthy dishes popular throughout the United States.

Healthy cooking relies on the freshness and perfection of good quality ingredients, as well as simplicity in preparation. Shopping for food is important, but it can also be fun, particularly when you are looking for new exciting ingredients.

Many of the lighter main course recipes focus cleverly on flavor development. For example, look at Scallop and Mushroom Brochettes, from France; Broiled Salmon with Dill Peach Sauce, from Russia; Baked Trout with Gremolata, from Switzerland; Tuna Sashimi on Cucumber, from Japan; Skewered Lamb, from Greece; Veal with Prosciutto, from Italy; Peppercorn Pork in Wine Sauce, from Spain; and Marinated Beef Steak, from the United States. Just add rice, pasta or potatoes and a green salad to any of these dishes for a delicious, well-balanced meal.

Other main courses are inspired by ethnic and peasant cultures using regional, seasonal foods from land and sea. Many contain a healthy high-fiber content in traditionally popular dishes. Examples include Stuffed Cabbage Rolls and Soya-roni with Pork and Red Cabbage, from Russia; Chickpea Casserole, from India; Turkey Louisiana with rice and okra, Roast Stuffed Chicken featuring wild rice and Tamale Pie made with cornmeal, all from the United States; and the inimitable *Chili con Carne* (with beans) from Mexico.

We also include some vegetarian main courses in this chapter. These provide a complete protein balance from nuts, legumes, seeds, dairy products and whole-grain cereals. There is tasty Tofu Mushroom and Bean Stir-Fry, from Japan; Stuffed Winter Squash and Vegetarian Loaf

with Red Pepper Coulis from the United States; Nut and Vegetable Enchiladas, from Mexico; and Phyllo with Cheese and Spinach, from Greece.

This Main Meals chapter assembles a variety of dishes—some have evolved from traditional cuisines, while others are from relatively new cuisines. All feature healthy ingredients. This wide and exciting selection of healthy international dishes offers further proof that we really can enjoy delicious food that is good for us too!

Above: *Native to tropical America, chilies are now an essential ingredient in cuisines as diverse as Indian and Mexican; sorting chilies in India.* Right: *Fruits are a good low-fat source of fiber, vitamins and minerals; fruit shop, Italy.*

CHICKEN AND APRICOTS

Australia

*A*pricots are one of the world's favorite fruits. Originally cultivated in China, they are now grown in temperate zones throughout the world. The process of drying apricots was developed in the United States and soon spread to Australia and Turkey. Today, all three are major producers. This recipe uses both apricot nectar and dried apricots for intense flavor. Serve with a green vegetable and boiled new potatoes or rice.

TOTAL TIME: 40 MINUTES

SERVES 4

Allow 2 to 2½ hours additional time if the Chicken Stock is not already prepared. Use dry wine for cooking savory (main course) dishes—white wine for cooking fish, chicken or pork; red wine when cooking beef or lamb.

1 tablespoon margarine or butter
1 medium onion, finely chopped
1 garlic clove, minced
4 boneless, skinless chicken breasts (fillets), about 4 oz (125 g) each
½ cup (4 fl oz / 125 ml) Chicken Stock (see page 52)
½ cup (4 fl oz / 125 ml) apricot nectar
¼ cup (2 fl oz / 60 ml) plus 1 tablespoon dry white wine

½ cup (3 oz / 90 g) dried apricots
½ cup thinly sliced celery
8 scallions (spring onions), thickly sliced
1 tablespoon plus 1 teaspoon cornstarch (cornflour)

◆ Melt the margarine in a large, non-stick frying pan over medium heat. Add the onion and garlic and sauté, stirring occasionally, until the onion is softened, about 5 minutes.
◆ Move the onion to the edge of the pan and add the chicken breasts, smooth side down, and cook until the color changes to light golden, about 4 minutes. Turn the chicken breasts over and cook the other side until golden, about 4 minutes.
◆ Add the stock, apricot nectar, ¼ cup of the wine, apricots, celery and scallions to the frying pan. Stir and bring to a boil.

Reduce the heat to medium-low, cover and simmer until the chicken is tender and the juices run clear when pierced with a skewer, about 10 minutes.
◆ Combine the cornstarch and the remaining wine in a small bowl and blend to a smooth paste. Add to the frying pan and return to a boil, stirring constantly. Simmer until the cornstarch is cooked, about 1 minute.
◆ Serve immediately.

SAVORY ZUCCHINI PIE

Australia

Australian cuisine is relatively young and reflects the influences of many other nations. For example, this crustless pie is a cross between a French quiche and an Italian frittata. The eggs, cheese and milk make it a good source of protein, calcium and phosphorus, and zucchinis are rich in vitamin C. The recipe is so simple that even people with no cooking skills will find it easy to prepare. Serve with a seasonal green salad.

TOTAL TIME: 1 HOUR 10 MINUTES
SERVES 6

For best results, use a quiche dish made of ovenproof porcelain. Alternatively, use a 9 inch (23 cm) glass pie dish.

olive oil cooking spray
1½ cups (about 7 oz/220 g) wholewheat (wholemeal) flour
1½ teaspoons baking powder
1 small onion, finely chopped
2 cups coarsely grated zucchini
1 cup (4 oz/125 g) finely chopped reduced-sodium, low-fat ham
3 large, free-range eggs, lightly beaten
½ cup (4 fl oz/125 ml) reduced-sodium, low-fat cottage cheese
¾ cup (6 fl oz/185 ml) skim milk
2 tablespoons finely chopped parsley
¼ teaspoon dry mustard
¼ teaspoon ground nutmeg
1 cup (4 oz/125 g) freshly grated, reduced-fat Cheddar cheese
1 tablespoon sesame seeds

◆ Preheat the oven to 350°F (180°C). Lightly spray a 9 inch (23 cm) quiche dish with olive oil spray.
◆ Combine the flour, baking powder, onion, zucchini, ham, eggs, cottage cheese, milk, parsley, mustard and nutmeg in a large bowl. Mix together until evenly combined.
◆ Pour the mixture into the prepared dish. Sprinkle with the cheese and sesame seeds.
◆ Bake until puffed, golden brown and set, 40 to 50 minutes. Cool on a wire rack for 5 minutes.
◆ Cut the pie into 6 wedges and serve.

NUTRITION NOTES

PER SERVING: 274 calories/1149 kilojoules; 23 g protein; 11 g fat, 36% of calories (5.3 g saturated, 17.3% of calories; 3.9 g monounsaturated, 12.8%; 1.8 g polyunsaturated, 5.9%); 21 g carbohydrate; 4.8 g dietary fiber; 689 mg sodium; 2.1 mg iron; 140 mg cholesterol.

ROAST FILLET OF LAMB WITH VEGETABLE PURÉES

Australia

A roast leg of lamb used to epitomize Australian hospitality. Nowadays, with new trim cuts readily available, healthier lower-fat lamb dishes can be enjoyed. Here, the colorful vegetable purées add flavor, fiber and moist texture to the roast lamb. There is no need to serve a gravy! Accompany with baby new potatoes, which add more complex carbohydrate and dietary fiber.

TOTAL TIME: 55 MINUTES

SERVES 4

This cut of lamb comes from the eye fillet of the loin and should have no visible fat. If not available, use thick loin chops with the fat removed, and broil them.

1 teaspoon dry mustard
1 tablespoon plus 2 teaspoons mint jelly
1½ lb (750 g) butternut squash (butternut
   pumpkin), cut into 1 inch (2.5 cm)
   thick pieces
1 medium onion, cut into 8 wedges
8 oz (250 g) green beans, trimmed
8 oz (250 g) broccoli, trimmed and cut
   into florets

olive oil cooking spray
4 lamb loin fillets, about 4 oz (125 g) each
1 tablespoon plus 1 teaspoon margarine
   or butter
2 tablespoons buttermilk
½ teaspoon salt
¼ teaspoon freshly ground white pepper
mint sprigs, for garnish, optional
⅓ cup (3½ oz / 100 g) mint jelly for serving,
   optional

◆ Combine the mustard and mint jelly in a small heatproof bowl and stir well. Place the bowl in a small saucepan with enough water to reach halfway up the side of the bowl. Remove the bowl and bring the water to a gentle simmer. Set the bowl in the saucepan and simmer until the mint jelly is just softened, about 30 seconds. Remove the bowl from the water-bath and stir the mixture until the mustard is dissolved. Brush the mixture over the lamb fillets and refrigerate until needed.

◆ Bring water to a boil in 2 large steamers. Place the pumpkin and onion in one and the beans and broccoli in the other. Steam both over medium-high heat until tender, about 20 minutes.

◆ Preheat the oven to 400°F (200°C). Place a rack in a roasting pan and spray it lightly with vegetable oil cooking spray.

◆ Place the pumpkin and onion in a blender or food processor. Process until smooth, stopping and scraping down the sides as needed. Transfer the purée to a medium-sized saucepan. Add half each of the buttermilk, margarine, salt and pepper to the pumpkin purée. Repeat this process with the broccoli and beans.

◆ Place the lamb fillets on the rack in the roasting pan. Roast the lamb until cooked but still slightly pink inside, 12 to 13 minutes. Remove from the oven, cover with foil and set aside for 5 minutes.

◆ Meanwhile, heat the saucepans of pumpkin purée and bean and broccoli purée over medium-low heat, stirring constantly, until heated through, about 5 minutes each.

◆ Transfer the lamb fillets to a carving board. Cut each fillet into ½ inch (1 cm) thick slices. Arrange on a warm serving platter or on 4 warm dinner plates. Spoon the vegetable purées onto the platter. Add the mint sprigs and extra mint jelly, if using. Serve immediately.

GREEN BEANS

A perennial plant that is grown as an annual, the green bean (Phaseolus vulgaris) was one of the New World vegetables taken to Europe by explorers in the sixteenth century. The whole pod of the fresh green bean is edible. Although this vegetable is often referred to as "green bean," there are several types. The most commonly eaten is the French bean, also known as the string bean or snap bean. There is also a yellow variety that is called the wax or butter bean. Other similar beans that are sometimes referred to as green beans are the runner bean (very popular in Britain) and the snake bean (often used in Asian cuisine). The green bean can vary in shape from round to flat, thick or thin. Green beans are a favorite hot vegetable, but can be cooked briefly, refreshed and then included in a salad. They are easy to grow at home. When buying fresh, choose green beans that are small, firm and even in color. The pod should snap easily with a crisp sound and should preferably be stringless. Available fresh all year round from supermarkets and farmer's markets, green beans should be stored in the crisper section of the refrigerator and used within a week. Green beans can also be purchased canned or frozen.

NUTRITION NOTES

PER SERVING (Analysis uses monounsaturated margarine): 336 calories / 1410 kilojoules; 37 g protein; 10 g fat, 27% of calories (3.6 g saturated, 9.7% of calories; 5 g monounsaturated, 13.5%; 1.4 g polyunsaturated, 3.8%); 24 g carbohydrate; 7.2 g dietary fiber; 414 mg sodium; 4.5 mg iron; 83 mg cholesterol.

BARBECUED GARLIC SHRIMP

Australia

Garlic has long been credited with health-giving properties. Roman soldiers used to eat it as a stimulant before going into battle. It is claimed to protect the digestive and respiratory system and to reduce blood cholesterol levels. A native of Asia, garlic is grown in warm climates all over the world. Large shrimp, barbecued with garlic, are often served on special occasions in Australia. Accompany with crisp warm bread and a green salad for a balanced meal.

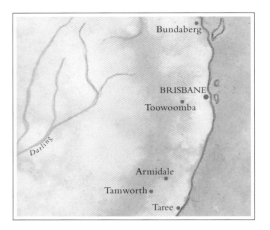

TARRAGON

Tarragon is a perennial herb native to Asia and southern Europe. Its name is thought to have come from a snake-eating bird called drakontion *by the Greeks—tarragon was reputed to help in cases of snakebite. There are two important species of tarragon, French (Artemisia dracunculus) and Russian (Artemisia dracunculoides). It is the French, with its more subtle flavor, that is highly prized. The herb must be treated with care as it can overpower a dish. Tarragon, together with parsley, chives and chervil, makes up the classic* fines herbes *which are added to omelets, stuffings and marinades. Store fresh tarragon in the crisper section of the refrigerator, and use within one week.*

TOTAL TIME: 1 HOUR 20 MINUTES

SERVES 4

When buying whole fresh shrimp (prawns), remember that shelled shrimp weigh half as much as unshelled shrimp.

4 wooden skewers, about 10 in (25 cm) long

*16 raw jumbo shrimp (green king prawns)
    (about 2 lb / 1 kg)*
⅓ cup (3 fl oz / 90 ml) dry white wine
2 tablespoons virgin olive oil
4 garlic cloves, minced
olive oil cooking spray
1 tablespoon snipped chives
1 tablespoon finely chopped tarragon or parsley

◆ Soak the skewers in cold water for 30 minutes.

◆ Meanwhile, shell and devein the shrimp, leaving the last segment of the shell and the tail attached.

◆ Combine the wine, oil and garlic in a shallow glass dish and mix well. Add the shrimp and turn to coat well. Cover with plastic wrap and marinate in the refrigerator for 1 hour.

◆ Heat the barbecue until the coals are white hot, or preheat the broiler and adjust the rack so that the pan is 3–5 inches from the source of heat (or preheat the grill on High). Lightly spray the cooking surface with olive oil cooking spray.

◆ Thread the shrimp neatly onto the drained skewers, 4 shrimp per skewer.

◆ Grill for 1 minute, turn, brush with the remaining marinade and grill until the shrimp turn pinkish orange, 1 or 2 minutes longer.

◆ Transfer to a warm serving platter and sprinkle the chives and tarragon on top. Serve at once.

NUTRITION NOTES

PER SERVING: 148 calories / 621 kilojoules; 16 g protein; 7.8 g fat, 46% of calories (1.3 g saturated, 7.7% of calories; 5.5 g monounsaturated, 32.4%; 1 g polyunsaturated, 5.9%); 0.5 g carbohydrate; 0.7 g dietary fiber; 272 mg sodium; 0.7 mg iron; 113 mg cholesterol.

CHAOU KAI LAOU

Chicken Stir-Fry—China

*M*odern nutritional experts stress eating fresh food whenever possible, and if it has to be cooked, then only very lightly. The Chinese first developed the stir-fry method of cooking in order to conserve their limited resources of fuel. In solving this problem they developed a quick and healthy cooking technique that uses a minimum of fat! In this recipe, a little meat is combined with a mixture of crisp vegetables. Serve with steamed rice.

SNOW PEAS

*The snow pea (*Pisum sativum *var.* macrocarpon) *is an entirely edible vegetable which is why it is also known as mangetout meaning "eat it all." Its crisp, thin, flattened, almost translucent bright green pod contains tiny peas and the pod only needs to be topped and tailed before cooking. The snow pea is widely used in stir-fry dishes and as a green vegetable. Overcooking will destroy its crisp texture. Snow peas can also be used raw in salads. Store snow peas, unwashed, in the crisper section of the refrigerator and use as soon as possible, washing just before use.*

TOTAL TIME: 20 MINUTES

SERVES 4

Allow 2 to 2½ hours additional time if the Chicken Stock is not already prepared.

1 tablespoon plus 1 teaspoon peanut or canola oil
1 medium onion, cut into 12 wedges
1 garlic clove, minced
1 teaspoon finely chopped fresh ginger
8 oz (250 g) boneless skinless chicken breasts (fillets), cut lengthwise into thin 3 inch (8 cm) strips
2 medium carrots, thinly sliced diagonally
1 cup (about 4 oz/125 g) trimmed green beans, cut into 3 inch (8 cm) pieces
1 cup (about 2½ oz/75 g) halved button mushrooms
1 cup (about 2½ oz/75 g) trimmed snow peas (mangetout)
1 cup (8 fl oz/250 ml) Chicken Stock (see page 52)
1 tablespoon plus 1 teaspoon cornstarch (cornflour)
1 tablespoon cold water
2 tablespoons reduced-sodium soy sauce
2 tablespoons mirin or dry sherry

◆ Heat the oil in a non-stick wok or large, non-stick frying pan over medium-high heat. Add the onion, garlic and ginger and stir-fry for 1 minute.

◆ Add the chicken and stir-fry until it has changed color from pink to cream, about 3 minutes.

◆ Add the carrot and stir-fry for 1 minute, then add the beans, mushrooms and snow peas. Stir-fry for 2 minutes longer.

◆ Stir in the stock and bring to a boil. Reduce the heat to low, cover and simmer for 3 minutes.

◆ Blend the cornstarch with the water in a small bowl until smooth. Add this mixture, and the soy sauce and mirin to the wok, stirring constantly until boiling and the sauce thickens. Simmer for 1 minute longer.

◆ Serve immediately in a warm serving bowl.

NUTRITION NOTES

PER SERVING: 171 calories/720 kilojoules; 18 g protein; 6.7 g fat, 35% of calories (1 g saturated, 5.2% of calories; 3.8 g monounsaturated, 19.9%; 1.9 g polyunsaturated, 9.9%); 8 g carbohydrate; 3.6 g dietary fiber; 307 mg sodium; 1.2 mg iron; 31 mg cholesterol.

CHAOU GAI LAN FAR AOU YUK

Beef and Broccoli Stir-Fry—China

Stir-frying is a classic Chinese cooking style that is amazingly versatile. An endless variety of ingredients can be used based on personal preference and market availability. A premium cut of beef, such as tenderloin, is best for a stir-fry. Because this recipe calls for a small amount of beef, it is not expensive. Here, the tenderloin is combined with colorful crisp vegetables which add dietary fiber, vitamins and minerals. Serve with rice for a well-balanced meal.

TOTAL TIME: 25 MINUTES

SERVES 4

Allow an extra 2 to 2½ hours additional time if the Vegetable Stock is not already prepared. Use a non-stick wok to help cut down on the oil required for stir-frying, or use a large, non-stick frying pan.

---

12 oz (375 g) lean, trimmed beef
   tenderloin fillets (fillets), cut ½ inch
   (1 cm) thick
1 tablespoon peanut or canola oil
1 large onion, cut into 12 wedges
2 garlic cloves, minced
1 tablespoon finely cut strips fresh ginger
1 medium red bell pepper (capsicum),
   seeded and cut into thin strips
2 cups broccoli florets

1 cup asparagus spears cut into 2 inch
   (5 cm) pieces
2 teaspoons cornstarch (cornflour)
1 cup Vegetable Stock (see page 52)
2 tablespoons oyster sauce or hoisin sauce
2 tablespoons mirin or dry sherry
watercress sprigs, for garnish

◆ Slice the beef across the grain into thin strips about 4 inches (10 cm) long.
◆ Heat the oil in a non-stick wok over medium-high heat. Add the onion and garlic and stir-fry for 1 minute.
◆ Add the beef and stir-fry for 1 minute. Sprinkle the ginger over the beef and stir-fry for 1 minute longer.
◆ Add the bell pepper and stir-fry for 3 minutes, then add the broccoli and asparagus and stir-fry for 2 minutes longer.

◆ Blend the cornstarch with 1 tablespoon of the stock in a small bowl until smooth. Add the remaining stock, the oyster sauce and the mirin to the wok and stir-fry until it comes to a boil.
◆ Add the cornstarch mixture to the wok and cook, stirring constantly, until the sauce thickens. Reduce the heat to low and simmer, to let the flavors blend, for 1 minute.
◆ Transfer to a warm serving bowl, garnish with the watercress and serve immediately.

NUTRITION NOTES

PER SERVING: 196 calories/825 kilojoules; 26 g protein; 6.7 g fat, 30% of calories (1.6 g saturated, 7.2% of calories; 3.5 g monounsaturated, 15.6%; 1.6 g polyunsaturated, 7.2%); 6 g carbohydrate; 3.1 g dietary fiber; 440 mg sodium; 3.9 mg iron; 63 mg cholesterol.

BROCHETTES DE COQUILLES SAINT-JACQUES AUX CHAMPIGNONS

Scallop and Mushroom Brochettes—France

The scallop takes its French name (coquille Saint-Jacques) from the patron saint of fishermen. Scallops provide protein and are an excellent source of iron, zinc, iodine, calcium and phosphorus. Mushrooms are low in calories, contain no fat and are a good source of B-complex vitamins. Serve the brochettes with rice and a green salad. This is a light main course, ideal for a summer lunch.

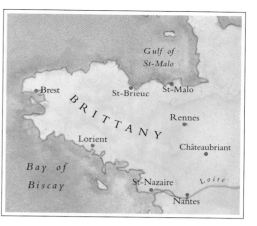

TOTAL TIME: 1 HOUR 10 MINUTES

SERVES 4

The orange coral is served as part of the scallop in France—in the United States scallops are sold without their coral. Lime zest may be julienned with a citrus zester.

8 wooden skewers, about 10 in (25 cm) long

32 small sea scallops, about 12 oz (375 g) (shelled weight)
40 button mushrooms, about 11 oz (345 g)
thyme sprigs, for garnish, optional

MARINADE

⅓ cup (3 fl oz/90 ml) freshly squeezed lime juice
2 tablespoons virgin olive oil
2 tablespoons dry white wine
¼ cup finely chopped shallots (French shallots)
zest of 2 limes, thinly julienned
1 tablespoon thyme leaves
1 garlic clove, minced

◆ Trim away any brown marks from the scallops.
◆ To make the marinade, combine the lime juice, oil, wine, shallots, lime zest, thyme and garlic in a shallow glass dish. Mix well.
◆ Add the scallops to the marinade and stir to coat well. Cover with plastic wrap and refrigerate for 1 hour.
◆ Meanwhile, soak the skewers in cold water for at least 30 minutes.
◆ Trim the ends of the mushroom stalks then brush the mushrooms clean with a dry pastry brush.
◆ Preheat the broiler and adjust the rack so that the pan is 3–5 inches from the source of heat (or preheat the grill on High). Line the broiler pan with foil.
◆ Thread the mushrooms and scallops alternately on each skewer, using 5 mushrooms and 4 scallops per skewer. Place the brochettes on the broiler pan and brush with half the marinade.

◆ Broil the brochettes until the scallops change to a dense white color, about 2½ minutes, turn them over, brush with the remaining marinade and broil until cooked through, about 2½ minutes longer.
◆ Transfer the brochettes to a serving dish, garnish with the thyme sprigs, if using, and serve at once.

NUTRITION NOTES

PER SERVING: 150 calories/629 kilojoules; 15 g protein; 8.2 g fat, 48% of calories (1.5 g saturated, 8.8% of calories; 5.5 g monounsaturated, 32.2%; 1.2 g polyunsaturated, 7%); 3 g carbohydrate; 2.8 g dietary fiber; 177 mg sodium; 1.1 mg iron; 33 mg cholesterol.

SOLE VÉRONIQUE

Sole with Grapes—France

This renowned French dish celebrates both the fresh and the fermented fruits of the grape vine. Narrow fillets of lean fish are rolled up and poached in flavorful white wine. The wine is used to make a tasty low-fat sauce, which is poured over the fish and garnished with fresh grapes. Fish is a useful source of iodine, magnesium and phosphorus. Serve with rice and a green vegetable or steamed baby carrots.

TOTAL TIME: 35 MINUTES

SERVES 4

Use narrow fish fillets for this dish, or wider fillets, cut lengthwise along the center.

1½ lb (750 g) fillets of sole or whiting or porgy (bream), cut into 8 narrow fillets, skin removed
16 baby spinach (English spinach) leaves
1 cup (8 fl oz/250 ml) plus 3 teaspoons cold water
1 cup (8 fl oz/250 ml) dry white wine
6 peppercorns
4 parsley sprigs
2 whole cloves
1 bay leaf

2 cups (10 oz/315 g) halved seedless green grapes
1 tablespoon plus 1 teaspoon cornstarch (cornflour)
3 teaspoons snipped chives, plus extra, for garnish
¼ teaspoon salt
pinch of white pepper
2 tablespoons light (fat-reduced) cream
extra grapes, for garnish
thinly julienned red bell pepper (capsicum), for garnish, optional

◆ Rinse the fish fillets in cold water and pat dry with paper towels. Place the fillets, skinned side up, on a flat surface. Place 2 spinach leaves on top of each fillet. Starting at the widest end, roll the fillets up neatly, enclosing the spinach leaves. Secure the rolls with wooden toothpicks.

◆ Combine 1 cup of the water, the wine, peppercorns, parsley sprigs, cloves and bay leaf in a large frying pan. Bring to a boil over medium-high heat. Stand the fish rolls upright in the pan. Reduce the heat to medium-low, cover and simmer until the fish turns opaque, 7 to 8 minutes.

◆ Carefully transfer the fish rolls to a warm plate. Cover and keep warm.

◆ Increase the heat to high and boil the wine mixture rapidly until it is reduced by a quarter, about 5 minutes. Drain and reserve the liquid. You should have about 1½ cups of liquid.

◆ Meanwhile, place 1½ cups of the grape halves in a blender or food processor. Process until puréed. Strain the purée through a sieve and discard the skins.

◆ Blend the cornstarch with the remaining 3 teaspoons of cold water in a small bowl until smooth.

◆ Add the grape purée and cornstarch mixture to the wine mixture and bring to a boil over medium heat, stirring constantly. Reduce the heat to medium-low and simmer, to blend, for 1 minute.

◆ Add the remaining halved grapes, 3 teaspoons of the chives, salt and pepper and heat through, 1 to 2 minutes. Stir in the cream, return the fish rolls to the sauce, spoon the sauce over the rolls and heat through, 1 to 2 minutes.

◆ Place the fish rolls upright on warm plates and carefully pour the sauce over. Garnish with the extra grapes, the extra chives and bell pepper, if using. Serve immediately.

SPINACH

A dark green, leafy vegetable, spinach (Spinacia oleracea) originally grew in Persia and is known to have been cultivated in southern Europe during the eleventh century. A favorite throughout Europe, it was taken to America by the Spanish and there it quickly gained popularity. Spinach is a good source of vitamins A and C. Although its iron content is high, spinach is also rich in oxalic acid which inhibits the body's absorption of iron and calcium and gives the vegetable its distinctive taste. Spinach (also known as English spinach) has either flat or curly leaves. It is available fresh throughout the year—be sure to choose leaves that are dark green and crisp. Traditionally served as a vegetable to accompany white meats and eggs, spinach is also used to make soups and quiches. Young, tender spinach leaves are becoming popular as a salad green. When using fresh leaves, always wash them thoroughly to remove any sand or grit. Store in the crisper section of the refrigerator, and use within 3 days as the leaves can wilt quite quickly. Spinach can also be purchased frozen, canned or bottled.

NUTRITION NOTES

PER SERVING: 296 calories/1243 kilojoules; 41 g protein; 3.5 g fat, 12% of calories (1.8 g saturated, 6% of calories; 1.1 g monounsaturated, 4%; 0.6 g polyunsaturated, 2%); 14 g carbohydrate; 1.1 g dietary fiber; 266 mg sodium; 1.2 mg iron; 199 mg cholesterol.

SPANAKÓPITA

Phyllo with Cheese and Spinach—Greece

Spanakópita *is a traditional Greek dish made with phyllo pastry filled with cheese and spinach. These ingredients combine to provide protein, vitamin C and beta-carotene. Here, lemon juice replaces some of the butter usually used to layer the pastry. The result is delightfully crisp and much lower in total fat than the traditional recipe. Serve with brown rice sprinkled with lemon juice and a Greek Salad (see page 76).*

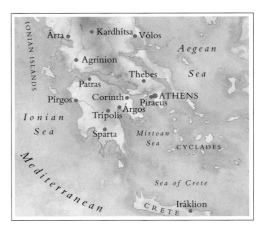

TOTAL TIME: 55 MINUTES
SERVES 6

When working with phyllo dough, keep the stack of thin sheets of fragile pastry covered with a sheet of waxed (greaseproof) paper topped with a cold, damp cloth. This prevents the pastry from becoming dry and brittle.

1 tablespoon virgin olive oil
1 small leek, thinly sliced
6 scallions (spring onions), thinly sliced

2 lb (1 kg) spinach (English spinach) or Swiss chard (silverbeet) leaves, trimmed from stalks and thinly shredded
½ cup thinly sliced celery
¼ cup shredded mint
1 tablespoon coarsely chopped oregano, optional
4 oz (125 g) reduced-sodium, low-fat cottage cheese
4 oz (125 g) feta cheese, crumbled
2 tablespoons soy grits or oat bran
2 teaspoons brown mustard seeds
¼ cup (1 oz/30 g) slivered almonds
2 tablespoons margarine or butter, melted
2 tablespoons freshly squeezed lemon juice
8 sheets phyllo pastry

◆ Heat the oil in a large, non-stick frying pan over medium heat. Add the leek and scallions. Sauté, stirring occasionally, until the leek is softened, about 5 minutes.
◆ Add the spinach to the frying pan and stir constantly until the leaves have softened, 3 to 5 minutes.
◆ Stir in the celery, mint and oregano. Cover and cook for 1 minute. Remove the frying pan from the heat and set aside to slightly cool.
◆ Combine the cottage cheese, feta cheese, soy grits and mustard seeds in a large bowl and mix well.
◆ Reserve 1 tablespoon of the almonds. Lightly toast the remaining almonds in a dry, non-stick frying pan over medium

heat, about 1 minute. Stir the toasted almonds into the cheese mixture.
◆ Add the spinach mixture to the cheese mixture and mix well.
◆ Combine the melted margarine and lemon juice in a small bowl.
◆ Place a sheet of phyllo pastry on a cool, dry work surface. Lightly brush with the lemon juice mixture. Working quickly, place a second sheet of phyllo on top. Continue brushing and layering all the phyllo pastry sheets.
◆ Place the cheese and spinach mixture along one of the long edges of the phyllo pastry and roll up firmly, jelly-roll (Swiss-roll) style.
◆ Carefully transfer the roll to a baking tray, seam side down. Brush with the remaining lemon juice mixture and sprinkle the reserved almonds on top.
◆ Bake until the pastry is crisp and golden brown, 20 to 25 minutes. Cut into 6 thick slices with a serrated knife.
◆ Serve on 6 individual warm dinner plates.

NUTRITION NOTES

PER SERVING (Analysis uses monounsaturated margarine): 260 calories/1093 kilojoules; 14 g protein; 17 g fat, 57% of calories (5.2 g saturated, 17.4% of calories; 8.7 g monounsaturated, 29.2%; 3.1 g polyunsaturated, 10.4%); 14 g carbohydrate; 4.5 g dietary fiber; 476 mg sodium; 3.8 mg iron; 17 mg cholesterol.

FETA CHEESE

This soft, white, uncooked cheese, traditionally made from sheep's or goat's milk, has its origins in Ancient Greece where it was made by shepherds in the hills around Athens. Feta even rates a mention in the Odyssey. *Milk curds are drained into block molds that give it its characteristic shape. The large blocks are then stored in brine, which contributes to the cheese's salty taste and ensures a rindless cheese. Although feta cheese is still made with traditional ingredients, there are also factory-produced types, which may include cow's milk. These are usually firmer and do not cost as much as those made with sheep's or goat's milk. Feta is now made in many countries including the United States, Australia and Denmark. Sold either loose by weight or in prepacked cartons, it should be kept in its own brine in the refrigerator to ensure freshness. Feta is an excellent cheese for cooking and is used in spinach and cheese pies, gratin dishes, and also as a stuffing. Traditional Greek salad is a combination of tomatoes, olives, cucumber and feta. Feta should always be very well drained before using, to avoid mixing the brine into the finished dish.*

SOUVLÁKIA ME ARNÍ

Skewered Lamb—Greece

Lamb is popular and readily available in Greece where it is prepared in many different ways. Lemons, too, are used extensively in Greek cooking. Here, lamb is trimmed of all visible fat, marinated in lemon juice and threaded onto skewers—the lemon is used as a tenderizer and for flavor. This dish is an excellent source of protein, vitamin C, niacin, iron and zinc. Serve with Greek Salad (see page 76) and rice.

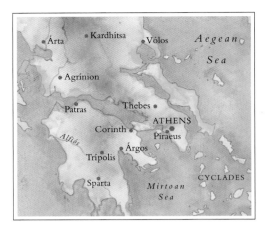

TOTAL TIME: 1 HOUR 40 MINUTES

SERVES 4

Marinate the meat for up to 24 hours if time allows. Try fresh lemon or lime leaves instead of the bay leaves for a slightly different flavor.

---

8 metal skewers, at least 10 inches (25 cm) long

1½ lb (750 g) boned leg of lamb, well trimmed
¼ cup (2 fl oz/60 ml) dry white wine
grated zest and juice of 1 lemon
1 tablespoon virgin olive oil
8 fresh or dried bay leaves
2 tablespoons finely chopped oregano or marjoram
2 garlic cloves, minced
¼ teaspoon freshly ground black pepper

oregano or marjoram sprigs, for garnish
lemon wedges, for serving, optional

◆ Cut the lamb into forty 1 inch (2.5 cm) neat cubes.
◆ Combine the wine, lemon zest and juice, oil, bay leaves, oregano and garlic in a shallow glass dish and mix well.
◆ Add the lamb to the marinade and stir until all the pieces are evenly coated. Cover with plastic wrap and marinate in the refrigerator for at least 1 hour, stirring once.
◆ Preheat the broiler and adjust the rack so that the pan is 3–5 inches from the source of heat (or preheat the grill on High). Line the broiler pan with foil.
◆ Thread 5 pieces of lamb and 1 bay leaf onto each skewer.
◆ Place the lamb on the broiler rack and broil until lightly browned, about 2 minutes per side. Lower the rack about 2 more

inches from the source of heat (or reduce the heat to Medium) and broil for 3 minutes longer per side. Brush the lamb with the remaining marinade and broil until cooked through, about 2 minutes longer per side. To test for doneness, cut a piece of lamb in half—it should be brownish pink and juicy inside.
◆ Transfer the lamb to a warm serving platter, garnish with the oregano sprigs and serve immediately with the lemon wedges, if using.

NUTRITION NOTES

PER SERVING: 261 calories/1095 kilojoules; 43 g protein; 7.8 g fat, 27% of calories (2.6 g saturated, 9% of calories; 4.5 g monounsaturated, 15.6%; 0.7 g polyunsaturated, 2.4%); 1 g carbohydrate; 1.1 g dietary fiber; 124 mg sodium; 4.3 mg iron; 123 mg cholesterol.

CHHOLE

Chickpea Casserole—India

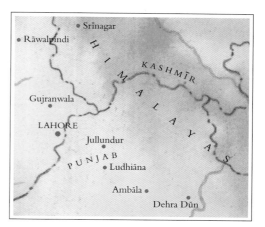

In India the chickpea is used in a multitude of ways. Roasted chickpeas are sold by street vendors as a nourishing snack. Ground chickpeas are used to make a flour (called besan*) that binds patties, pancakes and meatballs. Whole chickpeas are used in Indian vegetarian curry dishes like this one. Chickpeas are a good source of value-for-money protein and an excellent source of potassium, iron and dietary fiber. Serve with rice and curry condiments.*

TOTAL TIME: 40 MINUTES

SERVES 4

Use drained, canned chickpeas to save time—otherwise start preparing the chickpeas a day in advance. This is a simple and easily prepared curry, made more interesting and elegant with the addition of cubes of juicy, ripe mango.

1 tablespoon canola or safflower oil
2 large onions, thinly sliced
4 garlic cloves, minced
2 small green chilies, seeded and thinly
   sliced
1 teaspoon ground coriander
1 teaspoon ground cumin
1 teaspoon garam masala
1 teaspoon ground turmeric
3 large, vine-ripened tomatoes, coarsely
   chopped
1 teaspoon light brown sugar
2 tablespoons chopped cilantro (coriander)
   or parsley
2 tablespoons shredded mint
½ cup (4 oz / 125 g) dried chickpeas, cooked
   (see page 57)
1 large, ripe mango (about 1 lb / 500 g),
   peeled and cubed (see page 86)
½ cup (about 3 oz / 90 g) low-fat, plain
   yogurt, for serving

◆ Heat the oil in a large, heavy-bottomed pan over medium heat. Add the onions and sauté, stirring frequently, until soft and transparent, 3 to 5 minutes.
◆ Add the garlic, chilies, coriander, cumin, garam masala and turmeric. Reduce the heat to medium-low and cook, stirring constantly, to develop the flavor of the curry spices, about 2 minutes.
◆ Add the tomatoes, sugar, half of each of the cilantro and mint and stir well. Reduce the heat to low and simmer, stirring occasionally, until the tomatoes are soft, about 10 minutes.
◆ Gently stir in the chickpeas and simmer,

covered, until heated through, about 8 minutes. Carefully stir in the mango and simmer, covered, until it is heated through, about 2 minutes.
◆ Pour the mixture into a warm serving bowl and sprinkle with the remaining cilantro and mint. Serve immediately with the yogurt.

NUTRITION NOTES

PER SERVING: 213 calories / 895 kilojoules; 11 g protein; 5.8 g fat, 25% of calories (0.9 g saturated, 3.9% of calories; 2.7 g monounsaturated, 11.6%; 2.2 g polyunsaturated, 9.5%); 29 g carbohydrate; 8.3 g dietary fiber; 47 mg sodium; 3.8 mg iron; 2 mg cholesterol.

GUSHTABA

Lamb Meatballs in Curried Yogurt Sauce—India

Yogurt is believed to have originated in the Balkans. Its culinary uses have spread to many countries including India. Often used there as a meat tender-izer, as a salad dressing, as a drink, a marinade and as a dessert, yogurt is a good source of protein and is rich in calcium and phosphorus. Here, lean, spicy lamb meatballs are simmered in a delicious yogurt sauce. Chickpea flour is an excellent source of dietary fiber, iron and zinc. Serve with rice and condiments.

TOTAL TIME: 1 HOUR 10 MINUTES
SERVES 6

The meatballs are poached in water before simmering in the sauce to reduce the fat content. Ghee may be replaced with butter or oil, but some of the traditional flavor will be lost. Chickpea flour is available in Indian stores and in some health food stores.

2 lb (1 kg) finely ground (minced) lean lamb
⅓ cup (about 1 oz/30 g) cornstarch (cornflour)
1 teaspoon garam masala or curry powder

1 teaspoon salt
1 tablespoon cold water, plus extra if needed
4 cups (32 fl oz/1 liter) water
2 tablespoons ghee or butter
2 tablespoons canola or safflower oil
1 large onion, thinly sliced
2 teaspoons finely chopped fresh ginger
¼ cup (about 1 oz/30 g) chickpea flour
3 cups (20 oz/600 g) low-fat, plain yogurt
1 cinnamon stick, broken in half
¼ cup shredded mint or cilantro (coriander)
lime zest, thinly julienned, for garnish,
  optional
lime wedges, for garnish
mint or cilantro (coriander) sprigs, for garnish

◆ Place the lamb, cornstarch, garam masala salt and water in a large bowl. Mix together with your hands to combine. Add more water, a teaspoon at a time, as necessary, to help bind the mixture.

◆ Divide the lamb mixture into 30 portions. With cold hands, roll each portion into a ball about the size of a large walnut, 1–1½ inches (2.5–3 cm) in diameter.

◆ Bring the 4 cups of water to a boil in a large wide saucepan. Using a slotted spoon, carefully add the meatballs to the saucepan, cover and simmer over low heat until the meatballs are firm and have shrunk slightly in size, about 10 minutes.

◆ Transfer the meatballs to a warm plate. Reserve ½ cup of the cooking liquid and discard the rest. Refrigerate the reserved

liquid and discard the fat that rises quickly to the surface.

◆ Heat the ghee and oil in a large, heavy-bottomed saucepan over medium heat. Add the onion and ginger, reduce the heat to medium-low and sauté, stirring occasionally, until the onion is soft and golden brown, 7 to 10 minutes.

◆ Remove the saucepan from the heat and stir in the flour. Cook over medium heat, stirring constantly, until the flour is blended, about 1 minute.

◆ Add the yogurt and continue stirring just until the oil separates from the yogurt, 3 to 5 minutes.

◆ Reduce the heat to medium-low, add the meatballs, cooking liquid and cinnamon. Cover and simmer, stirring twice, until the meatballs are tender and cooked through, about 20 minutes.

◆ Transfer the meatballs to a warm serving platter, spoon the sauce on top and sprinkle with the shredded mint and lime zest, if using. Garnish with the lime wedges and mint sprigs and serve.

NUTRITION NOTES

PER SERVING (Analysis uses ghee): 384 calories/ 1611 kilojoules; 45 g protein; 14.9 g fat, 35% of calories (6.7 g saturated, 15.7% of calories; 6.6 g monounsaturated, 15.5%; 1.6 g polyunsaturated, 3.8%); 16 g carbohydrate; 1.2 g dietary fiber; 563 mg sodium; 4.2 mg iron; 128 mg cholesterol.

GARAM MASALA

Garam masala, the best known of the masalas, is an aromatic blend of a variety of dry-roasted ground spices used predominantly in Indian cooking. Garam is the Indian word for "hot" and masala means "spices." There are many different versions of garam masalas, some containing up to twenty different spices, and they can vary in flavor from hot to fragrant and slightly sweet. Garam masala may include black peppercorns, cinnamon, cloves, cardamom, coriander, cumin, mace, nutmeg and other spices. Other ingredients, such as saffron and fennel seeds, may also be included. It can be easily made at home or bought in some specialty markets. Commercial versions tend to use less of the more expensive cardamom, often replacing it with larger amounts of coriander and cumin. It is used in curries, as a condiment and on braised meats. In order to retain its aroma, garam masala is often added to a dish just before serving. Stored in an airtight container in a cool, dry place, it will maintain its flavor and fragrance for up to 6 months.

MEE GORENG UDANG

Spicy Noodles with Shrimp—Indonesia

*I*ndonesian cooking has been strongly influenced by its migrant population which originated predominantly in India and China. Kecap manis, *the thick sweet soy sauce of Indonesia, is a local variation of traditional Chinese soy sauce. A spicy, high-fiber dish, this recipe will revitalize your spirits in very hot weather. It is quick to cook, once everything is prepared, and is a complete meal in itself.*

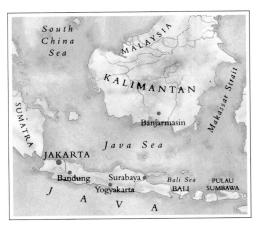

TOTAL TIME: 1 HOUR

SERVES 4

Allow 2 to 2½ hours additional time if the stock is not already prepared. Kecap manis, sambal ulek and Hokkien noodles are available from Asian food stores. Hokkien noodles (parboiled wheat noodles) are also known as "wet" noodles. Wear rubber gloves to prevent your hands from burning when preparing the chili flower.

1 smooth, well-shaped, small, red chili,
    for garnish
4 scallions (spring onions), for garnish
6 small raw shrimp (green prawns), about
    8 oz (250 g), shelled and deveined
2 tablespoons peanut or canola oil
1 large onion, thinly sliced
2 garlic cloves, minced
1 medium carrot, cut into thin julienne
    strips (about 1 cup)
¾ cup thinly sliced red bell pepper
    (capsicum)
1 stalk celery, thinly sliced diagonally
    (about 1 cup)
1 teaspoon ground chili paste (sambal ulek)
8 oz (250 g) Hokkien noodles
1 tablespoon kecap manis or reduced-sodium
    soy sauce
½ cup (4 fl oz / 125 ml) Chicken or
    Vegetable Stock (see page 52)
1 cup (2 oz / 60 g) soy bean sprouts

MARINADE

1 teaspoon kecap manis or reduced-sodium
    soy sauce
1 teaspoon mirin or dry sherry
1 teaspoon sesame oil
2 teaspoons cornstarch (cornflour)
1 teaspoon finely chopped fresh ginger

◆ Wear rubber gloves to make the chili flower. Use a sharp vegetable knife to cut a cross lengthwise down through the tip to ½ inch (1 cm) from the base of the chili. Make extra lengthwise cuts as necessary, depending on the size of the chili. Scrape away any white membrane, including the seeds. Place the chili in a bowl of iced water in the refrigerator until it opens out to form an attractive flower shape, about 45 minutes.

◆ To make scallion brushes, remove the outer layer from the scallions and trim off the root end. With a sharp vegetable knife, make a slit through the center of each scallion from the top, about 2 inches (5 cm) long. Cut down to make another slit at right angles to the first slit. Gently cut each quarter slit in half again lengthwise. Place the scallions in a bowl of iced water and chill in the refrigerator until the ends curl, about 45 minutes.

◆ Meanwhile, to make the marinade, combine the kecap manis, mirin, sesame oil, cornstarch and ginger in a small bowl and mix well. Add the shrimp and turn to coat with the marinade. Cover with plastic wrap and marinate in the refrigerator for about 20 minutes.

◆ Heat 1 tablespoon of the oil in a wok over medium heat or in an electric wok set at 300°F (150°C). Add the onion and garlic and stir-fry for 2 minutes.

◆ Add the carrot, bell pepper and celery and stir-fry for 2 minutes. Using a slotted spoon, transfer the vegetables to a plate.

◆ Heat the remaining oil in the wok, then add the shrimp with its marinade and stir-fry, about 2 minutes.

◆ Return the vegetables to the wok. Add the chili paste, noodles, kecap manis, stock and bean sprouts and stir-fry until the mixture is heated through, about 5 minutes.

◆ Place the noodle mixture on a warm serving platter or in a deep Asian serving bowl. Garnish with the chili flower and scallions, and serve at once.

NUTRITION NOTES

PER SERVING: 376 calories / 1579 kilojoules; 14 g protein; 13 g fat, 30% of calories (2.2 g saturated, 5.1% of calories; 5.6 g monounsaturated, 12.9%; 5.2 g polyunsaturated, 12%); 53 g carbohydrate; 5.6 g dietary fiber; 192 mg sodium; 1.7 mg iron; 59 mg cholesterol.

SALTIMBOCCA

Veal with Prosciutto—Italy

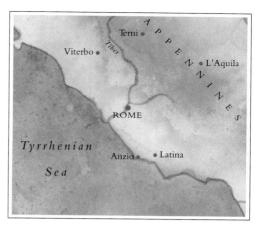

This classic veal dish, often associated with the most elegant restaurants in Rome, is cooked so quickly that it is supposed to "jump" into your mouth! Only the best and freshest veal will do. Veal is tender, low in fat, an excellent source of protein, niacin and zinc and is a valuable source of iron. Serve this delicious dish with noodles and a seasonal green vegetable like asparagus for a well-balanced meal.

TOTAL TIME: 15 MINUTES

SERVES 4

Butter will give a better color to the veal than olive oil.

4 thin slices veal scallopini (steak), about
   13 oz (410 g)
4 wafer thin slices prosciutto, about 3 oz (90 g)
8 sage leaves
1 tablespoon plus 1 teaspoon virgin olive oil
   or butter
2 vine-ripened tomatoes, coarsely chopped
½ cup (4 fl oz / 125 ml) dry white wine
¼ teaspoon freshly ground black pepper
sage sprigs, for garnish

◆ Cut the veal in half lengthwise. Place between two sheets of waxed (greaseproof) paper and pound into thin rounds with a mallet. Cut the slices of prosciutto in half.
◆ Place a slice of prosciutto and then a sage leaf on top of each piece of veal. Pin the layers together by inserting a wooden toothpick through the sage leaf, prosciutto and out through the veal. Then weave the toothpick back up through the layers so that it lies flat.
◆ Heat the oil in a large, non-stick frying pan over medium heat. Add the veal, prosciutto-side down, and cook for 1 minute. Turn over and cook until the veal changes to a light golden color, about 1 minute.
◆ Add the tomatoes, wine and pepper and bring to a boil. Reduce the heat to low and simmer, stirring frequently, until the veal is tender, about 3 minutes.
◆ Transfer to warm plates, garnish with the sprigs of sage and serve immediately.

NUTRITION NOTES

PER SERVING: 210 calories/881 kilojoules; 27 g protein; 8.1 g fat, 34% of calories (2 g saturated, 8.4% of calories; 5.1 g monounsaturated, 21.4%; 1 g polyunsaturated, 4.2%); 1.7 g carbohydrate; 1 g dietary fiber; 429 mg sodium; 2.4 mg iron; 92 mg cholesterol.

LASAGNE LENTICCHIE ROSSO

Red Lentil Lasagne—Italy

Lentils and other legumes are often used in traditional southern Italian recipes because meat and fresh vegetables can be expensive in this area. This lasagne recipe uses protein-rich, high-fiber lentils as a nourishing alternative to ground meat. Low-fat dairy products help to keep the fat content down. High in phosphorus, iron and B vitamins, the red lentil is one of the oldest varieties of legume known to be cultivated. Serve with a seasonal salad.

LENTILS

The lentil (Lens esculenta) is a small annual legume related to the pea. There are several varieties of lentils varying in color from green to brown to bright orange-red. Known to have been cultivated since ancient times, lentils have been found in settlements near Lake Biel in Switzerland which date from the Bronze Age. Today lentils are widely used in many parts of Asia, the Middle East and North Africa. An excellent source of vegetable protein and some B vitamins, lentils are also low in fat and do not contain any cholesterol. They do not need to be soaked before cooking, but doing so will speed up the cooking time. Lentils are most frequently used in soups and stews. The puréed dahl of India is justly famous. Lentils can also be ground to produce flour. Salads, too, can be enhanced by adding cooked lentils. Lentils will keep for about 6 months, stored in a cool, dark place. Rinse well before using.

TOTAL TIME: 1 HOUR 15 MINUTES

SERVES 8

If you do not have an attractive ovenproof baking dish, use a small roasting pan. In this case, cut the cooked lasagna into individual portions and serve on warmed plates.

olive oil cooking spray
2 tablespoons virgin olive oil
2 medium carrots, chopped
1 large onion, chopped
2 garlic cloves, minced
2 cups (12 oz/375 g) red lentils, washed, rinsed and drained
2 large, vine-ripened tomatoes, coarsely chopped
½ cup sundried tomatoes, coarsely chopped
1 tablespoon finely chopped oregano
1 bay leaf
4 cups (32 fl oz/1 liter) water
¼ teaspoon salt
¼ cup (2 oz/60 g) plus 1 tablespoon margarine or butter
¼ cup (1 oz/30 g) plus 1 tablespoon all-purpose (plain) flour
2½ cups (20 fl oz/600 ml) skim milk
1 lb (500 g) reduced-sodium, low-fat cottage cheese or ricotta cheese
½ teaspoon ground nutmeg
½ teaspoon freshly ground black pepper
8 oz (250 g) instant lasagne noodles
¼ cup (1 oz/30 g) freshly grated Parmesan cheese

◆ Lightly spray a 9 × 14 inch (23 × 35 cm) oven-to-table baking dish with olive oil cooking spray.

◆ Heat the oil in a large, heavy-bottomed saucepan over medium heat. Add the carrots, onion and garlic. Sauté, stirring occasionally, until softened, about 5 minutes.

◆ Add the lentils, tomatoes, sundried tomatoes, oregano, bay leaf and water. Mix well. Increase the heat to medium-high and bring to a boil, stirring frequently. Reduce the heat to medium-low, cover and simmer, stirring occasionally, until the lentils are tender, about 30 minutes. Discard the bay leaf. Stir in the salt.

◆ Preheat the oven to 350°F (180°C).

◆ Melt the margarine in a medium-sized saucepan over medium heat. Add the flour and stir constantly until lemon colored and grainy in texture, 1 to 2 minutes. Pour in the milk and bring to a boil, stirring constantly, until the sauce has thickened. Remove from the heat. Add the cottage cheese, nutmeg and pepper and stir well.

◆ Pour one-third of the cheese sauce into the baking dish. Spread to cover the bottom. Layer one-third of the lasagne noodles on top. Spread half the lentil mixture over the noodles. Repeat this process once more. Cover with the remaining noodles. Top with the remaining cheese sauce. Sprinkle the Parmesan cheese lightly over the top.

◆ Bake until bubbling and golden brown, about 30 minutes.

◆ Cut into 8 portions and serve immediately from the dish.

NUTRITION NOTES

PER SERVING (Analysis uses monounsaturated margarine): 458 calories/1925 kilojoules; 30 g protein; 16 g fat, 31% of calories (4.2 g saturated, 8.1% of calories; 8.8 g monounsaturated, 17.1%; 3 g polyunsaturated, 5.8%); 50 g carbohydrate; 9.4 g dietary fiber; 404 mg sodium; 4.2 mg iron; 14 mg cholesterol.

PIZZA INTEGRALE DI VERDURE FRESCHE

Wholewheat Pizza with Garden Vegetables—Italy

Pizza can have a countless variety of toppings. Here, zucchini and asparagus, which are both native to Italy, are used with other "adopted" vegetables like the tomato. Wholewheat flour, used to make this yeastless dough, provides more dietary fiber and B-complex vitamins than white flour. Serve the pizza with a fresh green salad.

TOTAL TIME: 1 HOUR

SERVES 4

It is advisable to store wholewheat flour in the refrigerator in hot weather.

PIZZA CRUST

2¼ cups (10 oz/300 g) wholewheat
    (wholemeal) flour
2½ teaspoons baking powder
pinch of salt
pinch of white pepper
2 tablespoons margarine or butter, cut into
    small pieces and chilled
scant cup (about 7½ fl oz/230 ml) cold water

TOPPING

1 tablespoon virgin olive oil
1 cup (about 3 oz/90 g) thinly sliced leek
2 garlic cloves, minced
1 cup (4 oz/125 g) grated carrot
4 anchovy fillets, soaked in milk for
    30 minutes and drained
2 medium, vine-ripened tomatoes, cut into
    ¼ inch (6 mm) thick slices

1 small zucchini, about 2 oz (60 g),
    thinly sliced
1 cup (4 oz/125 g) asparagus pieces,
    about 1½ inches (4 cm) long
1 cup (4 oz/125 g) freshly grated, low-fat
    mozzarella cheese
2 tablespoons freshly grated Parmesan cheese
4 black olives, halved and pitted

◆ Preheat the oven to 400°F (200°C).

◆ To make the pizza crust, sift the flour, baking powder, salt and pepper into a large bowl and add the bran left in the sieve to the bowl. Add the margarine and rub in with cold fingertips until the mixture resembles fine bread crumbs. Gradually add the water and cut through the flour mixture using a round-bladed knife until a stiff dough is formed. The dough should be firm enough to support the knife for a few seconds. Take care not to overwork the dough or it will become tough.

◆ Alternatively, the dough can be made in a food processor. Combine the flour, baking powder, salt, pepper and margarine in the processor. Process until the mixture

resembles fine bread crumbs. Add the water gradually and process until a stiff dough is formed which leaves the sides of the bowl.

◆ Turn the dough out onto a cool, lightly floured surface and sprinkle with flour. Lightly flour a rolling pin and roll the dough out to make a 10 inch (25 cm) round. Lift the dough onto an 11 inch (28 cm) pizza pan and press down the edges. Prick the dough with a fork in several places.

◆ Bake the pizza crust for 10 minutes, then remove from the oven and set aside.

◆ Meanwhile, prepare the topping. Heat the oil in a small, non-stick frying pan over medium heat. Add the leek and garlic and sauté, stirring occasionally until the leek is soft, about 5 minutes. Stir in the carrot and cook for 1 minute longer. Set aside to cool.

◆ Spoon the leek and carrot mixture onto the middle of the pizza base and spread to within ¾ inch (2 cm) of the edge.

◆ Arrange the anchovy fillets and sliced zucchini over the center of the pizza in a single layer. Arrange the slices of tomato around the outside edge and place the asparagus pieces on top of the tomatoes.

◆ Sprinkle the mozzarella cheese over the center of the pizza, allowing the color of the various vegetables to show through around the edge. Sprinkle with the Parmesan cheese, then scatter the olives over the top.

◆ Reduce the oven temperature to 375°F (190°C) and bake the pizza until the crust is cooked and the topping is golden brown, about 25 minutes.

◆ Cut the pizza into 4 portions and serve immediately.

ASPARAGUS

Asparagus (Asparagus officinalis) is a member of the lily family and believed to be native to the eastern Mediterranean region and Asia Minor. Long valued for its medicinal properties, asparagus is reputed to help eyesight, soothe toothaches and cure insect stings. Asparagus is also said to have diuretic and laxative qualities. There are two basic varieties of asparagus, the green and the white, and each variety has many different forms. Rich in vitamins A and C, asparagus is a versatile vegetable and can be served as a side dish or used in soups, quiches, stir-fry dishes, savory dishes and gourmet pizzas. Asparagus spears make a decorative garnish for hors d'oeuvre platters too. Select firm, straight, bright green or white spears with tight tips. Asparagus is highly perishable and should be cooked (and eaten) the same day it is purchased. However, it will keep in the crisper section of the refrigerator for 2 to 3 days. Asparagus is also available canned.

NUTRITION NOTES

PER SERVING (Analysis uses monounsaturated margarine): 421 calories/1768 kilojoules; 24 g protein; 17.3 g fat, 38% of calories (6.1 g saturated, 13.2% of calories; 8.8 g monounsaturated, 19%; 2.7 g polyunsaturated, 5.8%); 45 g carbohydrate; 12 g dietary fiber; 1189 mg sodium; 3.4 mg iron; 30 mg cholesterol.

MAGURO NO SASHIMI TO KYURI

Tuna Sashimi on Cucumber—Japan

Japanese chefs are world famous for their artistic presentation of food, and sashimi is no exception. It is an offering of raw fish served in several different ways, usually accompanied by soy sauce for dipping. The fish must be extremely fresh, ideally only 4 to 12 hours out of the water. Raw fish is easy to digest and delicious. Tuna is rich in protein, phosphorus, magnesium and iron. Serve as a light meal with a rice salad.

TOTAL TIME: 30 MINUTES

SERVES 4

Some fish markets and fish shops employ sashimi experts who will slice the raw fish for you. If you are doing it yourself, make sure you use a very sharp knife. Mizuna leaves are Japanese mustard greens and have a distinctive, mild flavor. Look for mizuna, wasabi paste and pickled ginger in Asian food stores.

⅓ cup (2 oz/60 g) low-fat, plain yogurt
2 tablespoons reduced-fat (light) sour cream
½ teaspoon wasabi paste (Japanese horseradish)
8 oz (250 g) very fresh (sashimi-grade) tuna steak, about 1 inch (2.5 cm) thick, cut from the center of the fish

16 cucumber slices, about ½ inch (1 cm) thick
16 cilantro (coriander) leaves
2 tablespoons thinly sliced Japanese pickled ginger, drained
16 baby mizuna leaves or watercress sprigs
soy sauce, for serving, optional

◆ Combine the yogurt, sour cream and wasabi in a small bowl and mix together.
◆ Trim the tuna and discard any dark-colored pieces. Slice the tuna as thinly as possible, into 16 slices, along the grain. Use your fingers or chopsticks to gently roll the tuna slices up into 16 small neat rolls.
◆ Place the slices of cucumber on a smooth work surface. Place a roll of tuna on top of each slice of cucumber.
◆ Top each roll of tuna with 1 teaspoon of

the yogurt mixture, allowing it to flow down attractively.
◆ Place a cilantro leaf on top of the yogurt mixture, then a slice of pickled ginger on top of the cilantro leaf. Finally, top each sashimi with a baby mizuna leaf.
◆ Divide the sashimi among 4 individual Japanese serving plates and serve immediately, accompanied by a bowl of soy sauce for dipping, if desired.

NUTRITION NOTES

PER SERVING: 119 calories/499 kilojoules; 18 g protein; 3.4 g fat, 28% of calories (1.3 g saturated, 10.7% of calories; 1 g monounsaturated, 8.2%; 1.1 g polyunsaturated, 9.1%); 2 g carbohydrate; 0.5 g dietary fiber; 62 mg sodium; 1.8 mg iron; 34 mg cholesterol.

TOFU, HOSHIJITAKE, MAME NO ITAMAMONO

Tofu, Mushroom and Bean Stir-Fry—Japan

Tofu, also known as soy bean curd, is widely used in Japanese cooking. Its taste is fairly bland, and so it is usually marinated for additional flavor before being added to soups, savory stir-fries and some noodle dishes. A nourishing food, rich in protein, calcium and iron, tofu is eaten regularly in a country like Japan where meat and fish are relatively expensive.

TOTAL TIME: 50 MINUTES

SERVES 4

Tofu comes in three different textures: silken tofu is very smooth, slippery and shiny; soft tofu is firmer but will crumble fairly easily; firm or hard tofu is well pressed to remove as much moisture as possible and slices more easily than silken or soft tofu. If chrysanthemum leaves are available use them instead of bok choy.

1 lb (500 g) firm tofu
1 tablespoon sesame oil
1 medium onion, cut into 12 wedges
6 scallions (spring onions), cut into 1 inch
   (2.5 cm) pieces
2 stalks celery, thinly sliced diagonally
2 garlic cloves, minced
2 teaspoons thinly sliced fresh ginger
1 cup (4 oz/125 g) green beans, trimmed
   and cut in half diagonally
4 dried shiitake mushrooms, soaked in
   warm water for 15 minutes, drained, and
   sliced into ¼ inch (6 mm) thick pieces
1 lb (500 g) bok choy or chrysanthemum
   leaves, thick stalks removed and thinly
   sliced

MARINADE

2 tablespoons tamari or reduced-sodium
   soy sauce
1 tablespoon mirin or dry sherry
juice of ½ lemon or 1 lime
1 tablespoon sesame oil

◆ Cut the tofu into ½ inch (1 cm) cubes.
◆ To prepare the marinade, combine the tamari, mirin, lemon juice and sesame oil in a small bowl and mix well.
◆ Pour the marinade mixture into a shallow glass or ceramic dish. Add the tofu in a single layer, then turn to coat all sides evenly. Cover with plastic wrap and marinate in the refrigerator for 30 minutes or overnight.
◆ Heat the sesame oil in a large wok or heavy-bottomed frying pan over medium heat. Add the onion and stir-fry until softened, about 5 minutes. Add the scallions and stir-fry for 1 minute.
◆ Add the celery, garlic and ginger to the wok and stir-fry for 1 minute.
◆ Add the beans, shiitake mushrooms and bok choy and stir-fry for 2 minutes.
◆ Gently stir in the tofu and the marinade, reduce the heat, cover and simmer until the tofu is heated through, about 2 minutes.
◆ Serve immediately in individual Japanese serving bowls.

NUTRITION NOTES

PER SERVING: 204 calories/856 kilojoules; 14 g protein; 13 g fat, 56% of calories (2.5 g saturated, 10.8% of calories; 4.7 g monounsaturated, 20.2%; 5.8 g polyunsaturated, 25%); 7 g carbohydrate; 5.2 g dietary fiber; 296 mg sodium; 6.6 mg iron; 0 mg cholesterol.

ENCHILADAS DE NUEZ CON VERDURAS

Nut and Vegetable Enchiladas—Mexico

Tortillas have long been a staple food in Mexico, a country that can boast one of the world's most interesting cuisines. Tortillas are the basis of many delightful and ingenious Mexican dishes like the enchilada, which consists of a tortilla wrapped around a prepared filling, then baked. Serve with a hot, spicy salsa for more intense flavor.

WALNUTS

The delicious walnut is shaped in two hemispheres which look rather like the two halves of the human brain. This is believed to be why the Greeks and Romans thought walnuts could cure headaches. The Romans thought so highly of walnuts that they planted trees wherever they established settlements. The walnut tree (genus Juglans) grows today in most temperate regions of the world. High in polyunsaturated oil, protein, vitamins B and D and phosphorus, walnuts are a good food for vegetarians. There are many species but the most popular are the yellow-brown English or Persian walnut and the black walnut. The English walnut is most widely available. It is also sold in its unripe state, pickled in vinegar. Walnuts are an important ingredient in the Mexican national dish, chiles en nogada. The lighter colored the kernel, the more delicate the flavor. Walnut oil is highly prized for its rich, fruity flavor and is excellent for salads. Ripe walnuts are eaten as a snack, used in desserts and in salads. The distinctive taste complements a variety of savory and sweet dishes. For freshness, buy walnuts in the shell and crack open just before use. Because of their high oil content, shelled walnuts should be stored in the refrigerator where they may be kept for up to 6 months. Walnuts in the shell will keep for 3 months.

TOTAL TIME: 25 MINUTES

SERVES 4

If the tortillas are too brittle to fold or roll around the filling, sprinkle or spray them with some hot water to soften.

¼ cup sundried tomatoes
1 tablespoon virgin olive oil
1 medium onion, finely chopped
1 garlic clove, minced
1 small red chili, seeded and thinly sliced
2 large zucchini, about 8 oz (250 g), coarsely grated
¼ cup (1 oz/30 g) chopped walnuts or pecans
¾ cup (3 oz/90 g) freshly grated, reduced-fat Cheddar cheese
8 corn tortillas, about 6 inches (15 cm) wide
1 cup shredded lettuce
½ cup halved cherry tomatoes
¾ cup Tofu and Avocado Dip (see page 53), for serving, optional
avocado slices, for garnish, optional

◆ Preheat the oven to 300°F (150°C).
◆ Soak the sundried tomatoes in boiling water for 20 minutes, then drain and chop.
◆ Heat the oil in a large, non-stick frying pan over medium heat. Add the onion and sauté, stirring occasionally, until transparent, about 5 minutes.
◆ Add the garlic and chili and cook, stirring constantly, until the flavors are developed, about 1 minute.

◆ Stir in the zucchini and sundried tomatoes. Cover and simmer until the zucchini is soft and tender, about 5 minutes.
◆ Meanwhile, spread the tortillas out on a large baking tray, overlapping if necessary. Bake until heated, about 5 minutes.
◆ Remove the frying pan from the heat. Add the walnuts and ½ cup of the cheese to the zucchini mixture and stir until evenly combined.
◆ Remove the tortillas from the oven. Working quickly, spoon the zucchini mixture along the center of each tortilla, dividing equally. Fold the sides of the tortillas over or roll like a thick cigar to enclose the filling.
◆ Place the stuffed tortillas in one flat layer on the bottom of a large baking dish. Bake until heated through, 10 to 15 minutes.
◆ Transfer the enchiladas to dinner plates, sprinkle with the remaining cheese and top with the lettuce and tomatoes, dividing equally. Garnish with the avocado slices, if using. Serve at once with the Tofu and Avocado Dip on the side, if using.

NUTRITION NOTES

PER SERVING: 334 calories/1401 kilojoules; 14 g protein; 18 g fat, 47% of calories (5.5 g saturated, 14% of calories; 6.3 g monounsaturated, 17%; 6.2 g polyunsaturated, 16%); 32 g carbohydrate; 3.9 g dietary fiber; 339 mg sodium; 1.7 mg iron; 18 mg cholesterol.

CHILE CON CARNE

Chili with Beef—Mexico

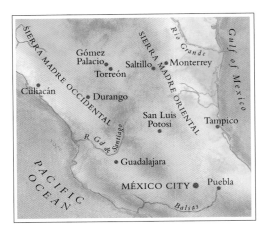

While some traditional Mexican dishes are high in fat, this one is not. It combines a protein-rich, high-fiber legume with a reasonable amount of lean ground beef, a rich source of iron. Dried chilies are ground and made into chili powder, the ingredient which gives this dish its distinctive color and flavor. Spicy hot and satisfying, Chili Con Carne *can be served with rice, warm tortillas and a fresh garden salad.*

TOTAL TIME: 1½ HOURS

SERVES 4

Add chili powder to taste. If preferred, cooked dried kidney beans can be used for this dish (see instructions for cooking red beans on page 33).

1 tablespoon virgin olive oil
1 large onion, finely chopped
1 medium green bell pepper (capsicum), seeded and finely chopped
2 stalks celery, finely chopped
2–4 teaspoons chili powder
1 lb (500 g) coarsely ground (minced) lean beef
3 large, vine-ripened tomatoes, coarsely chopped

10 oz (300 g) canned red kidney beans, drained but not rinsed
½ cup (4 fl oz/125 ml) water or Vegetable Stock (see page 52)
pinch salt

◆ Heat the oil in a large, heavy-bottomed saucepan over medium heat. Add the onion and sauté, stirring frequently, until slightly softened, about 3 minutes.
◆ Add the bell pepper, celery and chili powder. Cook, stirring frequently, until the bell pepper is firm but tender, about 5 minutes. Use a slotted spoon to transfer the vegetables to a plate.
◆ Increase the heat to medium-high and add the beef to the saucepan. Cook, stirring constantly, until browned, about 5 minutes.

Drain off any fat from the pan and discard.
◆ Return the vegetables to the saucepan. Add the tomatoes, kidney beans, water and salt. Bring to a boil over medium heat, stirring constantly. Reduce the heat and simmer, covered, stirring occasionally, until the beef is tender, about 1 hour.
◆ Transfer the mixture to a warm serving bowl or individual plates and serve at once.

NUTRITION NOTES

PER SERVING: 282 calories/1185 kilojoules; 34 g protein; 9.3 g fat, 29% of calories (3 g saturated, 9.4% of calories; 4.9 g monounsaturated, 15.3%; 1.4 g polyunsaturated, 4.3%); 16 g carbohydrate; 7.4 g dietary fiber; 522 mg sodium; 5.6 mg iron; 75 mg cholesterol.

MILLET PATTIES

Morocco

Millet is a useful source of complex carbohydrate, iron and vitamins A and B. Grown by the Chinese as long ago as 4500 BC, it is still used widely in many African and Asian cuisines. It is often ground into flour or used as a whole grain in many savory dishes, or brewed as a drink. This recipe combines millet with some hearty Mediterranean flavors. Serve with an assortment of salads for a well-balanced meal.

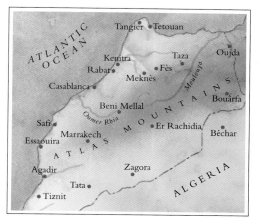

TOTAL TIME: 1 HOUR 20 MINUTES

SERVES 4

Millet is available from leading health food stores. Try using it as a substitute for couscous in other recipes.

¾ cup (5 oz/155 g) millet
1½ cups (12 fl oz/375 ml) water
2 tablespoons plus 1 teaspoon virgin olive oil
4 scallions (spring onions), thinly sliced
1 tablespoon capers, coarsely chopped
1 tablespoon finely sliced black olives
1 tablespoon poppy seeds
1 tablespoon finely chopped sundried tomato
1 tablespoon no-added-salt tomato paste
½ teaspoon dried oregano
1 tablespoon freshly squeezed lemon juice
⅓ cup (1½ oz/45 g) sesame seeds

◆ Combine the millet and water in a medium-sized, heavy-bottomed saucepan and bring to a boil over high heat. Cover, reduce the heat to medium-low and simmer until the millet is tender and all the water is absorbed, about 25 minutes. Transfer to a bowl and set aside to cool for 20 to 30 minutes.

◆ Heat 1 tablespoon of the oil in a small frying pan over medium heat. Add the scallions and sauté until softened, about 1 minute. Drain on paper towels.

◆ Add the scallions, capers, olives, poppy seeds, sundried tomato, tomato paste, oregano and lemon juice to the millet. Mix thoroughly.

◆ Divide the mixture into 4 equal portions. Spread the sesame seeds on a sheet of waxed (greaseproof) paper.

◆ With cold hands, shape each portion of the millet mixture into a round. Dip each patty into the sesame seeds, coating evenly.

◆ Place the patties on a plate, cover with plastic wrap and refrigerate until firm, about 1 hour.

◆ Heat the remaining oil in a large, nonstick frying pan over medium heat. Add the patties and cook until golden on both sides, about 1 minute per side. Reduce the heat to medium-low and cook until heated through, 3 minutes longer on each side.

◆ Drain the patties on paper towels and serve immediately.

NUTRITION NOTES

PER SERVING: 299 calories/1255 kilojoules; 5 g protein; 16 g fat, 50% of calories (2.6 g saturated, 8.1% of calories; 9.2 g monounsaturated, 28.8%; 4.2 g polyunsaturated, 13.1%); 32 g carbohydrate; 5.2 g dietary fiber; 86 mg sodium; 3.1 mg iron; 0 mg cholesterol.

COUSCOUS B'DJAJ

Couscous with Chicken—Morocco

Couscous, a grain-like cereal made from durum wheat, is a staple food in Moroccan cuisine. In this recipe, couscous is combined with colorful and flavorful Mediterranean ingredients and topped with spicy, fragrant, broiled chicken. This dish provides plenty of protein and carbohydrate as well as vitamin C. Serve with a green salad or a salad featuring Mediterranean ingredients, such as Caponata (see page 78).

TOTAL TIME: 1 HOUR 20 MINUTES
SERVE 4

Nowadays, instant or pre-steamed couscous is widely available. Harissa is available from leading specialty food stores. Fenugreek seeds are available from health food stores and specialty food stores.

¼ teaspoon saffron threads
1 tablespoon hot water
4 boneless, skinless chicken breasts (fillets), about 4 oz (125 g) each

¼ cup shredded mint
1 teaspoon ground cumin
1 teaspoon fenugreek seeds
1 garlic clove, minced
1 cup (6 ½ oz/200 g) low-fat, plain yogurt
juice of ½ lemon
1 teaspoon harissa sauce
1⅓ cups (8 oz/250 g) instant (pre-steamed) couscous
2 teaspoons margarine or butter
1 cup (8 fl oz/250 ml) boiling water
1 tablespoon virgin olive oil
¼ cup finely chopped shallots (French shallots)
¼ cup thinly sliced scallions (spring onions)
1 medium, vine-ripened tomato, cut into ¼ inch (6 mm) dice
⅓ cup cooked chickpeas (see page 57) or pomegranate seeds
mint sprigs, for garnish

◆ Gently crush the saffron threads and soak in the hot water for 10 minutes.
◆ Place the chicken breasts in a large, shallow glass dish.
◆ Mix together the saffron and its soaking liquid, the mint, cumin, fenugreek seeds, garlic, yogurt, lemon juice and harissa in a small bowl. Spread the mixture over the chicken pieces and turn to coat. Cover with plastic wrap and marinate in the refrigerator for at least 1 hour, or up to 8 hours.
◆ Place the couscous and the margarine in a small bowl. Pour over the boiling water and stir with a fork. Cover and set aside until the couscous grains are swollen and tender, about 2 minutes.
◆ Heat the oil in a large, heavy-bottomed frying pan over medium heat. Add the shallots and sauté, stirring frequently, until transparent, about 3 minutes.
◆ Add the scallions and cook, stirring constantly, until firm but tender, about 1 minute.
◆ Stir in the tomato and bring to a boil, stirring constantly.
◆ Add the chickpeas and couscous to the frying pan and mix well with a fork. Remove from the heat and set aside while cooking the chicken.
◆ Preheat the broiler. Adjust the rack so that the pan is 3–5 inches from the source of heat (or preheat the grill on High). Line the broiler pan with foil.
◆ Place the chicken breasts on the rack in the broiler pan and broil each side for 4 minutes until the yogurt mixture is slightly set. Lower the rack about 2 more inches from the source of heat (or reduce the heat to Medium). Broil until the chicken is pale yellow and cooked through, about 4 minutes longer per side.
◆ Transfer the cooked chicken to a plate and cover to keep warm.
◆ Return the pan containing the couscous mixture to medium-high heat and stir constantly until heated through, about 2 minutes. Remove from the heat and fluff with a fork.
◆ Slice the chicken pieces crosswise into thick slices.
◆ Spoon the couscous onto a warm serving platter or individual plates and arrange the chicken slices over the top. Garnish with the mint and serve at once.

NUTRITION NOTES

PER SERVING (Analysis uses monounsaturated margarine): 394 calories/1654 kilojoules; 38 g protein; 9.7 g fat, 22% of calories (2.2 g saturated, 4.9% of calories; 5.8 g monounsaturated, 13.2%; 1.7 g polyunsaturated, 3.9%); 40 g carbohydrate; 3.9 g dietary fiber; 174 mg sodium; 4.9 mg iron; 65 mg cholesterol.

HARISSA SAUCE

This very hot sauce is widely used in North African cooking, particularly in Morocco, Tunisia and Algeria. Its ingredients usually include dried hot chilies, olive oil, garlic, cumin, coriander and caraway seeds. Traditionally used as an accompaniment to couscous, harissa sauce is also used to add flavor to soups, casseroles and other dishes. This versatile sauce can be served with bread and olives at the beginning of a meal and can also be used as a condiment. It is available in cans and jars from specialty food stores and in some supermarkets. Once open, harissa sauce can be stored in a covered glass container in the refrigerator for several weeks. Add some olive oil to cover the top of the paste to prevent it from drying out.

SOYARÓNI S KRÁSNOY KAPÚSTOY, GOLUBTSY

Soyaroni with Pork and Red Cabbage and
Stuffed Cabbage Rolls—Russia

The combination of cabbage, lean pork and soy-bean based pasta is full of protein and fiber. Hijiki seaweed is a natural food of the sea and adds valuable iodine to this dish. The sauerkraut (pickled cabbage) in the cabbage rolls contributes vitamin B_{12} (difficult for vegetarians to obtain) and vitamin C.

Soyaroni with Pork and Red Cabbage (top) and Stuffed Cabbage Rolls

SOYARÓNI S KRÁSNOY KAPÚSTOY

Soyaroni with Pork and Red Cabbage

TOTAL TIME: 45 MINUTES

SERVES 4

Allow 2 hours additional time if the stock is not already prepared. If soyaroni pasta is unavailable, replace it with wholewheat pasta. Cut the core from the cabbage before shredding the leaves, then remove any remaining white center "ribs".

⅓ oz (10 g) hijiki seaweed strips, optional
8 oz (250 g) soyaroni, preferably spiral-shaped
1 tablespoon virgin olive oil
8 oz (250 g) lean pork (leg steak or fillet), cut into ½ inch (1 cm) wide strips
8 scallions (spring onions), thinly sliced
2 garlic cloves, minced
2 cups thinly shredded red cabbage
1 medium carrot, cut into thin julienne strips
1 medium parsnip, cut into thin julienne strips
¼ teaspoon caraway seeds or dill seeds
2 tablespoons apple cider vinegar
1 tablespoon apple juice
1 tablespoon prepared horseradish
2 cups (16 fl oz / 500 ml) Chicken or Vegetable Stock (see page 52)
2 tablespoons finely chopped parsley, for garnish

◆ Soak the hijiki seaweed in a bowl of cold water for 15 minutes. Drain.
◆ Meanwhile, bring a large saucepan of water to a boil over high heat. Slowly add the soyaroni, stir well and boil rapidly, uncovered, until tender, about 10 minutes. Drain well.
◆ Meanwhile, heat the oil in a large, non-stick frying pan over medium-high heat. Add the pork and sauté, stirring constantly, until browned, about 4 minutes.
◆ Add the scallions and garlic, reduce the heat to medium and sauté, stirring frequently, until softened, about 2 minutes.
◆ Add the cabbage, carrot, parsnip and caraway seeds. Reduce the heat to medium-low, cover and cook until the vegetables are firm but tender, about 6 minutes.
◆ Stir in the vinegar, apple juice and horseradish and heat through.
◆ Pour the stock into a large saucepan and bring to a boil over high heat. Reduce the heat to medium, add the soyaroni, hijiki, if using, and the pork and cabbage mixture. Stir until heated through, 3 to 5 minutes.
◆ Divide the mixture among 4 warm bowls, sprinkle the parsley on top and serve immediately.

PAPRIKA

Paprika is one of the several varieties of the bell pepper (Capsicum annuum). Taken to Europe after their discovery in the New World, peppers can vary in spiciness from mild and sweet (paprika) to hot (bird's eye chilies), depending on the soil and climatic conditions of the areas in which they are cultivated. Paprika, the pepper that flourishes in Hungary and Eastern Europe, is sweeter than other peppers. After harvesting, it is then dried and crushed to produce a bright orange to brick-red powder. The ground flesh of the pepper produces a mild, sweet spice, but when the seeds are also crushed and added, the spice can become very hot. Excellent with tomatoes, it is used to season casseroles, sauces and soups. Paprika is also added to a dish as a garnish as its lovely color is one of its main attractions. Paprika can turn brown when exposed to sunlight, so store in a dark, cool place to preserve its bright color.

GOLUBTSY

Stuffed Cabbage Rolls

TOTAL TIME: 1 HOUR 20 MINUTES

SERVES 4

For a vegetarian version of this recipe, omit the meat and add ½ cup of coarsely chopped almonds to the filling.

---

1 cup (6 oz / 185 g) brown rice
1 tablespoon plus 1 teaspoon canola or safflower oil
1 large onion, finely chopped
8 oz (250 g) finely ground (minced) lean pork or beef
4 oz (125 g) mushrooms, coarsely chopped
2 cups (13 oz / 410 g) prepared or canned sauerkraut, rinsed and drained
3 tablespoons no-added-salt tomato paste
1 teaspoon caraway seeds or poppy seeds
¼ teaspoon paprika, plus extra, for garnish
¼ teaspoon salt
8 large cabbage leaves
olive oil cooking spray
¼ cup (2 fl oz / 60 ml) dry white wine
1 large, vine-ripened tomato, coarsely chopped
1 cup (6½ oz / 200 g) low-fat, plain yogurt

◆ Bring a large saucepan of water to a boil. Add the rice, stir, reduce the heat and boil, uncovered, until tender, about 30 minutes. Drain well.
◆ Heat the oil in a large, non-stick frying pan over medium heat. Add the onion and sauté, stirring occasionally, until soft and golden, about 8 minutes.
◆ Add the pork and cook, stirring constantly, until browned, about 5 minutes.
◆ Add the mushrooms and cook until soft, about 3 minutes.
◆ Remove the pan from the heat. Stir in the rice, half the sauerkraut, the tomato paste, caraway seeds, paprika and salt.

◆ Preheat the oven to 350°F (180°C).
◆ Bring a large saucepan of water to a boil over high heat. Add 4 of the cabbage leaves and cook until softened, about 1 minute. Transfer the cabbage leaves to a plate. Repeat the process with the remaining cabbage leaves. Set aside to cool.
◆ Remove the hard core or rib from the center of each cabbage leaf, so that each leaf is pliable.
◆ Spoon the rice mixture onto the center of the cabbage leaves, dividing equally. Fold the top of each leaf over the filling, fold in the sides, then roll the leaf up neatly to enclose the filling.
◆ Spray a large casserole dish with cooking spray. Spread the remaining sauerkraut over the bottom of the dish. Arrange the stuffed cabbage rolls on top of the sauerkraut. Pour the wine on top and sprinkle with the chopped tomato. Spoon the yogurt evenly over the top.
◆ Cover the casserole dish and bake until the cabbage rolls are tender, about 1 hour.
◆ Transfer the cabbage rolls to a warm serving platter. Stir the sauerkraut mixture and spoon around the rolls and garnish with a sprinkle of paprika. Serve immediately.

NUTRITION NOTES

PER SERVING—Soyaroni with Pork and Red Cabbage: 363 calories / 1526 kilojoules; 29 g protein; 6.7 g fat, 16% of calories (1.6 g saturated, 4% of calories; 3.7 g monounsaturated, 9%; 1.4 g polyunsaturated, 3%); 52 g carbohydrate; 6.9 g dietary fiber; 227 mg sodium; 1.3 mg iron; 32 mg cholesterol.

PER SERVING—Stuffed Cabbage Rolls: 404 calories / 1695 kilojoules; 27 g protein; 7.7 g fat, 17% of calories (1.3 g saturated, 3% of calories; 4.1 g monounsaturated, 9%; 2.3 g polyunsaturated, 5%); 54 g carbohydrate; 12 g dietary fiber; 808 mg sodium; 4 mg iron; 34 mg cholesterol.

ZHARENNAYA NO VERTELÉ GÓRBUSHA

Broiled Salmon with Dill Peach Sauce—Russia

Salmon is recognized as one of the world's finest fish for eating. In Russia salmon is often served in aspic on a special zakuska buffet. Here, it is prepared in a simpler fashion. Salmon is a rich source of protein, vitamins A and D and niacin, and is a valued source of omega-3 oils. A light fruit-based sauce complements this richly flavored fish.

TOTAL TIME: 35 MINUTES

SERVES 4

Select the end pieces of salmon fillet for the most delicate flavor. These will cook under a hot broiler (grill) in 8 minutes. If thicker slices, cut from higher up the fillet, are used, 10 to 12 minutes cooking time is required.

4 pieces salmon fillet, about 6 oz (185 g) each
½ cup (4 fl oz/125 ml) dry white wine
¼ teaspoon freshly ground black pepper
¼ cup finely chopped dill

DILL PEACH SAUCE

2 tablespoons light brown or turbinado (raw) sugar
¼ cup (2 fl oz/60 ml) dill-flavored white wine vinegar
2 large ripe peaches, peeled and cut into ¼ inch (6 mm) dice
2 scallions (spring onions), thinly sliced
2 tablespoons finely chopped dill
dill sprigs, for garnish
peach wedges, for garnish

◆ Place the salmon in a single layer in a large shallow glass dish. Pour the wine over and sprinkle with the pepper and dill. Cover with plastic wrap and marinate in the refrigerator while preparing the sauce.

◆ To prepare the sauce, combine the sugar and vinegar in a small nonreactive saucepan. Cook over medium-low heat until the sugar is dissolved, about 1 minute. Pour the syrup into a small bowl and set aside to cool.

◆ Place the diced peaches, scallions and chopped dill in a medium-sized bowl. Add the vinegar syrup and lightly fold together until evenly mixed.

◆ Preheat the broiler. Adjust the rack so that the pan is 3–5 inches from the source of the heat (or preheat the grill on High). Line the broiler pan with foil.

◆ Place the salmon fillets, skin-side down, on the rack in the broiler pan. Cook for about 4 minutes. Brush with the remaining marinade and broil until firm and cooked through, about 4 minutes for tail end fillets, or about 6 minutes for thicker fillets.

◆ Transfer the salmon to a warm serving platter or individual plates. Garnish with the sprigs of dill and peach wedges. Spoon a small amount of the sauce on the side of the salmon. Serve immediately.

NUTRITION NOTES

PER SERVING: 342 calories/1437 kilojoules; 41 g protein; 12 g fat, 32% of calories (3.6 g saturated, 9.6% of calories; 4.8 g monounsaturated, 12.8%; 3.6 g polyunsaturated, 9.6%); 11 g carbohydrate; 1 g dietary fiber; 197 mg sodium; 2.3 mg iron; 144 mg cholesterol.

CERDO CON GRANO DE PIMIENTA EN SALSA DE VINO

Peppercorn Pork in Wine Sauce—Spain

*R*ecent developments in raising pigs have led to the production of leaner pork. Now recognized by nutritional authorities as another "white" meat, there are many new cuts available. Pork is rich in thiamin and a good source of protein, niacin, iron and zinc. Here, it is combined with the Mediterranean flavors of Spain. Serve with rice or potatoes and steamed mixed vegetables.

TOTAL TIME: 35 MINUTES

SERVES 4

If pork loin steaks are unavailable, tenderloin medallions may be used instead.

4 pork loin steaks or tenderloin medallions, well trimmed, 5 oz (155 g) each
1 tablespoon plus 1 teaspoon virgin olive oil
¼ cup thinly sliced scallions (spring onions)
½ cup (4 fl oz / 125 ml) freshly squeezed orange juice
½ cup (4 fl oz / 125 ml) dry sherry
1 tablespoon plus 1 teaspoon canned (preserved) green peppercorns, well drained
2 tablespoons golden raisins (sultanas)
2 tablespoons (⅔ oz / 20 g) ground almonds
1 tablespoon finely chopped sage
orange slices, for garnish, optional
sage sprigs, for garnish

◆ Arrange the pork steaks on a chopping board and pound with a meat mallet or cleaver to an even thickness, about ½ inch (1 cm) thick.
◆ Heat 1 teaspoon of the olive oil in a large, heavy-bottomed frying pan over medium heat. Add the scallions and sauté until softened, stirring constantly, about 2 minutes. Remove the scallions from the frying pan with a slotted spoon and drain well on paper towels.
◆ Add the remaining oil to the frying pan, and heat over medium-high heat. Add the pork and cook until opaque, about 2 minutes per side.
◆ Add the orange juice and sherry to the frying pan and bring to a boil, stirring to pick up any scrapings from the bottom of the pan. Reduce the heat, cover and simmer until the pork is tender, 6 to 8 minutes.
◆ Transfer the pork to a plate and cover with foil to keep warm.
◆ Boil the sauce, uncovered, over medium heat, and reduce to approximately ¾ cup, about 4 minutes.

◆ Add the peppercorns, raisins, ground almonds and sage. Reduce the heat to low, return the pork to the frying pan and simmer until heated through, about 2 minutes.
◆ Transfer the pork to a serving platter or individual plates. Spoon the sauce over the pork, garnish with the orange slices, if using, and sprigs of sage and serve at once.

NUTRITION NOTES

PER SERVING: 303 calories/1271 kilojoules; 36 g protein; 11 g fat, 32% of calories (2.1 g saturated, 6.1% of calories; 7.1 g monounsaturated, 20.7%; 1.8 g polyunsaturated, 5.2%); 7 g carbohydrate; 1 g dietary fiber; 104 mg sodium; 2 mg iron; 81 mg cholesterol.

TERNERA ASADA CON PURÉ DE PATATA, PUERRO Y ALMENDRA

Roast Veal with Potato, Leek and Almond Purée—Spain

Spanish cooks use ground almonds, rich in monounsaturated oil and vitamin E, to thicken and flavor dishes. In this recipe, the almonds are added to a purée of leeks and high-fiber pear and potatoes and served with a veal roast. Bright green and gold vegetables like green beans, spinach purée, yellow squash or baby winter squash make colorful accompaniments.

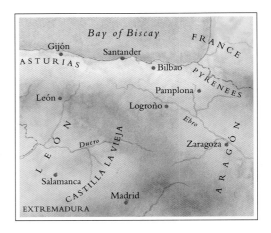

LEEKS

The leek (Allium porrum) *is a member of the onion family, and has long been prized by gourmets. Originating in the eastern Mediterranean more than 3000 years ago, the leek was taken to Britain by the Ancient Romans. It later became the national emblem of Wales, following a victory by King Cadwallader against the Saxons (in battle his troops each wore a leek as a way of identifying each other). Leeks are cultivated for their pale white, bulbous stalks and are widely used in both French and British cookery. Leeks have a mild tangy flavor and are often served as a first course with a vinaigrette sauce. They are also often teamed with potatoes in savory pies, casseroles and soups. Before using, the base and leaves should be trimmed and thoroughly washed under cold running water to remove the dirt that tends to accumulate between the leaves. Leeks are rich in vitamin C and dietary fiber. They should only be bought when they are firm and fresh; small to medium-sized leeks tend to be sweeter and more tender.*

TOTAL TIME: 1½ HOURS

SERVES 6

Allow 1½ to 2 hours additional time if the Chicken Stock is not already prepared. A boneless rump roast of veal is very lean and tender. A good butcher will tie the veal and prepare it for roasting.

olive oil cooking spray
1½ lb (750 g) boneless rump roast (nut)
   of veal, trimmed
2 tablespoons virgin olive oil
2 teaspoons dark brown sugar
2 tablespoons low-fat, plain yogurt
1½ cups (about 5 oz/155 g) thinly sliced leeks
1 cup (8 fl oz/250 ml) Chicken Stock
   (see page 52)
1 lb (500 g) small russet potatoes, scrubbed
1 medium pear, quartered, cored, peeled
   and sliced
¼ cup (1 oz/30 g) ground almonds, toasted
herbs, for garnish, optional

◆ Preheat the oven to 400°F (200°C). Spray the bottom of a roasting pan with olive oil cooking spray.
◆ Tie the veal into a neat roll with string and place in the roasting pan. Combine the oil, sugar and yogurt in a small bowl and mix well. Brush the mixture over the veal.
◆ Roast the veal for 30 minutes, remove from the oven and transfer to a plate.
◆ Arrange the sliced leeks over the bottom of the roasting pan and pour the stock over the top. Set a rack over the leeks in the roasting pan and place the veal securely on the rack.

◆ Return the veal to the oven, reduce the temperature to 350°F (180°C) and roast until the veal is cooked through and the juices run clear when pierced with a skewer in the center, about 40 minutes.
◆ Meanwhile, bring a large saucepan of water to a boil. Add the potatoes and boil, covered, over medium heat until tender, 20 to 25 minutes. Drain the potatoes and place in a potato ricer and purée (or remove the skins and mash until smooth.) Return the purée to the saucepan.
◆ Place the veal on a plate and cover with foil to keep warm. Drain off ¼ cup of the cooking liquid from the leeks and reserve for another use. Combine the leeks and the remaining cooking liquid in a blender or food processor and process until smooth. Add the pear and purée again until smooth.
◆ Add the leek and pear purée to the potato purée. Place over medium–low heat and mix well. Add the ground almonds and cook, stirring constantly, until the mixture is heated through, 3 to 4 minutes.
◆ Carve the veal into slices about ½ inch (1 cm) thick. Arrange on a warm serving plat-ter and surround them with the potato, leek and almond purée. Garnish with herbs, if using, and serve at once.

NUTRITION NOTES

PER SERVING: 290 calories/1217 kilojoules; 32 g protein; 9.8 g fat, 30% of calories (1.7 g saturated, 5.2% of calories; 6.4 g monounsaturated, 19.6%; 1.7 g polyunsaturated, 5.2%); 18 g carbohydrate; 3.4 g dietary fiber; 125 mg sodium; 3 mg iron; 103 mg cholesterol.

TRUITE AU FOUR À LA SAUCE "GREMOLATA"

Baked Trout with Gremolata—Switzerland

Although Switzerland has no coastline, its rivers and lakes are home to a variety of fish, including trout. Rich in protein, vitamins A and D as well as phosphorus and iodine, fresh trout is quick and easy to cook. Here, it is prepared with mushrooms, which are a good source of niacin and contribute dietary fiber and other B-complex vitamins.

TOTAL TIME: 35 MINUTES

SERVES 4

Trout is usually purchased eviscerated with the head and tail intact. Experiment with the many varieties of trout available.

4 small trout, cleaned, about 12½ oz
    (400 g) each
1 tablespoon plus 1 teaspoon margarine
    or butter
3 cups (8 oz/250 g) sliced button
    mushrooms or mushroom caps
juice of 1 lemon
freshly ground black pepper
¼ cup (1 oz/30 g) wholewheat (wholemeal
    plain) flour
olive oil cooking spray
flat-leaf parsley sprigs, for garnish

GREMOLATA

¼ cup chopped flat-leaf parsley
4 scallions (spring onions), thinly sliced
1 tablespoon capers
1 tablespoon finely grated lemon zest
1 garlic clove, minced
juice of 1 lemon

◆ Wash the trout in a large bowl of cold, lightly salted water, rinse in cold water and pat dry with paper towels.
◆ Preheat the oven to 425°F (220°C).
◆ Melt the margarine in a large, heavy-bottomed frying pan over medium heat. Add the mushrooms and lemon juice and sauté, stirring occasionally, until soft, about 3 minutes.
◆ Transfer the mushrooms to a large baking dish or roasting pan.
◆ Preheat the broiler. Adjust the rack so that the pan is 3–5 inches from the source of heat (or preheat the grill on High). Line the broiler pan with foil.
◆ Using the point of a sharp knife, make small incisions to score the trout diagonally 3 times on each side. Sprinkle a little pepper inside the cavity of each trout.

◆ Spread the flour on a piece of waxed (greaseproof) paper. Coat the fish in flour and shake off the excess.
◆ Place the trout on the broiler pan, without the rack. Spray lightly with the cooking spray and broil for 2 minutes. Turn over, again spraying the trout lightly, and broil until light golden, about 2 minutes.
◆ Transfer the trout to the baking dish, carefully arranging them in a single layer on top of the mushrooms.
◆ Bake until the flesh flakes easily when the fish is tested with a fork in the thickest part, about 10 minutes.
◆ Meanwhile, make the gremolata. Combine the parsley, scallions, capers, lemon zest and garlic in a blender or food processor.

Process until a coarse-textured paste forms, 5 to 10 seconds. Add the lemon juice and process briefly to mix well.
◆ Transfer the trout to a warm serving platter. Spoon the mushrooms around the trout, spread the gremolata over the trout and garnish with the sprigs of parsley. Serve immediately.

NUTRITION NOTES

PER SERVING (Analysis uses monounsaturated margarine): 401 calories/1686 kilojoules; 54 g protein; 17 g fat, 38% of calories (3.9 g saturated, 8.7% of calories; 7.5 g monounsaturated, 16.8%; 5.6 g polyunsaturated, 12.5%); 7 g carbohydrate; 4 g dietary fiber; 139 mg sodium; 4.7 mg iron; 156 mg cholesterol.

GAI YANG

Broiled Marinated Game Hens—Thailand

Use small (1½ lb to 2½ lb) young birds, that are quick and easy to cook—Rock Cornish game hens are ideal. This marinade of Asian spices and fresh lime juice makes them tender and gives the meat an exotic flavor. Game hens are an excellent source of protein and niacin. They also contain small quantities of iron and zinc, too. Serve with rice and a green salad or a medley of colorful steamed vegetables.

TOTAL TIME: 1 HOUR 50 MINUTES

SERVES 4

Use heavy duty kitchen scissors or poultry shears to cut the birds in half. Remove and discard the backbone. Alternatively, ask your supplier to do this for you. Ingredients such as lemongrass, purple basil and Asian mint are available in Asian food stores and in some supermarkets.

2 Rock Cornish game hens (poussins), about 1½ lb (750 g) each
juice of 2 limes
¼ teaspoon salt
1 tablespoon peanut or canola oil
8 shallots (French shallots), finely chopped
2 small green chilies, seeded and finely chopped
2 small red chilies, seeded and finely chopped
2 garlic cloves, minced
1 tablespoon finely chopped fresh ginger
1 stalk lemongrass, thinly sliced
1 teaspoon finely chopped cilantro (coriander) root
¼ cup shredded purple basil or sweet basil
¼ cup finely chopped cilantro (coriander)
¼ cup shredded mint, preferably Asian
basil and mint sprigs, for garnish
lime wedges, for serving

◆ Rinse the game hens under cold running water and pat dry with paper towels. Cut the birds in half lengthwise with kitchen scissors or poultry shears. Cut through the center of the breastbone, then as close as possible on both sides of the backbone. Discard the backbone. Trim the game hens neatly and remove any visible excess fat.
◆ Place the game hens, skin side up, in a shallow glass dish large enough to hold them in one flat layer. Sprinkle the lime juice and salt on top.
◆ Heat the oil in a small, non-stick frying pan over medium heat. Add the shallots, chilies, garlic, ginger, lemongrass and cilantro root and sauté, stirring constantly, until softened, about 2 minutes. Remove the pan from the heat and stir in the basil, cilantro and mint.
◆ Spread the shallot mixture over the game hens and turn to coat. Cover with plastic wrap and marinate in the refrigerator for about 1 hour.
◆ Preheat the broiler. Adjust the rack so that the pan is 4–5 inches from the source of heat (or preheat the grill on High). Line the broiler pan with foil.
◆ Place the game hens on the broiler pan, skin side down, and broil until the flesh turns pale golden, about 3 minutes; turn over and broil for 3 minutes longer. Adjust the rack so that the pan is 6 inches (15 cm) from source of heat. Brush the game hens with the marinade and broil for 12 minutes; turn over and broil until cooked through and the juices run clear when pierced with a skewer in the thigh, about 12 minutes longer.
◆ Transfer the game hens to a warm platter, garnish with the basil and mint sprigs and serve with the wedges of lime.

NUTRITION NOTES

PER SERVING: 262 calories/1101 kilojoules; 26 g protein; 17 g fat, 57% of calories (4.9 g saturated, 16.4% of calories; 8.8 g monounsaturated, 29.5%; 3.3 g polyunsaturated, 11.1%); 2 g carbohydrate; 1.5 g dietary fiber; 188 mg sodium; 2.2 mg iron; 88 mg cholesterol.

ROAST STUFFED CHICKEN

The United States

Wild rice, often called "the gourmet grain," is the seed of an aquatic grass native to the Great Lakes region of the United States. For hundreds of years, wild rice has been a staple food of the local Indians. It is higher in dietary fiber than brown rice and white rice, is low in fat, and is an excellent source of B-complex vitamins and complex carbohydrate. Green vegetables and cornbread (see page 108) complement this dish.

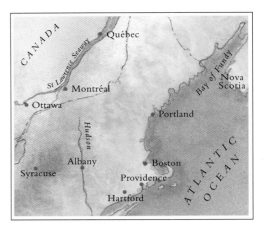

TOTAL TIME: 2 HOURS

SERVES 4

To truss the chicken, tie the chicken drumsticks together with string, then fold the neck skin over the opening and under the back. Secure the neck skin by folding the wing tips back underneath the chicken.

STUFFING

1 cup wild rice (5 oz / 155 g)
1 tablespoon margarine or butter
1 cup thinly sliced scallions (spring onions)
1 garlic clove, minced
2 tablespoons currants
2 tablespoons pine nuts
¼ teaspoon Chinese five-spice powder
1 tablespoon finely chopped oregano or marjoram
grated zest of 1 orange

1 small chicken, about 3 lb (1.5 kg)
¼ cup (about 1½ oz / 45 g) low-fat, plain yogurt
juice of 1 orange
oregano sprigs, for garnish

◆ Bring a large saucepan of water to a boil over high heat. Add the wild rice, stir, reduce the heat and boil, uncovered, until tender, 30 to 35 minutes. Drain well.

◆ Preheat the oven to 375°F (190°C). Wash the chicken under cold running water and pat dry with paper towels.

◆ To make the stuffing, heat the margarine in a small, non-stick frying pan over medium heat. Add the scallions and garlic and sauté, stirring constantly, until softened, about 3 minutes.

◆ Add the currants and the pine nuts and stir constantly until the pine nuts turn golden, about 2 minutes.

◆ Place the cooked wild rice in a large mixing bowl. Add the scallion mixture, the five-spice powder, oregano and orange zest. Mix well.

◆ Spoon half the stuffing into the chicken cavity, then truss the chicken.

◆ Place the chicken on a rack in a roasting pan and brush the yogurt over it.

◆ Roast the chicken in the oven for 15 minutes then reduce the temperature to 350°F (180°C) and roast until cooked through and the juices run clear when pierced with a skewer in the thigh, about 1 hour longer. Transfer the remaining stuffing to a small baking dish. When the chicken has 20 minutes cooking time left, pour the orange juice on top of the extra stuffing, place the dish in the oven and cook until heated through, about 20 minutes.

◆ Transfer the roast chicken to a warm serving platter and surround with the extra stuffing. Garnish with the oregano sprigs and serve immediately.

WILD RICE

Wild rice (Zizania aquatica) is the long-grained seed of a water grass native to the Great Lakes region of North America. It is not even closely related to rice. For centuries wild rice has been used as a staple food by the Chippewa and Sioux Indians—in some areas they are the only ones permitted to harvest it. It is still mainly grown in Minnesota though there is some commercial cultivation in California. Difficult to grow and harvest (this is still done by hand in certain areas), wild rice is therefore expensive. However, when cooked, it expands to about three times its original volume, so a little goes a long way. It may also be used in combination with the cheaper white or brown rice. The reddish brown to black stick-like grains are sought after for their rich nutty flavor and chewy texture. Wild rice is used as a delicious accompaniment to, or a stuffing for, poultry and fish. It also adds flavor and texture to soups and salads. It is higher in dietary fiber than brown or white rice, low in fat and is an excellent source of protein, B-complex vitamins and complex carbohydrate. Wild rice is available in different grades, parboiled and in a multi-grain mix—a blend of wild and brown rice. It may be purchased from specialty food stores and some supermarkets. Always wash the rice thoroughly before cooking.

NUTRITION NOTES

PER SERVING (Analysis uses monounsaturated margarine): 495 calories/2080 kilojoules; 50 g protein; 13 g fat, 23% of calories (2.9 g saturated, 5% of calories; 6.3 g monounsaturated, 11%; 3.8 g polyunsaturated, 7%); 47 g carbohydrate; 5 g dietary fiber; 154 mg sodium; 2.8 mg iron; 113 mg cholesterol.

Note: This analysis is based on removing the skin from the chicken before eating. Leaving the skin on doubles the fat content.

CHICKEN CREOLE

The United States

Creole cooking has its origins in the Mississippi Delta area of the American South. It is reported to be a medley of French, Spanish and West African cuisines. Creole sauces are versatile and are used to complement fish, chicken, game and pork. Here, a healthy mixture of vegetables are spiced with hot peppers and flavored with white wine. There is no need for salt to be added, which makes this dish low in sodium. Serve with rice.

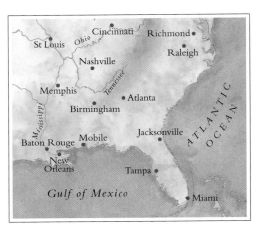

TOTAL TIME: 45 MINUTES

SERVES 4

If leftover table wine is to be saved for cooking purposes, pour it into a smaller container, cover and store in the refrigerator until required.

4 boneless, skinless chicken breasts (fillets), about 4 oz (125 g) each
2 tablespoons canola or safflower oil
1 large onion, coarsely chopped
2 garlic cloves, minced
1 cup (2½ oz/75 g) coarsely chopped mushroom caps
1 medium green bell pepper (capsicum), seeded and coarsely chopped
2 large, vine-ripened tomatoes, coarsely chopped
½ cup (4 fl oz/125 ml) dry white wine
½ teaspoon finely chopped dried red chili, or ¼ teaspoon dried red pepper flakes
2 tablespoons finely chopped parsley

◆ Using a sharp knife, cut the chicken into 1 inch (2.5 cm) cubes.
◆ Heat 1 tablespoon of the oil in a large, non-stick frying pan over medium heat. Add the chicken and sauté, stirring frequently, until the pieces have changed from pink to cream on all sides, about 5 minutes. Using a slotted spoon, transfer to a plate, cover and set aside.
◆ Add the remaining oil to the frying pan and heat, then add the onion and garlic and sauté, stirring occasionally, until the onion is transparent, about 5 minutes.
◆ Add the mushrooms and cook, stirring frequently, until soft, about 2 minutes.
◆ Add the bell pepper and cook, stirring constantly, until softened, about 2 minutes.
◆ Add the tomatoes, wine and chili. Stir well, and bring to a boil. Reduce the heat to low and simmer, uncovered, to blend the flavors, about 5 minutes.
◆ Return the chicken to the frying pan, cover and simmer until the chicken and vegetables are tender, about 10 minutes.
◆ Spoon onto individual plates or into a warm serving bowl and sprinkle with the parsley. Serve at once.

NUTRITION NOTES

PER SERVING: 252 calories/1059 kilojoules; 31 g protein; 10 g fat, 36% of calories (1.6 g saturated, 5.8% of calories; 5.9 g monounsaturated, 21.2%; 2.5 g polyunsaturated, 9%); 4 g carbohydrate; 2.4 g dietary fiber; 90 mg sodium; 1.6 mg iron; 62 mg cholesterol.

TURKEY LOUISIANA

The United States

The gumbos and jambalayas of New Orleans-style cooking often contain a larger proportion of rice and vegetables to meat, which is a good rule to adopt for a healthy diet. They also have a delicious mix of flavors. This dish combines lean turkey with rice and vegetables, popular ingredients in the sunny South. The recipe provides protein and carbohydrate and is a good source of fiber, B-complex vitamins, iron and zinc.

TOTAL TIME: 1 HOUR

SERVES 4

Allow 2 to 2½ hours additional time if the Chicken Stock is not already prepared. A Dutch oven or a ceramic-lined, cast-iron casserole is the best utensil for cooking this dish, so that the rice does not stick to the bottom. The finished dish may be served in the casserole at the table.

---

8 oz (250 g) boneless, skinless turkey breast, cut into 1½ inch (about 4 cm) pieces
juice of 2 limes
1 tablespoon chopped oregano, plus extra, for garnish
¼ teaspoon freshly ground white pepper
1 tablespoon plus 1 teaspoon canola or safflower oil
1 small onion, coarsely chopped
1 garlic clove, minced
1½ cups thickly sliced mushrooms
1 large, vine-ripened tomato, coarsely chopped
1 cup (6 oz/185 g) long-grain rice
½ cup thickly sliced okra
1¾ cups (14 fl oz/425 ml) boiling Chicken Stock (see page 52)
½ cup thinly sliced green bell pepper (capsicum)
½ cup thinly sliced red bell pepper (capsicum)
1 tablespoon capers

◆ Place the turkey in a shallow glass dish. Pour the lime juice on top, sprinkle with 1 tablespoon of the oregano and the pepper and turn to coat. Cover with plastic wrap and chill in the refrigerator until needed.
◆ Heat the oil in a Dutch oven or a large, heavy-bottomed saucepan over medium heat. Add the onion and garlic and sauté, stirring occasionally, until softened, about 5 minutes.
◆ Add the pieces of turkey and cook, stirring constantly, until lightly browned, 3 to 4 minutes.

◆ Stir in the mushrooms, tomato, rice and okra. Pour in the boiling stock. Cover and cook over medium–low heat until the rice is almost tender, about 25 minutes. Stir in the bell peppers, cover and cook until the rice is tender, about 10 minutes longer.
◆ Stir in the capers, sprinkle the remaining oregano on top and serve immediately.

NUTRITION NOTES

PER SERVING: *326 calories/1368 kilojoules; 20 g protein; 7.9 g fat, 22% of calories (1.2 g saturated, 3.3% of calories; 3.9 g monounsaturated, 10.9%; 2.8 g polyunsaturated, 7.8%); 43 g carbohydrate; 3.9 g dietary fiber; 161 mg sodium; 1.3 mg iron; 28 mg cholesterol.*

MARINATED BEEF STEAK AND LEAN BEEF HAMBURGERS

The United States

Lean beef is low in fat, high in protein, a good source of iron, zinc and B-complex vitamins, making it a good choice for people with a busy lifestyle. Here, beef steak is presented with a choice of marinades. The ground beef used to make the hamburgers is mixed with fresh, healthy vegetables. About three ounces of lean beef will provide all the vitamin B_{12} you need each day.

Marinated Beef Steak and Lean Beef Hamburgers (top)

MARINATED BEEF STEAK

TOTAL TIME: 2 HOURS 20 MINUTES

SERVES 4

Beef steak can be broiled to a rare, medium or well-done stage, according to individual taste. A marinade usually has a high acid content which helps to tenderize and add flavor to meats. A properly balanced marinade makes beef juicy and is well worth the time and effort involved. Never use a fork to turn meat when broiling as the juices and nutrients escape when the meat is pierced.

4 tenderloin (fillet) or rib-eye (Scotch fillet) steaks, trimmed of all visible fat, about 6 oz (185 g) each

WINE MARINADE

2 tablespoons finely chopped parsley
1 tablespoon finely chopped tarragon or thyme
1 tablespoon wholegrain mustard
2 garlic cloves, minced
¼ teaspoon freshly ground black pepper
¼ teaspoon salt
½ cup (4 fl oz / 125 ml) dry red wine
2 teaspoons virgin olive oil
¼ teaspoon Tabasco sauce, optional

CHINESE MARINADE

1 teaspoon Chinese five-spice powder
2 garlic cloves, minced
1 teaspoon finely chopped fresh ginger
¼ cup (2 fl oz / 60 ml) dry sherry or mirin (rice wine)
2 tablespoons honey
1 tablespoon plus 1 teaspoon reduced-sodium soy sauce
1 teaspoon sesame oil

◆ Place the steaks in a large, shallow glass dish in a single layer.
◆ To make the wine marinade, combine the parsley, tarragon, mustard, garlic, pepper, salt, wine, oil and Tabasco sauce, if using, in a small bowl. Mix well.
◆ To make the Chinese marinade, combine the five-spice powder, garlic, ginger, sherry, honey, soy sauce and sesame oil in a small bowl. Mix well.
◆ Pour your chosen marinade mixture over the steaks; turn to coat well. Cover with plastic wrap and marinate the steaks in the refrigerator for at least 2 hours or overnight, basting with the marinade occasionally.
◆ Preheat the broiler. Adjust the rack so that the pan is 3-5 inches from the source of heat (or preheat the grill on High). Line the broiler pan with foil.
◆ Place the steaks on the rack in the pan and broil until light brown, about 2

minutes per side. Turn the steaks, brush with the marinade, and broil 1 minute longer for rare steak and 4 minutes longer for medium steak. For well-done steak broil 4 minutes longer on each side.
◆ Transfer the steaks to warm dinner plates and serve immediately.

LEAN BEEF HAMBURGERS

TOTAL TIME: 40 MINUTES

SERVES 4

Vegetables added to the ground beef in this recipe are finely chopped to help hold the hamburgers together during mixing and cooking.

2 teaspoons virgin olive oil
¾ cup finely chopped mushrooms
¼ cup finely chopped onion
1 lb (500 g) finely ground (minced) lean beef
¼ cup finely chopped cooked beet (beetroot)
1 tablespoon chopped capers
½ teaspoon freshly ground black pepper
1 large egg white
4 hamburger buns
4 lettuce leaves
1 large, vine-ripened tomato, sliced
4 dill pickles (pickled cucumbers), sliced

◆ Heat the oil in a small, non-stick frying pan over medium heat. Add the mushrooms and onion and sauté, stirring frequently, until softened, about 5 minutes. Remove from the heat and set aside to cool.
◆ Place the ground beef in a large mixing bowl. Add the beet, capers, pepper and the cooled onion and mushroom mixture. Mix well with a fork.
◆ Place the egg white in a medium-sized bowl and whisk until soft peaks form. Add to the beef mixture and gently fold through until well combined.

MUSTARD

Mustard is made from the seeds of annual plants belonging to the cabbage family (genus Brassica). There are three varieties of seed: black, brown and white. Mustard seeds can be bought whole, but are normally sold as prepared mustards. The seeds are crushed and then usually mixed with water or vinegar to produce a sharp pungent condiment. The many exotic varieties now available derive from the addition of herbs, spices and other liquids like wine and lemon juice. Store prepared mustards in the refrigerator and powders in a cool cupboard.

◆ Divide the mixture into quarters. Working on a cool surface, with damp hands, shape each quarter into a round or patty, 3 inches (about 8 cm) in diameter and ¾ inch (2 cm) high.
◆ Heat a large, non-stick frying pan over medium-high heat for about 1 minute. Add the hamburgers and cook until lightly browned, about 2 minutes per side. Reduce the heat to medium-low and cook, turning once, until cooked through, about 5 minutes longer for rare, and 8 minutes longer for medium-rare.
◆ Drain the cooked hamburgers on paper towels.
◆ Meanwhile, preheat the broiler (grill). Slice the hamburger buns in half and toast the cut sides until golden and crisp.
◆ Place the bottom halves of the toasted hamburger buns on individual plates, top each with a cooked hamburger. Add a lettuce leaf, tomato slice and dill pickle slices to each one and cover with the top of the bun. Serve immediately.

NUTRITION NOTES

PER SERVING—Steak with Wine Marinade: 280 calories / 1177 kilojoules; 41 g protein; 10 g fat, 33% of calories (3.8 g saturated, 12.5% of calories; 5.3 g monounsaturated, 17.5%; 0.9 g polyunsaturated, 3%); 1 g carbohydrate; 0.5 g dietary fiber; 250 mg sodium; 6.9 mg iron; 126 mg cholesterol.

PER SERVING—Steak with Chinese Marinade: 07 calories / 1290 kilojoules; 41 g protein; 9.1 g fat, 26% of calories (3.8 g saturated, 10.9% of calories; 4.1 g monounsaturated, 11.7%; 1.2 g polyunsaturated, 3.4%); 12 g carbohydrate; 0.3 g dietary fiber; 264 mg sodium; 6.6 mg iron; 126 mg cholesterol.

PER SERVING—Lean Beef Hamburgers: 410 calories / 1723 kilojoules; 38 g protein; 8.9 g fat, 19% of calories (3 g saturated, 6.4% of calories; 4.3 g monounsaturated, 9.2%; 1.6 g polyunsaturated, 3.4%); 44 g carbohydrate; 4.7 g dietary fiber; 702 mg sodium; 4.2 mg iron; 61 mg cholesterol.

BROILED TUNA WITH FRESH TOMATO SALSA

The United States

Fresh tuna is rich in protein, vitamin E, phosphorus and niacin. It is also a good source of omega-3 oils, known to be essential for the heart and brain. Here, the tuna is marinated with Asian flavorings, cooked quickly and then served with a refreshing tangy tomato sauce. The result is delicious. Serve with a mixed green salad and boiled or steamed new potatoes.

TOTAL TIME: 45 MINUTES

SERVES 4

When it is available, try substituting swordfish for tuna in this recipe—it's delicious.

4 tuna steaks, ¾ inch (2 cm) thick,
    about 6 oz (185 g) each
2 garlic cloves, minced
2 teaspoons thin strips fresh ginger
juice of 4 limes
1 teaspoon finely chopped cilantro
    (coriander) root
½ cup chopped cilantro (coriander) leaves
½ cup shredded mint
julienne of lime zest, for garnish
cilantro (coriander) and mint sprigs, for
    garnish
lime wedges, for serving, optional

TOMATO SALSA

2 medium, vine-ripened tomatoes, quartered
    and seeds removed
2 tablespoons Trim French Dressing
    (see page 75)
2 tablespoons low-fat, plain yogurt
1 tablespoon chopped cilantro (coriander)
1 tablespoon shredded mint

◆ Place the tuna in a single layer in a large shallow glass dish. Sprinkle with the garlic and ginger, pour the lime juice on top, then sprinkle with the cilantro root, cilantro leaves and mint. Cover with plastic wrap and marinate in the refrigerator for at least 30 minutes.

◆ Meanwhile, to make the salsa, cut the tomato flesh into ¼ inch (6 mm) dice.

◆ Combine the tomato, French dressing, yogurt, cilantro and mint in a medium-sized bowl. Mix with a fork or balloon whisk until well combined. Cover with plastic wrap and refrigerate until ready to serve.

◆ Preheat the broiler. Adjust the rack so that the pan is 3–5 inches from the source of heat (or preheat the grill on High). Line the broiler pan with foil.

◆ Place the tuna on the rack in the broiler pan. Broil for about 2 minutes on each side. Brush the tuna with the marinade and broil until the flesh flakes easily when tested with the point of a sharp knife, about 2 minutes per side.

◆ Transfer the tuna to a warm serving platter or individual dinner plates. Garnish with the lime zest and the sprigs of cilantro and mint. Spoon the tomato salsa beside the tuna. Serve with the lime wedges, if using.

CILANTRO (CORIANDER)

Cilantro (Coriandrum sativum) is also known as coriander and Chinese parsley. A member of the carrot family, its leaves, stalks, roots and seeds all have their culinary uses. Originating in the Mediterranean area, cilantro was used by the Egyptians 3500 years ago and 500 years later by the Persians, who grew it in the famous Hanging Gardens of Babylon. Cilantro was taken to Britain by the Romans and later was one of the first herbs grown by the early British colonists in America. It has a distinctive flavour and is used in South American, Middle Eastern and Asian (particularly Thai) cuisines. In Western cuisine, the sweet aromatic seeds, whole and ground, are more likely to be used, especially in cakes, breads and pastries. They also partner citrus-flavored foods well. An important ingredient in curries, their flavor is quite distinct from the green leaves. Fresh cilantro leaves and roots are generally available, as are dried leaves and whole and ground dried seeds. Store fresh cilantro in the refrigerator. Use the leaves in moderation as the flavor can become overpowering. Ground cilantro loses its aroma quickly so it is preferable to grind it just before use.

NUTRITION NOTES

PER SERVING: 298 calories/1253 kilojoules; 47 g protein; 8.7 g fat, 27% of calories (1.3 g saturated, 4% of calories; 3.9 g monounsaturated, 12.1%; 3.5 g polyunsaturated, 10.9%); 3 g carbohydrate; 2.2 g dietary fiber; 156 mg sodium; 5.9 mg iron; 81 mg cholesterol.

STUFFED WINTER SQUASH

The United States

Species of winter squash were cultivated throughout America long before the arrival of white settlers. The many varieties have been used in a versatile fashion, from soups and stuffed pastas to curries, casseroles, pies and even cookies. This recipe combines winter squash, a rich source of beta-carotene and vitamins A and C, with a high-fiber savory brown rice stuffing which provides B-complex and C vitamins. Serve with a steamed green vegetable or a salad.

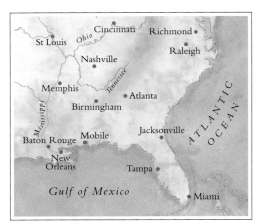

RICE

There are many varieties of this ancient grain which is a staple food in numerous countries, particularly in Asia. Evidence of rice cultivation dates back about 7000 years. The varieties of rice can be classified as long-grain (bottom left), medium-grain (top left) or short-grain (top right). Rice can be either white or brown. Both are eaten as an accompaniment to curries and other savory dishes. Basmati rice from India is an exotic variety of long-grain rice with a delicate flavor and perfumed aroma. Medium-grain rice tends to form clumps soon after it is cooked. Also known as glutinous rice and pearl rice, short-grain has plump, rounded grains. It has a higher starch content than long-grain and medium-grain rice. The Italian Arborio rice is a well-known example of short-grain rice and is the main ingredient in a risotto. Black and red forms are popular in Asian cuisines (bottom right). Brown and white rice differ in their cooking time: brown rice has a higher fiber content and takes longer to cook. White rice has fewer vitamins and minerals than brown rice (top right) and is not as good an energy source. It can also be bought parboiled. Instant or quick brown and white rice are also available. Brown rice is prone to become rancid and will therefore only last about 6 months. White rice will last indefinitely.

TOTAL TIME: 1 HOUR

SERVES 4

This stuffing can fill 4 to 6 acorn squash, depending on their size, but the nutritional analysis is based on 4 squash.

4 large acorn or golden nugget squash
   (pumpkins), about 9 oz (280 g) each
2 tablespoons virgin olive oil
pinch salt
½ cup (3 oz/90 g) brown rice
1 medium onion, finely chopped
2 garlic cloves, minced
1½ cups (about 4 oz/125 g) finely chopped
   mushroom caps
1 large, vine-ripened tomato, finely chopped
¼ cup chopped sundried tomatoes
¼ cup (1½ oz/45 g) golden raisins
   (sultanas)
¼ cup finely chopped parsley
¼ cup (1 oz/30 g) finely chopped walnuts
¼ teaspoon freshly ground black pepper
2 tablespoons freshly grated Parmesan
   cheese, for sprinkling

◆ Preheat the oven to 350°F (180°C). Cut a slice about ½ inch (1 cm) thick from across the top of each squash and scoop out the seeds with a metal spoon.
◆ Brush the exposed squash flesh and inside the cavities with 1 tablespoon of the olive oil. Place the squash on a baking tray and bake until the squash flesh is almost tender, about 30 minutes.
◆ Meanwhile, bring a large saucepan of water to a boil. Add the salt and rice and boil rapidly, uncovered, until the rice is tender, 35 to 40 minutes. Drain the rice, rinse under hot running water and drain thoroughly.
◆ Meanwhile, heat the remaining oil in a medium-sized, non-stick frying pan over medium-high heat. Add the onion and garlic and sauté, stirring frequently, until the onion is soft and golden, about 5 minutes.
◆ Reduce the heat to medium, add the mushrooms and cook, stirring frequently, until tender, about 3 minutes. Add the tomato and the sundried tomatoes and cook, stirring frequently, until the fresh tomatoes are cooked, about 2 minutes longer.
◆ Transfer the onion, mushroom and tomato mixture to a large bowl. Add the golden raisins, parsley, walnuts, pepper and the cooked rice. Mix well.
◆ Spoon the rice mixture into the squash shells, dividing evenly. Sprinkle a quarter of the grated Parmesan cheese over the stuffing in each squash.
◆ Bake until hot and the cheese is golden brown, about 20 minutes.
◆ Serve immediately.

NUTRITION NOTES

PER SERVING: 392 calories/1647 kilojoules; 15 g protein; 18 g fat, 40% of calories (3.4 g saturated, 7.6% of calories; 7.9 g mono-unsaturated, 17.6%; 6.7 g polyunsaturated, 14.8%); 44 g carbohydrate; 6.4 g dietary fiber; 124 mg sodium; 2.2 mg iron; 5 mg cholesterol.

TAMALE PIE

The United States

The cooking of the American Southwest has naturally been influenced by that of Mexico. The tamale, *a highlight of Mexican feasts, is traditionally served baked in a corn husk. Here, the tamale ingredients are made into a pie. A polenta-topped pie is much lower in fat than a pastry-covered pie and also supplies desirable fiber and iron. The high proportion of vegetables to meat makes this an even healthier dish. Serve with green vegetables and rice.*

TOTAL TIME: 1½ HOURS

SERVES 8

Soy grits are sold in leading health food stores. Brown the meat in two batches as described below for best results.

¼ *cup sundried tomatoes*
3¼ *cups (26 fl oz/about 800 ml) water*
1 *cup (6 oz/185 g) cornmeal*
¼ *cup (1½ oz/45 g) soy grits*
1 *tablespoon virgin olive oil*
1 *medium onion, finely chopped*
1 *lb (500 g) finely ground (minced) lean beef*
2 *teaspoons chili powder*
2 *large, vine-ripened tomatoes, coarsely chopped*
1 *medium ear corn, kernels removed, about ½ cup kernels*
½ *cup chopped green bell pepper (capsicum)*
½ *cup chopped mushrooms*
1 *tablespoon chopped oregano*
1 *tablespoon brown or white vinegar*
½ *teaspoon salt*
¼ *cup (1 oz/30 g) freshly grated Parmesan cheese*

◆ Place the sundried tomatoes in a small bowl and add boiling water to cover. Let stand for 30 minutes then drain well.
◆ Meanwhile, bring the water to a boil in a large saucepan. Reduce the heat to medium, add the cornmeal and stir constantly, using a wooden spoon, until the mixture thickens and is smooth, 3 to 5 minutes. Remove from the heat, add the soy grits and mix well. Set aside.
◆ Preheat the oven to 350°F (180°C).
◆ Heat the oil in a large, non-stick frying pan over medium heat. Add the onion and sauté, stirring occasionally, until softened, about 5 minutes. Use a slotted spoon to transfer the onion to a plate. Set aside.
◆ Increase the heat to medium-high, add half the beef and cook, stirring constantly, until browned, about 4 minutes. Transfer the beef to the plate with the onion. Add

the remaining beef to the frying pan and repeat the process of browning. After 4 minutes, return the onion and first half of the beef to the pan.
◆ Add the chili powder to the beef mixture and mix well. Add the tomatoes, corn kernels, bell pepper, mushrooms, sundried tomatoes, oregano, vinegar and salt. Stir well and bring to a boil. Reduce the heat to medium-low, cover and simmer until slightly thickened, about 15 minutes.
◆ Spoon half the polenta mixture into a 10 inch (25 cm) pie plate (dish). Press the mixture evenly over the bottom of the dish and up the sides.
◆ Spoon the beef mixture into the pie dish and sprinkle with the Parmesan cheese.

◆ Spoon the remaining polenta mixture over the top and gently press to make an even layer. Smooth the top of the polenta mixture with a wet knife, making sure all the beef mixture is covered.
◆ Bake until golden brown, about 35 to 40 minutes.
◆ Cut the pie into 8 neat wedges and serve at once.

NUTRITION NOTES

PER SERVING: 245 calories/1028 kilojoules; 21 g protein; 7.3 g fat, 27% of calories (2.5 g saturated, 9.2% of calories; 3.2 g monounsaturated, 11.8%; 1.6 g polyunsaturated, 6%); 24 g carbohydrate; 2.7 g dietary fiber; 241 mg sodium; 2.3 mg iron; 41 mg cholesterol.

VEGETARIAN LOAF WITH RED PEPPER COULIS

The United States

This dish combines a legume with delicious nuts, seeds, eggs and cheese to make a complete-protein dish. Soy beans are one of the most nutritionally valuable legumes because they contain eight of the essential nine amino acids. All legumes are low in fat, have no cholesterol and are a good source of dietary fiber. Serve with steamed mixed vegetables or salad and rice.

TOTAL TIME: 5½ HOURS

SERVES 7

If 2 cups canned soy beans are used in place of the dried beans, the total time will be reduced to 1 hour.

⅘ cup (5 oz/155 g) dried soy beans
olive oil cooking spray
¼ cup (1 oz/30 g) raw blanched almonds, coarsely chopped
¼ cup (1 oz/30 g) raw cashews, coarsely chopped
¼ cup (1 oz/30 g) raw macadamia nuts, coarsely chopped
¼ cup (1½ oz/45 g) sunflower seeds
2 tablespoons poppy seeds
1 teaspoon miso or ¼ teaspoon salt
¼ cup finely chopped parsley
1 tablespoon virgin olive oil or macadamia oil
½ cup sliced celery
½ cup sliced scallions (spring onions)
1 large, free-range egg, lightly beaten
¼ cup (1 oz/30 g) freshly grated Parmesan cheese, for sprinkling

RED PEPPER COULIS

2 teaspoons virgin olive oil
1 small onion, finely chopped
1 large red bell pepper (capsicum), seeded and chopped
¼ cup chopped parsley

◆ Place the soy beans with water to cover in a medium-sized saucepan and bring to a boil. Boil, uncovered, for 2 minutes. Remove from the heat, cover and set aside for 1 hour.
◆ Drain the beans, return them to the saucepan and cover with fresh water. Cover and bring to a boil over high heat. Reduce the heat to medium-low and boil gently until tender, about 3½ hours. Drain.
◆ Preheat the oven to 375°F (190°C). Line the bottom of a 9 × 4 inch (23 × 10 cm) loaf pan with parchment (non-stick baking) paper and spray the pan with cooking spray.

◆ Place the cooked soy beans in a blender or food processor and process to form a coarse texture.
◆ Add the almonds, cashews and macadamia nuts to the soy bean mixture. Process to form a coarse texture, stopping and scraping down the sides as needed. Transfer the mixture to a large bowl.
◆ Add the sunflower seeds, poppy seeds, miso and parsley to the soy bean and nut mixture, mix well and set aside.
◆ Heat the oil in a small, non-stick frying pan over medium heat. Add the celery and scallions and sauté, stirring occasionally, until softened, about 3 minutes.
◆ Add the scallion and celery mixture and the beaten egg to the soy bean and nut mixture. Stir to combine.
◆ Transfer the mixture to the loaf pan and spread the top evenly. Sprinkle with the grated cheese, if using. Bake until firm, and a skewer inserted into the center comes out clean, about 30 minutes.

◆ Meanwhile prepare the coulis. Heat the oil in a small, non-stick frying pan over medium heat. Add the onion and sauté, stirring frequently, until golden, about 5 minutes. Add the bell pepper and cook, stirring frequently, until soft, about 5 minutes. Place the mixture in a blender or food processor, add the parsley and process until puréed. Pour the coulis into a small saucepan and heat over medium heat until warmed through.
◆ Turn the cooked loaf out onto a wire rack, then invert onto a rectangular or oval serving plate. Cut into thick slices, and serve immediately with the coulis.

NUTRITION NOTES

PER SERVING: 230 calories/968 kilojoules; 13 g protein; 18 g fat, 68% of calories (3.8 g saturated, 14% of calories; 9.5 g mono-unsaturated, 36%; 4.7 g polyunsaturated, 18%); 6 g carbohydrate; 6.3 g dietary fiber; 110 mg sodium; 3.2 mg iron; 36 mg cholesterol.

CIOPPINO AND SALMON MOUSSE

The United States

*I*talian fishermen long ago introduced Cioppino to the San Francisco region of California. The combination of fresh vegetables and delicate fish flavors make it an appetizing dish. Traditionally, salmon mousse is made with heavy cream and plenty of eggs. Here, a healthy new variation is presented. Salmon is rich in protein and a good source of omega-3 oils which help protect against heart disease. Serve both dishes with a salad and warm pita or sourdough bread.

Cioppino and Salmon Mousse (top)

CIOPPINO

TOTAL TIME: 1 HOUR 40 MINUTES

SERVES 4

If large, cooked crab (such as the Dungeness variety) are not available, substitute 1 pound of lump crab meat, picked over, and add just before serving. If using cooked shrimp, reduce the cooking time to 5 minutes.

¼ cup sundried tomatoes
2 medium cooked crabs, about 1 lb 6 oz
    (685 g) total weight
2 tablespoons virgin olive oil
1 large onion, chopped
1 cup thinly sliced scallions (spring onions)
2 garlic cloves, minced
2 large, vine-ripened tomatoes, peeled and
    quartered
1 cup (8 fl oz/250 ml) water
1 cup (8 fl oz/250 ml) dry white wine
¼ cup shredded basil
¼ cup chopped flat-leaf parsley
½ teaspoon freshly ground black pepper
1 medium green bell pepper (capsicum),
    seeded and chopped
1 lb (500 g) medium raw shrimp (green
    prawns), shelled and deveined

◆ Place the sundried tomatoes in a small bowl and add boiling water to cover. Let stand for 30 minutes then drain well.
◆ Meanwhile, scrub the crabs clean in cold water. Twist the claws off and crack open with a hammer. Pry the top of the body shell away from the bottom shell with a knife, then pull apart carefully—the crabmeat is attached to the bottom shell. Remove the gills and the spongy parts from the body meat and discard. With poultry shears, cut the body of the crab into quarters. Cover with plastic wrap and chill in the refrigerator until needed.
◆ Heat the oil in a large, heavy-bottomed saucepan over medium heat. Add the onion, scallions and garlic and sauté, stirring frequently, until soft, about 5 minutes.
◆ Combine the sundried tomatoes and the quartered tomatoes in a blender or food processor. Process until smooth.
◆ Add the tomato purée, the water, wine, basil, parsley and pepper to the saucepan. Bring to a boil, stirring occasionally. Reduce the heat, cover and simmer for 30 minutes. Add the bell pepper to the tomato mixture and simmer 5 minutes longer.
◆ Place the crab in a large, heavy-bottomed saucepan, then place the shrimp on top of the crab. Pour the hot tomato sauce over the top, cover and simmer until the shrimp turn pinkish orange, about 10 minutes.
◆ Serve in warm soup bowls.

WATERCRESS

Watercress (Nasturtium officinale) *is a perennial aquatic plant belonging to the mustard family. It is valued for its fresh peppery taste and is rich in vitamins A and C, calcium and iron. Mainly used raw in salads, and as a garnish, watercress is often added to soups and stir-fry dishes. Choose short sprigs with crisp, deep green leaves that show no signs of yellowing or wilting. Best used fresh, it can be stored in the crisper section of the refrigerator for 2 to 3 days.*

SALMON MOUSSE

TOTAL TIME: 4¾ HOURS

SERVES 4

Do not discard the bones from canned fish as they are soft and are a good source of calcium. If the dissolved gelatine is too hot when added to the basic mixture, it will form threads and lumps instead of mixing in evenly. See Glossary concerning raw eggs.

26 oz (820 g) canned salmon, drained
1 large (telegraph) cucumber, about 1 lb (500 g)
1½ cups (12 oz/375 g) reduced-sodium,
    low-fat cottage cheese
1 cup watercress, finely chopped
finely grated zest of 1 lemon
¼ teaspoon freshly ground white pepper
juice of 1 lemon
2 tablespoons plus 2 teaspoons gelatine
2 large egg whites
chopped cucumber, for garnish
1 hard-boiled egg, with yolk sieved and
    white finely chopped, for garnish, optional
dill sprigs, for garnish

◆ Place the salmon on a plate, remove and discard the skin. Using a fork, flake the fish finely. Grind the bones in a mortar and pestle and add to the salmon. Cover with plastic wrap and set aside.
◆ Cut the cucumber in half lengthwise and scoop out the seeds. Cut the cucumber halves into ¼ inch (6 mm) dice. Place in a colander and set aside to drain until needed.
◆ Place the cottage cheese in a food processor and process until smooth.
◆ Combine the salmon, cottage cheese, watercress, lemon zest, pepper and diced cucumber in a large bowl. Fold together lightly with a plastic spatula until evenly combined.
◆ Combine the lemon juice and gelatine in a small heatproof bowl, stir well and let stand for 5 minutes to soften. Meanwhile, bring a small saucepan containing enough water to reach halfway up the side of the bowl to a boil. Set the bowl in the saucepan, reduce the heat and simmer until the gelatine is dissolved. Remove the bowl from the saucepan and set aside to cool until lukewarm, 5 to 10 minutes. Test the temperature with the tip of your little finger—the gelatine should be at body temperature.
◆ Add the gelatine mixture to the salmon mixture, stirring quickly to combine as evenly as possible.
◆ In a large bowl, whisk the egg whites until stiff peaks form. Add the egg whites to the salmon mixture and fold in evenly.
◆ Rinse a 5 cup (40 fl oz/1.25 liters) fluted ring mold with cold water. Pour the salmon mixture into the mold. Cover with plastic wrap and refrigerate until set, at least 4 hours, or overnight.
◆ To remove the mousse, loosen the top edges by gently pulling the ring mold away from the mousse. Dip the base and sides of the mold into a bowl of hot water for a few seconds. Quickly remove the mold from the water and dry. Place a serving platter over the mold, hold in place and invert. Shake well until the mousse turns out. If the mousse does not turn out, repeat this process.
◆ Garnish the mousse with the chopped cucumber, chopped hard-boiled egg white and sieved egg yolk, if using, and sprigs of dill. Serve immediately.

NUTRITION NOTES

PER SERVING—Cioppino:
264 calories/1111 kilojoules; 25 g protein; 8.6 g fat, 29% of calories (1.6 g saturated, 5.4% of calories; 5.7 g monounsaturated, 19.2%; 1.3 g polyunsaturated, 4.4%); 11 g carbohydrate; 3 g dietary fiber; 596 mg sodium; 3.1 mg iron; 190 mg cholesterol.

PER SERVING—Salmon Mousse:
344 calories/1444 kilojoules; 45 g protein; 15 g fat, 39% of calories (5.5 g saturated, 14.3% of calories; 6.5 g monounsaturated, 16.9%; 3 g polyunsaturated, 7.8%); 6 g carbohydrate; 2.2 g dietary fiber; 982 mg sodium; 2.1 mg iron; 87 mg cholesterol.

DESSERTS & CAKES

A dessert is a course of fruit or a sweet concoction served at the end of lunch or dinner. They also include delicious categories of comfort-food including old-fashioned puddings, tarts and pies. A cake is a mixture of flour, eggs, sugar and other ingredients baked in a defined shape. This is a simple definition that barely describes the huge variety of cakes, but we know from experience that some cakes have a light airy texture with a sweet, subtle flavor, while others have a denser texture with a luscious, rich flavor.

Desserts and cakes in general do not have a healthy image, but recipes that specify fresh fruits, dried fruits, protein-rich eggs, custard mixtures, low-fat yogurt, wholegrain cereal products, nuts (in moderation) and seeds are quite nutritious.

For a refreshing light fruit dessert, choose Cherry Compote, from France; Melon in Port Wine, from Spain; Nectar-

ines Poached in Wine, from Australia; oranges served with a delightful flavored yogurt sauce, from Morocco; Peaches in Fig Sauce, from Greece; Fresh Fruit Salad, from the United States or Dried Fruit and Nut Salad, from Lebanon. Many of these recipes are amazingly easy to prepare. They simply require careful selection of ingredients, good organization and a few basic skills.

Easy to digest nourishing desserts include Stirred Egg Custard Sauce, from Britain; Raspberry Ring with Fresh Berries, from Australia; Pumpkin Pie and the unusual but delicious Lime and Buttermilk Cheesecake, from the United States. These are all good choices for entertaining—they look impressive and taste good too.

High-fiber Carrot Cake and Oatmeal Cookies, from the United States, and Banana Cake, from Australia, are bursting with the goodness of wholesome wholewheat (wholemeal) flour. Try these with tea or coffee in the morning or at afternoon tea or dinner. They are also a popular sweet treat for children.

In the hotter countries of Asia, fresh fruit is invariably the typical finale to most

Left: *A cakeshop on Majorca, Spain. Rich cakes should be served very occasionally.*
Below: *Beehives in southern France—honey is a natural sweetener.*

meals. A simple sticky rice or black rice pudding made with fresh coconut milk is sometimes served too. However, most of the creative recipes featured here come from Europe where the preparation of desserts has combined art with skill. There are several recipes from Greece, for example, Custard Pie with Strawberry Purée, Semolina Cake with Rhubarb Purée and a wonderful Rice Cake. There is also a light and flaky Apple and Cheese Strudel, from Switzerland. Some of these recipes require a degree of skill, but don't let this put you off because they are very satisfying to make and you will be doubly rewarded by the praise of family and friends.

Ices are favorite treats with every age and nationality. A homemade ice cream or sorbet adds a touch of glamor and elegance to summertime entertaining. To make perfect ices, you have to be patient if you do not have an ice-cream maker. However, both sorbet and ice cream can be made well in advance. To tempt you there is a tangy, no-fat Strawberry Sorbet, from France; a fat-free, palate refreshing, icy, lemon-flavored *Granita*, from Italy; and a

memorable Pistachio and Apricot Frozen Yogurt, from Greece.

Many of the comfort-food puddings and traditional cakes come from Britain where these recipes have been handed down through generations of good home cooks. In colder weather, enjoy Apple Meringue Pie, Pear and Blackberry Crumble or Rice Pudding with Gooseberry Sauce for dessert, and Scottish Gingerbread or Rich Eggless Fruit Cake for afternoon tea—all featuring fruit and fiber-rich cereals. Freshness and quality are paramount; only use the freshest eggs, milk and fruit.

A beautiful dessert adds a happy finale to a family dinner or dinner party. It also gives a festive feeling to a celebratory meal. A homemade cake symbolizes caring and hospitality. This lovely selection of mouthwatering recipes illustrates that desserts and cakes don't have to be excluded from a healthy diet, just chosen more carefully!

Above: *An Indian melon-grower inspects his harvest. Watermelon makes a refreshing summertime dessert.*
Right: *Balinese woman with fruit, a popular healthy dessert in Indonesia.*

NECTARINES POACHED IN WINE AND RASPBERRY RING WITH FRESH BERRIES

Australia

The nectarine, a relative of the peach, is delicious on a hot summer's day. Its name is derived from the Greek word "nekter," meaning "the drink of the gods." Cooked nectarines are also delicious, particularly in a no-fat recipe like this one. Wild raspberries were first cultivated 400 years ago. Raspberries, now popular in modern Australian cooking, are a good source of fiber and vitamin C.

Nectarines Poached in Wine (right) and Raspberry Ring with Fresh Berries

NECTARINES POACHED IN WINE

TOTAL TIME: 2 HOURS

SERVES 8

To avoid discoloration, use a nonreactive pan when poaching fruit in an acidic wine mixture. There must be sufficient poaching liquid to cover, or almost cover, the fruit. The leftover liquid may be re-used for a repeat performance of this refreshing dessert. Add a small amount of extra wine to the liquid to enhance the flavor before re-using.

8 ripe nectarines, about 2 lb (1 kg)
3 cups (24 fl oz/750 ml) dry white wine
1 cup (8 fl oz/250 ml) water
½ cup (6 oz/185 g) honey
1 medium orange, thinly sliced
4 whole cloves
1 stick cinnamon
mint leaves, for decoration

◆ Wash the nectarines in cold water, drain, and pat dry with a clean cloth.
◆ Pour the wine, water and honey into a nonreactive saucepan large enough to allow the nectarines to fit in a single layer. Add the sliced orange, cloves and cinnamon. Cook over medium heat, stirring occasionally, until the honey is dissolved, about 5 minutes. Cover and bring to a boil.
◆ Add the nectarines, spoon the poaching liquid over and return to a boil. Cover, reduce the heat and simmer until the fruit is tender, about 10 minutes. Turn the nectarines carefully with 2 spoons after 5 minutes. Do not tear the delicate flesh.
◆ Transfer the nectarines and the poaching liquid to a heatproof bowl. Set aside to cool for 30 minutes. Cover with plastic wrap and transfer to the refrigerator for at least 1 hour or until chilled.
◆ Remove and discard the skins of the nectarines and return to the poaching liquid. Chill until ready to serve.
◆ Arrange the nectarines in a glass bowl, or in long-stemmed glasses, with some of the poaching liquid spooned over. Decorate with mint leaves just before serving.

RASPBERRY RING WITH FRESH BERRIES

TOTAL TIME: 3 HOURS 50 MINUTES

SERVES 8

Almond oil, used to coat the inside of the mold, adds a delicate flavor to gelatine desserts. If you can't find it, use an unflavored vegetable oil instead. See Glossary for information concerning raw eggs.

RASPBERRIES

The red raspberry (Rubus idaeus) is the fruit of the raspberry cane that grows wild in the woodland areas of temperate regions, in gardens, and is cultivated for commercial use. It is a soft, oval-shaped fruit with a sweet, slightly tart flavor. Its origins go back to the Middle Ages although it probably was not cultivated until the mid-sixteenth century. It was not until the twentieth century that the fruit became widely available. There are black and golden raspberries, but the red are most readily available. They are at their best at the end of a warm summer. Raspberries are very delicate and taste delicious eaten fresh, either alone or accompanied by yogurt or a liqueur. They can be puréed, then sweetened to taste with sugar and chilled, to make a quick and easy dessert sauce. High in vitamins A and C, iron and potassium, they are an extremely versatile fruit and can also be used in fruit salads, fruit tarts, puréed for sorbets and ice creams, and to make jam. Choose plump berries with no sign of mold. They can be stored in a moisture-proof container in the refrigerator for 2 to 3 days. They can also be bought frozen, but these will lack the strong aroma of the fresh berries.

almond oil
2 cups (16 fl oz/500 ml) whole (full cream) milk
2 tablespoons plus 2 teaspoons gelatine
2 large, free-range eggs, separated
¾ cup (6 oz/185 g) superfine (caster) sugar
1 cup red raspberries
1 tablespoon freshly squeezed lemon or lime juice
1½ cups mixed red raspberries, small halved strawberries, and blueberries
1 tablespoon confectioners' (icing) sugar
mint leaves, for decoration

◆ Lightly brush a fluted 7 cup ring mold with a little almond oil.
◆ Place the milk in a medium-sized saucepan and bring almost to a boil over medium heat. Remove the saucepan from the heat as soon as the first bubbles rise to the surface and sprinkle the gelatine over the surface of the milk. Stir until dissolved, then set aside.
◆ Combine the egg yolks and sugar in a medium-sized, heatproof bowl. Use an electric mixer to beat the mixture until light and creamy, about 3 minutes.
◆ Half fill the lower part of a double-boiler with water and bring to a boil.
◆ Add the warm milk mixture to the egg and sugar, stirring constantly. Pour the mixture into the top of the double-boiler. Reduce the heat and cook over the simmering water, stirring constantly, until the custard mixture is warm and slightly thickened, about 10 minutes.

◆ Remove from the heat, cover and set aside to cool at room temperature. Place in the refrigerator and chill until cold but not set, about 30 minutes.
◆ Meanwhile, combine the raspberries and the lemon juice in a blender or food processor. Process until smooth. (Do not sieve, as the seeds provide fiber.) Fold the berry purée into the cold custard mixture.
◆ Whisk the egg whites in a medium-sized bowl until stiff peaks form. Fold the whites into the berry mixture.
◆ Pour the mixture into the mold, cover with plastic wrap and refrigerate until set, about 3 hours.
◆ Just before unmolding the ring, place the mixed berries in a bowl and sift the confectioners' sugar over them.
◆ Unmold the ring onto a flat serving platter. Spoon the berries into the center of the ring and around the edge, decorate with mint leaves and serve immediately.

NUTRITION NOTES

PER SERVING—Nectarines Poached in Wine: 172 calories/721 kilojoules; 1 g protein; 0 g fat; 27 g carbohydrate; 2.2 g dietary fiber; 27 mg sodium; 0.3 mg iron; 0 mg cholesterol.

PER SERVING—Raspberry Ring with Fresh Berries: 181 calories/760 kilojoules; 6 g protein; 4.2 g fat, 20% of calories (2.3 g saturated, 11% of calories; 1.5 g monounsaturated, 7.1%; 0.4 g polyunsaturated, 1.9%); 31 g carbohydrate; 1.7 g dietary fiber; 55 mg sodium; 0.6 mg iron; 65 mg cholesterol.

BANANA CAKE AND APRICOT BRAN COFFEE CAKE

Australia

Bananas, a major crop in eastern Australia, are an excellent source of potassium, vitamins A and C and fiber. Banana cake can be served as an elegant dessert, to accompany a cup of tea or coffee, or as part of a picnic. This "coffee" cake features an unusual combination of dried apricots and All-Bran cereal. Serve with plain yogurt, flavored with vanilla extract, for a lovely dessert.

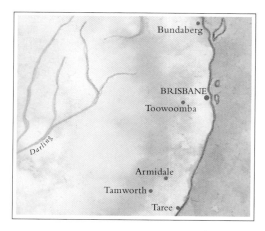

Banana Cake (top) and Apricot Bran Coffee Cake

BANANA CAKE

TOTAL TIME: 1 HOUR 25 MINUTES

SERVES 8

Ripe bananas develop brown "freckles" on the skin when ripe. Store bananas at room temperature until perfectly ripe, then use as soon as possible. This cake is prepared quickly and simply with the aid of a food processor.

1 cup (4 oz/125 g) self-rising (self-raising) flour
1 cup (about 5 oz/155 g) wholewheat (wholemeal plain) flour
2 teaspoons baking powder
¾ cup (6 oz/185 g) turbinado (raw) sugar
½ cup (4 oz/125 g) reduced-fat margarine spread or unsalted butter, cut into dice and softened
2 large, ripe bananas, peeled and quartered
2 large, free-range eggs
¼ cup (about 1½ oz/45 g) low-fat, plain yogurt
¼ cup (1 oz/30 g) skim milk powder
1 tablespoon confectioners' (icing) sugar, for sifting, optional

◆ Preheat the oven to 350°F (180°C). Line a deep, 8 inch (20 cm) round cake pan with parchment (non-stick baking) paper.
◆ Sift the flours and baking powder onto a sheet of waxed (greaseproof) paper. Add any bran left in the sieve to the flour mixture.
◆ Combine the sugar, margarine spread and bananas in a food processor. Process until the mixture is creamy and the bananas are puréed, stopping and scraping down the sides as needed.
◆ Add the eggs, one at a time, and process for about 30 seconds after each addition to blend. Add the yogurt and process again until combined.
◆ Add the sifted dry ingredients and the milk powder to the processor and process to combine.
◆ Pour the batter into the cake pan. Bake until a skewer inserted into the center comes out clean, 45 to 50 minutes. Transfer the pan to a wire rack and let stand for 5 minutes. Turn the cake out onto the rack and remove the paper.
◆ Transfer the cake to a serving plate and sift with confectioners' sugar, if using. Cool completely before slicing.

APRICOT BRAN COFFEE CAKE

TOTAL TIME: 3½ HOURS

MAKES 16 SLICES

The puréed fruit of 1 large orange is used instead of an egg in this recipe.

1 cup (1½ oz/45 g) All-Bran cereal
1 cup (6 oz/185 g) coarsely chopped dried apricots, tightly packed
1 cup (6 oz/185 g) golden raisins (sultanas)
½ cup (3 oz/90 g) light brown sugar, firmly packed
1½ cups (12 fl oz/375 ml) skim milk
vegetable oil cooking spray
1 cup (about 5 oz/155 g) wholewheat (wholemeal plain) flour
½ cup (1½ oz/45 g) soy flour
2 teaspoons baking powder
1 teaspoon ground cinnamon
1 large orange
½ cup (1⅔ oz/50 g) granola or muesli
1 tablespoon pumpkin seeds

◆ Combine the All-Bran, apricots, golden raisins, sugar and milk in a large bowl and mix well. Cover with plastic wrap and soak in the refrigerator for 2 hours.
◆ Preheat the oven to 375°F (190°C). Line a 9 × 5 inch (23 × 13 cm) loaf pan with waxed (greaseproof) paper and spray lightly with vegetable oil cooking spray.
◆ Sift the wholewheat flour, soy flour, baking powder and cinnamon into a large bowl, adding any bran left in the sieve to the bowl.

Make a deep well in the center.
◆ Remove the zest from the orange, and reserve. Remove the white pith from the fruit and separate into sections. Discard all seeds.
◆ Place the zest in a blender or food processor and process until well chopped. Add the orange sections and process until well combined.
◆ Add the apricot mixture and the orange mixture to the dry ingredients and stir quickly to mix well.
◆ Pour the batter into the loaf pan and spread the top to level. Mix the granola and pumpkin seeds together in a small bowl, then sprinkle over the top of the cake.
◆ Bake until a wooden skewer inserted in the center comes out clean, 1 to 1¼ hours.
◆ Stand the pan on a wire rack for 10 minutes, then turn out onto the rack and cool. Cut the cake into 16 slices to serve.

NUTRITION NOTES

PER SERVING—Banana Cake (Analysis uses monounsaturated margarine spread): 341 calories/1432 kilojoules; 8 g protein; 12 g fat, 30% of calories (2.3 g saturated, 6% of calories; 6.9 g monounsaturated, 17%; 2.8 g polyunsaturated, 7%); 53 g carbohydrate; 3.4 g dietary fiber; 372 mg sodium; 1.2 mg iron; 58 mg cholesterol.

PER SLICE—Apricot Bran Coffee Cake: 145 calories/610 kilojoules; 5 g protein; 1.5 g fat, 9% of calories (0.5 g saturated, 3% of calories; 0.4 g monounsaturated, 2.4%; 0.6 g polyunsaturated, 3.6%); 28 g carbohydrate; 5.6 g dietary fiber; 50 mg sodium; 2.2 mg iron; 0.7 mg cholesterol.

BANANAS

The banana tree (Musa spp.) originated in India and is now cultivated in most tropical regions. Probably one of the first fruits to be domesticated, the banana was taken to Africa by the Arabs and to Europe by Portuguese traders. It was then introduced into the Americas and is now one of the world's most important fruit crops. There are two main types of banana: the fruit banana and the cooking banana called the plantain. Bananas grow on a long stalk in bunches known as "hands" while the individual fruit are the "fingers." The fruit banana ripens from green to a deep yellow and then develops black and brown freckles. The plantain, which is larger and more fibrous, remains green. It has less sugar and contains more starch and is always served cooked. Very high in energy, vitamins A and C, and potassium, and easy to digest when ripe, bananas are an ideal food. Some cuisines, for instance in Africa, also treat the banana as a vegetable. Choose fruit that are a greenish yellow without any blemishes. They will ripen at home within a few days. When adding sliced banana to a dish, prepare at the last minute and sprinkle with lemon juice to prevent the slices from turning black.

COMPOTE DE CERISES, SORBET À LA FRAISE

Cherry Compote and Strawberry Sorbet—France

In France, this fruit compote is poached in wine, sweetened and flavored with cinnamon, cloves or vanilla, and served as a colorful, flavorful dessert. Cherries are a source of potassium and vitamins A and B. Sorbets have been enjoyed in China since about 1000 BC. A tangy, acidic berry is a good choice for a successful sorbet as chilling causes the intensity of the fruit's flavor to be lost.

Cherry Compote and Strawberry Sorbet (top)

COMPOTE DE CERISES
Cherry Compote

TOTAL TIME: 1 HOUR 20 MINUTES
SERVES 6

This compote may be stored in the refrigerator for up to a week or frozen for up to 6 months. Bing and William varieties of cherries are ideal for this dish.

1½ lb (750 g) sweet, dark red cherries
½ cup (4 fl oz/125 ml) dry red wine
¼ cup (3 oz/90 g) red currant jelly
1 tablespoon superfine (caster) sugar
grated zest and juice of 1 orange
pinch ground cinnamon
1 tablespoon plus 1 teaspoon arrowroot
   or cornstarch (cornflour)
3 tablespoons water

◆ Rinse the cherries and pat dry with a soft cloth. Pit the cherries with a cherry-pitter or the point of a vegetable knife.
◆ Combine the wine, red currant jelly, sugar, the orange zest and juice and the cinnamon in a medium-sized, nonreactive saucepan. Cook over medium-low heat, stirring occasionally, until the red currant jelly is melted, 1 to 2 minutes.
◆ Add the cherries to the saucepan, increase the heat to medium and bring to a boil, stirring occasionally. Cover, reduce the heat and simmer until the cherries are tender, about 5 minutes.
◆ Meanwhile, combine the arrowroot with the water in a small bowl and blend until smooth. Stir into the cherry mixture and return to a boil, stirring constantly, until the juice thickens, about 1 minute. Simmer for 1 minute longer to cook the starch taste out of the arrowroot. Remove from the heat and set aside to cool for 1 hour.
◆ Cherry compote is best served at room temperature, in a large glass bowl or divided among 6 elegant dessert dishes.

SORBET À LA FRAISE
Strawberry Sorbet

TOTAL TIME: 3 HOURS 20 MINUTES
SERVES 8

An electric ice-cream maker will give the best results when making sorbet. If you have one, do not add the tofu. Process the berries and lemon juice, cover and chill for 1 hour, then pour the berry mixture and the sugar syrup into the ice-cream maker and mix according to the manufacturer's directions. Spoon the sorbet into a freezer

STRAWBERRIES

The strawberry (Fragaria *spp.*) is a low-growing perennial plant much enjoyed for its bright red, flavorful berries. The Romans thought highly of the wild strawberry, both for its wonderful taste and its medicinal properties. It was not until the seventeenth century when a native North American strawberry (from Virginia) and a native Chilean strawberry were taken to France and there crossbred that the cultivated strawberry of today was first grown. The resulting strawberry is larger and juicier than the wild variety, though its flavor is not so strong. Low in sugar but high in vitamin C, folic acid, potassium and other minerals, strawberries are available all year but are at their best during the summer months. Strawberries are delicious eaten fresh, perhaps with a touch of sugar, or added to fruit salad. They also complement a cheese platter. Strawberries make excellent sorbets, frozen yogurt, flans, mousses, and of course, the ever-popular strawberry jam. For a refreshing low-fat dessert, serve halved strawberries splashed with orange liqueur. Choose unblemished, brightly colored berries with the hulls still attached. Store the strawberries unwashed and loosely packed in the refrigerator and eat within 2 days. Lightly rinse (if necessary) and hull just before serving. Strawberries are also available canned and frozen; these are best used for puréeing or cooking as they lose their shape when processed.

container, cover securely and store in the freezer until ready to serve. See Glossary for information concerning raw eggs.

1 cup (8 fl oz/250 ml) water
½ cup (4 oz/125 g) sugar
1 lb (500 g) strawberries or raspberries
8 oz (250 g) silken tofu
juice of 1½ lemons or 3 limes
1 large egg white
mint leaves, for decoration

◆ Combine the water and the sugar in a small saucepan over medium heat. Stir frequently until the sugar is dissolved. Increase the heat to medium-high and boil until slightly reduced, about 5 minutes. Remove from the heat and set aside until cool.
◆ Pour the syrup into a small bowl, cover and chill in the refrigerator for 1 hour.
◆ Meanwhile, rinse the strawberries, drain well and remove the hulls. Pat dry with a soft cloth. Reserve 8 berries for decoration, if desired, and refrigerate until needed.
◆ Combine the berries, tofu and lemon juice in a blender or food processor. Process until puréed, stopping and scraping down the sides as needed.
◆ Pour the berry purée into a medium-

sized bowl, cover and chill in the refrigerator for at least 1 hour.
◆ Pour the sugar syrup and the berry mixture into a shallow freezer container. Place in the freezer, uncovered, and freeze until crystals form 1¼ inches (3 cm) in from the edge of the container, about 1½ hours.
◆ Whisk the egg white in a small bowl until stiff peaks form. Fold the egg white into the icy berry mixture. Cover and freeze, occasionally mixing with a fork, until an even slushy texture forms, about 1½ hours. Store in the freezer until ready to serve.
◆ Scoop the sorbet into stemmed sorbet glasses or dessert bowls. Decorate with the reserved berries, if using, and the mint and serve immediately.

NUTRITION NOTES

PER SERVING—Cherry Compote:
124 calories/522 kilojoules; 1 g protein; 0 g fat; 26 g carbohydrate; 2.3 g dietary fiber; 6 mg sodium; 0.5 mg iron; 0 mg cholesterol.

PER SERVING—Strawberry Sorbet:
100 calories/419 kilojoules; 4 g protein; 1.3 g fat, 12% of calories (0.2 g saturated, 1.8% of calories; 0.3 g monounsaturated, 2.8%; 0.8 g polyunsaturated, 7.4%); 18 g carbohydrate; 1.8 g dietary fiber; 14 mg sodium; 1.2 mg iron; 0 mg cholesterol.

RICE PUDDING WITH GOOSEBERRY SAUCE AND MARBLED PRUNE WHIP

Britain

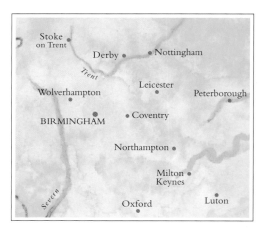

Rice pudding is one of the best known British desserts. Rich in protein, carbohydrate, calcium, phosphorus, fiber and vitamin C, this pudding is healthy and delicious. Often served stewed for breakfast, prunes make a delicious dessert, too. In Britain, this elegant, low-fat Prune Whip is often served as the perfect end to a dinner party.

Rice Pudding with Gooseberry Sauce and Marbled Prune Whip (right)

RICE PUDDING WITH GOOSEBERRY SAUCE

TOTAL TIME: 1½ HOURS

SERVES 8

Glutinous or short–grain rice is also known as pudding rice. If fresh gooseberries are not available, use canned gooseberries, puréed in their juice, as a substitute for the sauce. Use fresh or canned plums if gooseberries are unavailable.

RICE PUDDING

1 cup (8 fl oz / 250 ml) water
½ cup (3½ oz / 110 g) glutinous (short-grain) rice
1 tablespoon plus 1 teaspoon reduced-fat margarine spread or unsalted butter
4 cups (32 fl oz / 1 liter) skim milk
¼ cup (1 oz / 30 g) skim milk powder
1 stick cinnamon
1 bay leaf
finely grated zest of 1 lemon

finely grated zest of 1 orange
¼ cup (2 oz / 60 g) turbinado (raw) sugar
2 large, free-range eggs, separated
¼ cup (2 fl oz / 60 ml) Irish whiskey
¼ whole nutmeg, freshly grated, or
    ¼ teaspoon ground nutmeg, for sprinkling

GOOSEBERRY SAUCE

1 lb (500 g) gooseberries, topped and tailed
1 cup (8 fl oz / 250 ml) water
⅓ cup (3 oz / 90 g) sugar

◆ To make the rice pudding, combine the water and rice in a medium-sized, heavy-bottomed saucepan and stir well. Bring to a boil over medium-high heat. Remove from the heat and drain the rice.

◆ Preheat the oven to 350°F (180°C).

◆ Brush a 5 cup baking pan with 1 teaspoon of the margarine spread, melted.

◆ Whisk the milk with the skim milk powder in a large bowl until the powder is dissolved. Combine the rice, milk, cinnamon, bay leaf and the lemon and orange zest in a large, heavy-bottomed saucepan. Stir well.

◆ Bring the rice mixture to a boil over medium heat. Reduce the heat and simmer, stirring occasionally, until the rice is tender, about 10 minutes. Remove from the heat. Discard the cinnamon stick and bay leaf.

◆ Add the sugar and remaining margarine spread to the rice mixture. Mix well and set aside to cool.

◆ Add the egg yolks, one by one, to the rice mixture, and stir until combined. Stir in the whiskey.

◆ Beat the egg whites in a medium-sized bowl until stiff peaks form and gently fold into the rice mixture.

◆ Pour the rice mixture into the baking pan, and sprinkle the grated nutmeg over the top. Bake until the pudding sets, about 1 hour. (To test, gently press the center of the pudding with the back of a spoon—the texture should be firm.)

◆ Meanwhile, make the gooseberry sauce. Combine the gooseberries, water and sugar in a heavy-bottomed saucepan. Cover and bring to a boil over medium heat. Reduce the heat and simmer until the gooseberries burst, about 15 minutes. If you prefer a smooth sauce, process the cooked gooseberry mixture in a blender or food processor until puréed.

◆ Serve the rice pudding with the warm gooseberry sauce on the side.

MARBLED PRUNE WHIP

TOTAL TIME: 2¾ HOURS

SERVES 4

When cooking with gelatine, it is important to accurately measure all ingredients. Be sure to dissolve gelatine rather than cook it. Make sure that it is at body temperature when combining with the basic mixture and mix well. Crystallized violets or rose petals may be used for decoration instead of the berries, if desired. See Glossary for information concerning raw eggs.

1¼ cups (6½ oz/200 g) pitted prunes, about 32 small prunes
¾ cup (6 fl oz/185 ml) freshly squeezed orange juice
3 tablespoons port
½ cup (about 3 oz/90 g) low-fat, plain yogurt
3 tablespoons turbinado (raw) sugar
1 tablespoon gelatine
2 large egg whites
red berries or red currants for decoration, optional

◆ Combine the prunes, ½ cup of the orange juice and the port in a small bowl and stir well. Cover with plastic wrap and soak, stirring occasionally, until the prunes have absorbed all of the liquid, 2 to 3 hours.

◆ Transfer the prunes to a blender or food processor. Process until smooth, stopping and scraping down the sides as needed, then transfer to a large bowl. Add ¼ cup of the yogurt and mix well.

◆ Combine the sugar and the remaining orange juice in a small heatproof bowl. Sprinkle the gelatine over the surface and mix well until evenly combined.

◆ Place the bowl in a medium-sized saucepan and add enough boiling water to reach halfway up the side of the bowl. Boil the water over medium heat until the gelatine and the sugar have dissolved, about 3 minutes. Remove the bowl from the water-bath and cool to lukewarm or body temperature. (Test with the tip of your finger. When the mixture feels the same temperature as your finger, it is ready for the next step.)

◆ Pour the gelatine mixture into the prune mixture, stir quickly and constantly until well combined. Refrigerate the mixture until it begins to thicken slightly, about 5 minutes.

◆ Whisk the egg whites in a medium-sized bowl until stiff peaks form. Gently fold the egg whites into the prune mixture. Cover with plastic wrap and refrigerate for 5 minutes to chill.

◆ Divide the mixture among 4 tall glasses or attractive dessert dishes. Spoon the remaining yogurt over the tops, dividing equally, and draw a skewer through the mixture to give a marbled effect to the yogurt.

◆ Chill until set. Decorate with red berries or red currants, if using.

NUTRITION NOTES

PER SERVING—Rice Pudding with Gooseberry Sauce (Analysis uses monounsaturated margarine spread): 228 calories/957 kilojoules; 9 g protein; 3.5 g fat, 14% of calories (1 g saturated, 4% of calories; 1.7 g monounsaturated, 6.8%; 0.8 g polyunsaturated, 3.2%); 37 g carbohydrate; 1.7 g dietary fiber; 104 mg sodium; 0.6 mg iron; 61 mg cholesterol.

PER SERVING—Marbled Prune Whip: 201 calories/845 kilojoules; 7 g protein; 0.3 g fat, 1% of calories (0.15 g saturated, 0.5% of calories; 0.15 g monounsaturated, 0.5%; 0 g polyunsaturated, 0%); 40 g carbohydrate; 4 g dietary fiber; 72 mg sodium; 0.7 mg iron; 2 mg cholesterol.

PRUNES

The prune is a dried plum (Prunus spp.). Drying and preserving plums was popular as long ago as the Roman empire when fruit was often sun-dried. Many different types of plum are turned into prunes but the one that is the most sought after for flavor is the Agen plum. This was taken from France to California in the mid-nineteenth century and the United States is now the world's leading producer of prunes. Prunes are very rich in sugar, potassium, magnesium and calcium and are high in fiber. They can be eaten by themselves or used in winter fruit salads, compotes and tarts. Prunes are excellent for bringing out the flavor of meat when cooked in a savory dish; they combine particularly well with lamb, pork and game meats. Choose prunes that are soft and have a shiny black color. Store them in a cool, dry place and use within 6 months. Wash before cooking, then soak for a couple of hours. If the prunes are to be added to a casserole and then cooked for a long time, there is no need to soak them first.

Pear and Blackberry Crumble with Stirred Egg Custard Sauce

Britain

In Britain, high-fiber pears are popular in winter desserts. Blackberries add wonderful color and flavor as well as vitamin C to this crumble. The topping is rich in fiber and B-complex vitamins. Serve it with Stirred Egg Custard, an elegant dessert sauce. Its silken texture and velvety taste make it the ideal sauce for baked puddings or poached fruit.

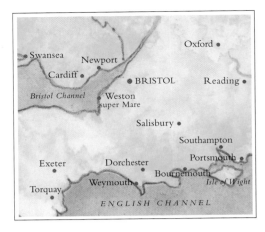

Pear and Blackberry Crumble with Stirred Egg Custard Sauce (right)

PEAR AND BLACKBERRY CRUMBLE

TOTAL TIME: 1 HOUR 5 MINUTES

SERVES 6

Boysenberries or blueberries may be used instead of blackberries, which are also known as brambles in Britain.

2 large, green-skinned pears, preferably
  Bartlett (or William), about 1 lb
  (500 g), peeled, cored and quartered
½ cup (4 fl oz/125 ml) water
¼ cup (2 oz/60 g) sugar
2 whole cloves
1½ cups (6½ oz/200 g) blackberries
1 teaspoon arrowroot or cornstarch (cornflour)

CRUMBLE

½ cup (2⅓ oz/70 g) wholewheat
  (wholemeal plain) flour
¼ cup (2 oz/60 g) reduced-fat margarine
  spread or unsalted butter, chilled and
  diced
¼ cup (2 oz/60 g) turbinado (raw) sugar
¼ cup (1 oz/30 g) oat bran
2 tablespoons dried (desiccated) coconut
2 tablespoons skim milk powder
1 tablespoon brewer's yeast
1 tablespoon wheatgerm
1 tablespoon confectioners' (icing) sugar,
  for sifting

◆ Preheat the oven to 350°F (180°C).
◆ Cut the pears into ¼ inch (6 mm) wedges.
◆ Combine the water, sugar and cloves in a large saucepan. Heat over medium heat, stirring occasionally, until all the sugar is dissolved. Add the pears, cover and bring to a boil. Reduce the heat and simmer until the pears are tender, about 10 minutes.
◆ Remove the saucepan from the heat. Remove and discard the cloves. Add the blackberries, and stir constantly until the syrup changes to a burgundy color, about 30 seconds.
◆ Use a slotted spoon to transfer the pears and blackberries to a deep, 3 cup pie dish. Add ¼ cup of the syrup to the fruit and set aside. Reserve the remaining syrup.
◆ To make the crumble, combine the flour and margarine spread in a food processor. Process until the mixture resembles coarse bread crumbs.
◆ Transfer the flour mixture to a large bowl. Add the turbinado sugar, oat bran, coconut, milk powder, brewer's yeast and wheatgerm. Mix well until combined, then sprinkle the mixture over the fruit.
◆ Bake until hot and golden brown, about 30 minutes.

WHEATGERM

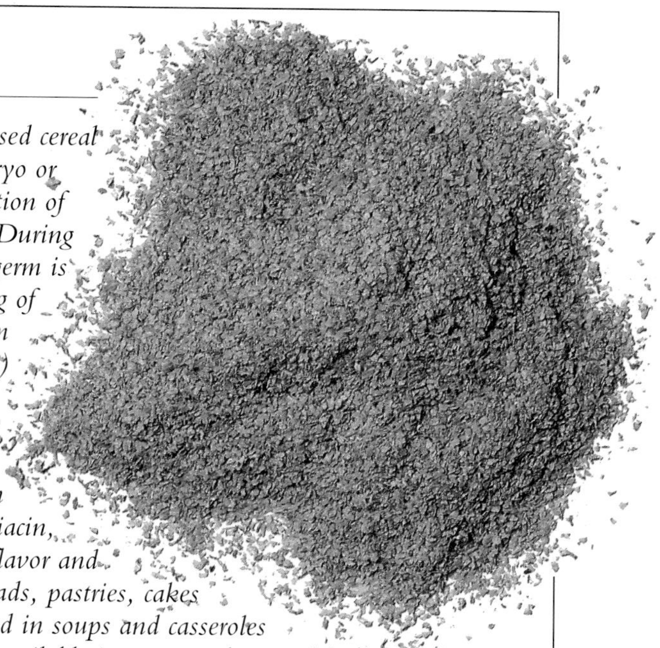

Wheat is the Western world's most used cereal and wheatgerm is essentially the embryo or germ of the wheat grain. (The proportion of germ in wheat is about two percent.) During the milling process of white flour the germ is removed from the grain. In the milling of wholewheat (wholemeal) flour the germ and the husk (also known as the bran) are retained. Although wheatgerm is very nutritious, its value has only been recognized since the early 1900s. It is a good source of thiamin and iron and also contains useful amounts of niacin, magnesium and zinc. It has a nutty flavor and is often added to breakfast cereals, breads, pastries, cakes and a variety of desserts. It is also used in soups and casseroles as a thickening agent. Wheatgerm is available in supermarkets and health food stores. Because of its high oil content the germ is often roasted and vacuum-packed to prevent it becoming rancid. Wheatgerm should be stored in the refrigerator in an airtight container where it will keep for up to 6 months. The oil from wheatgerm is sometimes pressed and sold as cooking oil.

◆ Meanwhile, use a wooden spoon to blend the arrowroot with the remaining syrup in a small saucepan. Bring to a boil over medium heat, stirring constantly. Reduce the heat and simmer until the sauce thickens, about 1 minute.
◆ Place the warm crumble on individual dessert plates. Sift the confectioners' sugar over the crumble, spoon some of the sauce over the fruit.

STIRRED EGG CUSTARD SAUCE

TOTAL TIME: 25 MINUTES

SERVES 6

Vanilla sugar is made by adding a split vanilla pod to 2 cups (1 lb/500 g) superfine (caster) sugar. Keep in a covered jar for at least 5 to 7 days or longer. Try using vanilla sugar in other dessert recipes.

2 cups (16 fl oz/500 ml) whole (full
  cream) milk
1 vanilla bean, split open lengthwise
6 large egg yolks
1 cup (8 oz/250 g) vanilla sugar
2 teaspoons vanilla extract (vanilla essence)

◆ Pour the milk into a medium-sized saucepan, add the vanilla bean and bring almost to a boil over medium-high heat. Remove the saucepan from the heat as soon as the first bubbles rise to the surface.
◆ Combine the egg yolks and vanilla sugar in a medium-sized bowl. Beat until thick, creamy and lemon-colored.
◆ Add ½ cup of the hot milk to the egg mixture and stir well. Pour in the remaining milk and stir until combined.
◆ Bring a double-boiler, half filled with water, to a slow boil.
◆ Pour the custard mixture into the top of the double-boiler and cook over the simmering water, stirring constantly, until the custard thickens slightly and coats the back of a spoon, about 10 minutes. Do not overcook or let the water boil rapidly or the custard will curdle and separate. As soon as the custard thickens, remove the top of the double boiler from the water.
◆ Remove the vanilla bean from the custard and discard. Stir in the vanilla extract.
◆ Serve the custard warm or cold.

NUTRITION NOTES

PER SERVING—Pear and Blackberry Crumble
(Analysis uses monounsaturated margarine spread):
257 calories/1079 kilojoules; 5 g protein;
8.1 g fat, 27% of calories (2.1 g saturated,
7% of calories; 4.2 g monounsaturated, 14%;
1.8 g polyunsaturated, 6%); 44 g carbohydrate;
6.5 g dietary fiber; 53 mg sodium; 1.5 mg iron;
0.8 mg cholesterol.

PER SERVING—Stirred Egg Custard Sauce:
277 calories/1163 kilojoules; 6 g protein;
8.8 g fat, 28% of calories (4.2 g saturated,
13% of calories; 3.6 g monounsaturated, 12%;
1 g polyunsaturated, 3%); 46 g carbohydrate;
0 g dietary fiber; 47 mg sodium; 0.9 mg iron;
221 mg cholesterol.

RICH EGGLESS FRUIT CAKE AND SCOTTISH GINGERBREAD

Britain

This healthy eggless British fruit cake recipe has been specially developed for people on low-cholesterol diets. Serve with a selection of dried or candied fruits. Scottish cooks are known for their delicious cakes and breads. As in the following recipe, genuine Scottish gingerbread uses honey or light molasses (treacle) as a sweetener. This gingerbread is so moist that it does not require icing.

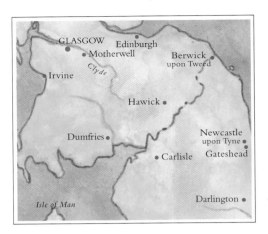

Rich Eggless Fruit Cake (top) and Scottish Gingerbread

RICH EGGLESS FRUIT CAKE

TOTAL TIME: 2 HOURS 15 MINUTES

MAKES 24 SLICES

To keep the fat content low in fruit cakes, use a reduced-fat margarine spread and limit the quantity of nuts.

6 large, tart, green cooking apples,
    preferably Granny Smith, peeled, cored
    and thinly sliced
1 tablespoon plus 1 teaspoon cold water
1 cup (8 oz/250 g) reduced-fat margarine
    spread
2 cups (16 oz/500 g) turbinado (raw)
    sugar
3 cups (about 15 oz/470 g) wholewheat
    (wholemeal plain) flour
1 tablespoon plus 1 teaspoon baking powder
1¼ teaspoons ground cinnamon
½ teaspoon ground nutmeg
¼ teaspoon ground cloves
1 cup (6 oz/185 g) golden raisins
    (sultanas)
1 cup (6 oz/185 g) raisins (seedless raisins)
½ cup (2 oz/60 g) hazelnuts, coarsely
    chopped
⅓ cup (2 oz/60 g) candied (glacé) cherries,
    quartered
⅓ cup (2 oz/60 g) mixed candied citrus
    peel, chopped

◆ Place the apples in a large, nonreactive saucepan. Add the water, cover and cook over medium heat until the apples start to bubble. Reduce the heat and simmer until the apples are soft, about 15 minutes. Remove from the heat and let cool for 10 minutes.
◆ Preheat the oven to 375°F (190°C). Line a deep, 9 inch (23 cm) round cake pan with parchment (non-stick baking) paper.
◆ Place the stewed apples in a blender or food processor. Process until smooth, stopping and scraping down the sides as needed.
◆ Pour 2½ cups of the apple purée into the rinsed saucepan. Refrigerate any remaining apple purée for another use.
◆ Add the margarine spread and sugar to the saucepan and stir well. Cook over medium heat, stirring constantly, until the margarine spread melts and the sugar dissolves, 5 to 8 minutes.
◆ Sift the flour, baking powder, cinnamon, nutmeg and cloves into a large bowl. Add any bran left in the sieve to the bowl.
◆ Make a well in the center of the dry ingredients. Pour the apple purée into the well, stirring until combined.
◆ Add the golden raisins, raisins, hazelnuts, cherries and mixed citrus peel. Mix well until combined.

◆ Spoon the mixture into the cake pan and spread to level with the back of a spoon.
◆ Bake until a skewer inserted into the center comes out clean, about 1½ hours.
◆ Place the cake pan on a wire rack and let stand for 30 minutes, then turn the cake out onto the rack and cool.
◆ Serve the cake thinly sliced. Makes 24 wedges, each about 1¼ inches (3 cm) thick.

SCOTTISH GINGERBREAD

TOTAL TIME: 1 HOUR 25 MINUTES

SERVES 12

Parchment (non-stick baking) paper is excellent for lining cake pans. If it is not available, use waxed (greaseproof) paper, lightly brushed with melted margarine or butter, to prevent the cake from sticking. Steel-cut oats and light molasses are available at health food stores.

½ cup (4 oz/125 g) reduced-fat margarine
    spread or unsalted butter
¾ cup (9 oz/280 g) light molasses (treacle)
⅔ cup (4 oz/125 g) dark brown sugar
¼ cup (2 oz/60 g) corn syrup or golden
    syrup
2 large, free-range eggs, lightly beaten
½ cup (4 fl oz/125 ml) skim milk
2 cups (8 oz/250 g) all-purpose (plain)
    flour
1 teaspoon baking soda (bicarbonate of soda)
1¼ teaspoons ground cinnamon
1 teaspoon ground ginger
½ teaspoon ground nutmeg
¼ teaspoon ground cloves
½ cup (3 oz/90 g) steel-cut oats

◆ Preheat the oven to 350°F (180°C). Line a deep, 8 inch (20 cm) round cake pan with parchment (non-stick baking) paper.
◆ Combine the margarine spread, molasses, sugar and corn syrup in a large saucepan. Cook over medium-low heat, stirring frequently, until the margarine has melted and the sugar has dissolved, 2 to 3 minutes. Set aside to cool. Stir in the eggs and the milk and mix well.
◆ Sift the flour, baking soda, cinnamon, ginger, nutmeg and cloves into a large bowl. Add the oats and mix well. Make a well in the center.
◆ Pour the milk mixture into the well and stir until combined. Beat the mixture with a spoon until smooth.
◆ Pour the mixture into the cake pan. Bake until a skewer inserted in the center comes out clean, about 1 hour.
◆ Transfer the cake pan to a wire rack and let stand for 5 minutes, then turn the gingerbread out onto the rack and cool.
◆ Cut into 12 wedges and serve.

NUTRITION NOTES

*PER SLICE—Rich Eggless Fruit Cake (Analysis uses monounsaturated margarine spread):
270 calories/1133 kilojoules; 3 g protein;
8.4 g fat, 28% of calories (1.2 g saturated,
4% of calories; 5.3 g monounsaturated, 17.7%;
1.9 g polyunsaturated, 6.3%); 47 g carbohydrate;
3.9 g dietary fiber; 116 mg sodium; 1.5 mg iron;
0 mg cholesterol.*

*PER SERVING—Scottish Gingerbread (Analysis uses monounsaturated margarine spread):
293 calories/1231 kilojoules; 5 g protein; 8.2 g fat,
25% of calories (1.5 g saturated, 4.6% of calories;
4.8 g monounsaturated, 14.6%; 1.9 g polyunsaturated, 5.8%); 52 g carbohydrate; 1.3 g dietary
fiber; 98 mg sodium; 2 mg iron; 38 mg cholesterol.*

GINGER

Ginger is the root or rhizome of the ginger plant (Zingiber officinale). It has a pungent, spicy aroma, a peppery, sweet flavor and a fresh, spicy fragrance. A native of southern Asia, it is now grown throughout the world's tropical areas. Ginger adds flavor to bland dishes, neutralizes fats and also aids digestion. It is found in various forms: fresh, ground, dried, minced, crystalized or candied, preserved and pickled. All these are available from Asian food stores and larger supermarkets and will last indefinitely, except for fresh ginger which will keep for up to 2 months if stored in a cool, dry cupboard.

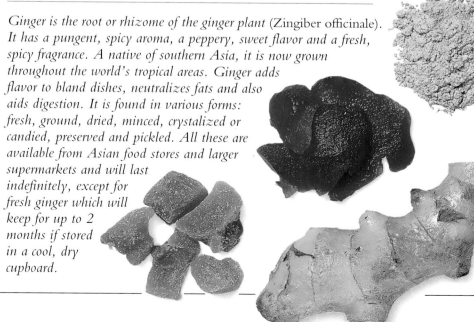

APPLE MERINGUE PIE

Britain

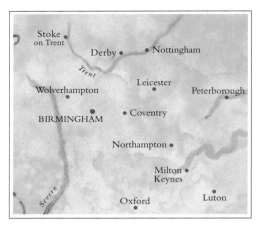

Pies, both savory and sweet, have been an important part of British cuisine since the Middle Ages. In those days the pies were very large—some were big enough to enclose live birds! This unusual apple pie is elevated from the homey classic to gourmet status by the addition of a light meringue. The pastry, made with wholewheat flour and wheatgerm, increases the carbohydrate, dietary fiber, vitamin and mineral content of the pie.

TOTAL TIME: 1 HOUR 15 MINUTES

SERVES 8

Only an approximate amount of water is given for pastry recipes. The actual amount depends on room temperature, humidity and the quality of the flour. Dried beans make excellent pie weights—the beans may be re-used several times.

WHOLEWHEAT PASTRY

1 cup (about 5 oz/155 g) wholewheat (wholemeal) flour
1 cup (1 ⅔ oz/50 g) wheatgerm
⅓ cup (3 oz/90 g) reduced-fat margarine spread, chilled
about ¼ cup (2 fl oz/60 ml) iced water

FILLING

4 large, tart, green cooking apples, preferably Granny Smith
¼ cup (2 oz/60 g) white sugar
grated zest and juice of 1 lemon
1 tablespoon fat-reduced margarine spread
2 large, free-range eggs, separated

vegetable oil cooking spray
¼ cup (2 oz/60 g) superfine (caster) sugar
mint leaves, for decoration, optional

◆ To make the pastry, combine the flour, wheatgerm and margarine spread in a food processor. Process until the mixture resembles fine bread crumbs. Add the iced water 1 tablespoon at a time and process for 10 seconds after each addition. Add water only as needed to form a stiff dough. The dough should leave the sides of the bowl and come together to form a ball around the center of the bowl when ready.

◆ Turn the dough out onto a cool, lightly floured surface and pat into a round. Wrap in waxed (greaseproof) paper and chill in the refrigerator for 30 minutes.

◆ Meanwhile, prepare the filling. Peel, core and thinly slice the apples. Place in a large nonreactive saucepan and add the sugar, lemon zest and juice. Cover and cook over medium heat until the apples begin bubbling. Reduce the heat and stew the apples until soft, about 15 minutes.

◆ Remove the apple mixture from the heat and cool. Pour into a blender or food processor and process until smooth. Add the margarine spread and egg yolks and process briefly until the margarine spread has melted and the egg yolks are evenly combined.

◆ Preheat the oven to 425°F (220°C). Lightly spray a deep, 8 inch (20 cm) flan pan or a 9 inch (23 cm) pie plate with cooking spray.

◆ Roll the dough out to make a 10 inch (25 cm) round. Lift and turn the dough between rolls to prevent sticking. If it does stick, loosen the dough with a pastry spatula (palette knife) and sprinkle extra flour over the work surface.

◆ Gently press the pastry into the pan, starting at the center and working out to the edges. Trim off the excess pastry and prick the bottom well with a fork.

◆ Line the pastry with a square of waxed (greaseproof) paper and add a single layer of dried beans. Bake for 10 minutes, then remove the paper and beans.

◆ Reduce the oven temperature to 350°F (180°C). Pour the apple mixture into the pastry shell. Bake until the filling is almost set, about 15 minutes.

◆ Place the egg whites in a bowl, and whisk with an electric mixer on high speed until stiff peaks form. Add the superfine sugar slowly but constantly—a teaspoon at a time—while whisking at high speed. The mixture will turn from a dull white to a shiny white.

◆ Spoon the meringue mixture over the apple filling, starting at the edge, and decoratively swirl with a plastic spatula.

◆ Return the pie to the oven and bake until the meringue is set and golden, about 15 minutes.

◆ Serve the pie warm, decorated with the mint leaves, if using.

NUTRITION NOTES

PER SERVING (Analysis uses monounsaturated margarine spread): 238 calories/998 kilojoules; 6 g protein; 10 g fat, 39% of calories (1.9 g saturated, 7.4% of calories; 5.8 g monounsaturated, 22.6%; 2.3 g polyunsaturated, 9%); 31 g carbohydrate; 5.2 g dietary fiber; 72 mg sodium; 1.6 mg iron; 56 mg cholesterol.

RIZÓGALO

Rice Cake—Greece

Acknowledged as one of the most important and popular grains in the world, rice is often associated with savory dishes. In Greece it is also used to make sweets like this magnificent cake. First the rice is cooked like a pudding, then combined with eggs, nourishing dried fruit, nuts and citrus fruit and baked. It is a good source of calcium, phosphorus and protein. Rice cake may be served warm or cold accompanied by low-fat, plain yogurt or wedges of ripe melon.

TOTAL TIME: 1 HOUR 20 MINUTES

SERVES 12

If fresh dates are not available, use the best quality dried dates. These are sometimes called "dessert" dates. To prepare the hazelnuts, roast them in a 180°F (350°C) oven until the skins are scorched, 10 to 15 minutes. Rub the skins off with a cloth. The nuts can then be finely ground in a food processor.

vegetable oil cooking spray

1 cup (7½ oz/210 g) glutinous (short-grain) rice

2 cups (16 fl oz/500 ml) skim milk

1 cup (8 fl oz/250 ml) whole (full cream) milk

½ cup (4 oz/125 g) turbinado (raw) sugar

12 fresh dates, pitted and halved lengthwise, or dried dates, coarsely chopped

¾ cup (3 oz/100 g) shelled hazelnuts, roasted, peeled and finely ground

finely grated zest and juice of 1 orange

2 large, free-range eggs, well beaten

confectioners' (icing) sugar, for sifting, optional

dates and orange slices, for decoration, optional

◆ Preheat the oven to 375°F (190°C).

◆ Line the base of an 8 inch (20 cm) springform pan or deep cake pan with parchment (non-stick baking) paper. Spray the inside of the pan lightly with vegetable oil cooking spray.

◆ Combine the rice, skim milk, whole milk and sugar in a large, heavy-bottomed saucepan and stir well. Bring to a boil over medium heat, stirring often. Reduce the heat and simmer very slowly, stirring frequently, until the rice is softened and half the liquid is absorbed, 10 to 15 minutes.

◆ Remove the saucepan from the heat and stir in the dates, hazelnuts, orange zest and juice. Add the eggs and stir well to combine.

◆ Pour the mixture into the springform pan and spread the top to level. Bake until golden brown and a skewer inserted into the center comes out clean, 40 to 45 minutes.

◆ Place the pan on a wire rack and let stand for 10 minutes. Remove the sides and base of the pan and place the cake on the rack.

◆ Transfer the cake to a serving plate, sift the confectioners' sugar over the top and decorate with the dates and orange slices, if using. Serve the cake warm or cold.

NUTRITION NOTES

PER SERVING: 222 calories/932 kilojoules; 6 g protein; 7.2 g fat, 28% of calories (1.3 g saturated, 5% of calories; 4.9 g monounsaturated, 19%; 1 g polyunsaturated, 4%); 35 g carbohydrate; 3.6 g dietary fiber; 43 mg sodium; 0.9 mg iron; 42 mg cholesterol.

Pagoméno Yiaoúrti me Fistikia ke Veríkoko, Rodákina me Sáltsa Síko

Pistachio and Apricot Frozen Yogurt and
Peaches with Fig Sauce—Greece

Pistachios and apricots are combined with honey and yogurt to create this delicious low-fat frozen dessert. The peach originally came from China, but is now grown around the world. Figs, native to the Mediterranean region, are rich in dietary fiber. Peaches and figs make a great combination.

Pistachio and Apricot Frozen Yogurt (top) and Peaches with Fig Sauce

PAGOMÉNO YIAOÚRTI ME FISTIKIA KE VERÍKOKO

Pistachio and Apricot Frozen Yogurt

TOTAL TIME: 4½ HOURS

SERVES 8

Prepare at least 6 hours in advance. This recipe may be made in an electric ice-cream maker. Follow the manufacturer's instructions for best results.

1 cup (4 oz/125 g) dried apricots, well packed
1 cup (8 fl oz/250 ml) water
⅓ cup (4 oz/125 g) honey
⅓ cup (2 oz/60 g) dark brown sugar
3 tablespoons margarine or butter
1 tablespoon plus 1 teaspoon freshly
    squeezed lemon juice
2 cups (13 oz/400 g) low-fat, plain yogurt
½ cup (2 oz/60 g) shelled pistachio nuts,
    peeled and coarsely chopped

◆ Combine the dried apricots and water in a small saucepan over medium heat and slowly bring to a boil. Cover, reduce the heat to medium-low and simmer until the apricots are tender, about 15 minutes. Remove from the heat, transfer to a small bowl and set aside to cool. Chill in the refrigerator for about 1 hour.
◆ Meanwhile, combine the honey, sugar and margarine in a small saucepan over medium heat. Stir occasionally until the sugar is dissolved and the margarine is melted. Remove from the heat.
◆ Add the lemon juice and stir to combine.
◆ Combine the yogurt and the honey mixture in a medium-sized bowl and mix well.
◆ Combine the apricots and their liquid in a blender or food processor. Process until puréed, stopping and scraping down the sides as needed.
◆ Pour half the apricot purée into the yogurt mixture and mix well to combine. Cover the remaining apricot purée with plastic wrap and refrigerate until ready to serve.
◆ Pour the yogurt mixture into a 4 cup shallow, rigid freezer container. Place in the freezer, uncovered, for 2 to 3 hours.
◆ Using a fork, stir the mixture from the center outwards to the edge of the container and then from the edge back to the center.
◆ Reserve 4 teaspoons of the chopped pistachios for decoration. Stir the remaining pistachios into the yogurt mixture.
◆ Cover the container and return to the freezer until firm, about 6 hours.
◆ Scoop the frozen yogurt into dessert bowls. Sprinkle with the reserved pistachios. Serve immediately with the remaining apricot purée on the side.

RODÁKINA ME SÁLTSA SÍKO

Peaches with Fig Sauce

TOTAL TIME: 1 HOUR 35 MINUTES

SERVES 6

Select freestone peaches, not clingstone peaches. It is easier to remove the pit cleanly without tearing the fruit.

6 large peaches
1 cup (8 fl oz/250 ml) water
1 cup (8 fl oz/250 ml) dry white wine
½ cup (4 oz/125 g) sugar
2 tablespoons brandy
6 plump figs, about 1 lb (500 g)
1 tablespoon confectioners' (icing) sugar,
    sifted
mint sprigs, for garnish
extra figs, for serving, optional

◆ Cut the peaches in half with a sharp knife and carefully remove the pits.
◆ Combine the water, wine and sugar in a nonreactive frying pan that is large enough to hold the peach halves in a single layer. Cook over medium heat, stirring constantly, until the sugar is dissolved. Bring to a boil, then reduce the heat to medium-low and simmer for 5 minutes.
◆ Add the peach halves and simmer, occasionally basting with the syrup, until tender, 5 to 10 minutes. Remove from the heat and set aside until cool enough to handle, about 15 minutes. Carefully remove the skins from the peaches with your fingers.
◆ Transfer the peaches to a serving bowl or individual dessert plates and sprinkle with the brandy. Cover with plastic wrap and cool at room temperature for about 1 hour.
◆ Meanwhile, cut the figs into quarters and remove the stalks. Place the figs in a blender or food processor. Process to a purée, stopping and scraping down the sides of the bowl as needed.
◆ Strain the fig purée through a fine mesh sieve into a small bowl and discard the seeds. Add the confectioners' sugar to the purée and mix well.
◆ Spoon the fig purée over or around the poached peaches, then decorate with the mint sprigs and extra figs, if using. Serve at room temperature for best flavor.

NUTRITION NOTES

PER SERVING—Pistachio and Apricot Frozen Yogurt: 214 calories/897 kilojoules; 6 g protein; 8.4 g fat, 35% of calories (1.2 g saturated, 5% of calories; 5 g monounsaturated, 21%; 2.2 g polyunsaturated, 9%); 29 g carbohydrate; 2.1 g dietary fiber; 74 mg sodium; 1 mg iron; 3 mg cholesterol.

PER SERVING—Peaches with Fig Sauce: 189 calories/793 kilojoules; 2 g protein; 0 g fat; 36 g carbohydrate; 3.3 g dietary fiber; 14 mg sodium; 0.5 mg iron; 0 mg cholesterol.

FIGS

One of the oldest fruits in cultivation, the fig (Ficus carica) *was a staple food of the Mediterranean region over 6000 years ago, and was talked about in the Old Testament. Figs are a member of the mulberry family which has over 600 species of vines, shrubs and trees. Today figs are gown commercially in California—where they were introduced during the eighteenth century—and throughout North Africa, the Middle East and southern Europe. Figs vary in color from greenish white to red to purple, and can be eaten fresh as a snack or cooked with meat or for dessert. Even more nourishing when dried, figs are high in natural sugar, iron and vitamins. They have long been prized for their digestive qualities. Fresh figs are available during the summer, and for the best flavor should be eaten at room temperature. Choose fruits that are firm to the touch, store them in the refrigerator and eat them as soon as possible. Dried figs are often sold in blocks and keep indefinitely when stored in the dark. Dried figs are sometimes ground into a paste and used in commercial baked goods.*

GALATÓPITA ME LIOMÉNES FRÁOULES, HALVÁS ME SIMIGDÁLI KE RAVANÍ

Custard Pie with Strawberry Purée and
Semolina Cake and Rhubarb Purée—Greece

In this delicious Greek pie, phyllo pastry is wrapped around a soft-textured semolina custard made with skim milk, yogurt and eggs. Semolina, an energy-boosting complex carbohydrate, is a popular ingredient in Greek desserts. Semolina Cake includes dried figs, a good source of calcium and magnesium.

Custard Pie with Strawberry Purée and Semolina Cake and Rhubarb Purée (top)

GALATÓPITA ME LIOMÉNES FRÁOULES

Custard Pie with Strawberry Purée

TOTAL TIME: 1 HOUR 30 MINUTES

SERVES 12

When using sheets of phyllo pastry, keep them covered with waxed (greaseproof) paper, topped with a cold damp cloth, to prevent them from becoming brittle. Vanilla sugar is easy to make at home and much cheaper than the store-bought variety.

CUSTARD

3 cups (24 fl oz/750 ml) skim milk
1 cup (8 oz/250 g) vanilla sugar (see Glossary)
¾ cup (4½ oz/140 g) fine semolina
5 large, free-range eggs, lightly beaten
1 cup (6½ oz/200 g) low-fat, plain yogurt
2 teaspoons vanilla extract (vanilla essence)
¼ cup (1 oz/30 g) coarsely chopped dried apricots

2 tablespoons margarine or unsalted butter, melted

2 tablespoons freshly squeezed orange juice
12 sheets phyllo pastry

SYRUP

½ cup (4 fl oz/125 ml) water
½ cup (4 oz/125 g) sugar
1 cinnamon stick
1 long strip of lemon zest
juice of 1 large lemon

STRAWBERRY PURÉE

2 cups strawberries, washed, dried and hulled
2 tablespoons confectioners' (icing) sugar
2 tablespoons ouzo, optional

◆ Preheat the oven to 350°F (180°C).
◆ To make the custard, combine the milk and vanilla sugar in a large, heavy-bottomed saucepan over medium heat. Stir frequently until the sugar is dissolved. Bring to a boil and immediately pour in the semolina, stirring quickly. Reduce the heat to low and cook, stirring constantly, until the mixture thickens, about 5 minutes.
◆ Remove the saucepan from the heat. Add the eggs, one at a time, beating after each addition until evenly combined.
◆ Add the yogurt, vanilla and apricots and beat well.
◆ Place a piece of plastic wrap directly on the surface of the custard to prevent a skin from forming. Set aside until lukewarm.
◆ Meanwhile, prepare the pastry. Combine the melted margarine and orange juice in a small bowl.
◆ Place a sheet of phyllo pastry on a cool, dry work surface. Lightly brush with the orange juice mixture. Working quickly, carefully place the pastry sheet in a 10 inch (25 cm) round, ceramic, ovenproof dish. There will be a slight overlap.
◆ Brush a second sheet of phyllo pastry and gently ease it into place in the dish at right angles to the first sheet.
◆ Continue brushing and layering 4 more sheets of phyllo, placing at right angles, as directed.

◆ Pour the custard filling into the phyllo-lined dish. Brush the remaining sheets of phyllo pastry and layer over the filling, allowing the edges to overhang.

◆ Using kitchen scissors, trim the overhanging edge neatly, leaving a ¾ inch (2 cm) wide border. With a very fine sharp knife, score a pattern of diagonal lines, about 1¼ inch (3 cm) apart, on top of the pie. Brush any remaining orange juice mixture over the top.

◆ Bake until the pastry is puffed and golden brown, and the point of a fine knife inserted in the center comes out clean, 45 to 50 minutes. Transfer the dish to a wire rack.

◆ Meanwhile, make the syrup. Combine the water, sugar, cinnamon, lemon zest and lemon juice in a small saucepan over medium heat and stir until the sugar is dissolved.

◆ Bring to a boil, then reduce the heat to medium-low and simmer until slightly thickened, about 10 minutes.

◆ Remove and discard the cinnamon stick and lemon zest. Set the syrup aside until lukewarm, about 10 minutes.

◆ Pour the syrup slowly over the pie, so that it is gradually absorbed by the pastry— do not flood or the syrup may overflow. After all of the syrup has been absorbed, set the pie aside for about 10 minutes.

◆ To make the strawberry sauce, combine the strawberries, confectioners' sugar and ouzo, if using, in a blender or food processor. Process until a smooth purée is formed, stopping and scraping the sides down as needed.

◆ Transfer the sauce to a serving bowl or pitcher.

◆ Cut the pie into 12 wedges and serve with the strawberry sauce.

HALVÁS ME SIMIGDÁLI KE RAVANÍ

Semolina Cake and Rhubarb Purée

TOTAL TIME: 1 HOUR 20 MINUTES

SERVES 8

Orange-flower water, also called orangeblossom water, is available at pharmacies, health food stores and in the gourmet sections of some supermarkets.

CAKE

¼ cup (2 oz/60 g) reduced-fat margarine spread
½ cup (4 oz/125 g) superfine (caster) sugar
2 large, free-range eggs
1 cup (6 oz/185 g) semolina

RHUBARB

Rhubarb (Rheum rhaponticum) is a hardy perennial vegetable that has been cultivated for about 4000 years. Originally grown in China and Siberia, it was sought after by western traders for its medicinal properties. During the eighteenth century the English discovered its delights as a cooked dessert and since then it has been treated as a fruit. Rhubarb has long, fleshy stalks varying in color from light pink to deep red, and large green leaves that are poisonous. The flavor of cooked rhubarb is complemented by citrus fruits, particularly lemon and orange, and by spices such as cinnamon and cloves. High in calcium, potassium and iron, the stalks should have a bright fresh color and should be crisp and not fibrous. Available fresh from late summer to early winter, rhubarb stalks should be stored in the crisper section of the refrigerator and used within 4 days.

1 cup (4 oz/125 g) self-rising (self-raising) flour, sifted
⅓ cup (3 fl oz/90 ml) freshly squeezed orange juice
½ cup (3 oz/90 g) dried figs, sliced ½ inch (1 cm) thick
24 blanched almonds

SYRUP

1 cup (8 fl oz/250 ml) freshly squeezed orange juice
½ cup (4 oz/125 g) sugar
2 teaspoons orange-flower water

RHUBARB PURÉE

1 lb (500 g) trimmed red rhubarb
1 cup (8 fl oz/250 ml) water
½ cup (4 oz/125 g) sugar

◆ Preheat the oven to 350°F (180°C).

◆ Line an 8 inch (20 cm) springform pan or deep cake pan with parchment (non-stick baking) paper.

◆ To make the cake, combine the margarine spread and superfine sugar in a large bowl and beat with an electric mixer until light and creamy. Add the eggs, one at a time, and beat well after each addition.

◆ Add the semolina and flour and gently stir to combine. Stir in the orange juice.

◆ Spoon two-thirds of the batter into the cake pan and spread the top to level. Arrange the figs on top, then cover with the remaining batter and spread the top to level. Arrange the almonds on top of the cake.

◆ Bake until a skewer inserted into the center comes out clean, 35 to 40 minutes. Transfer to a wire rack and cool for about 10 minutes.

◆ Meanwhile, make the syrup. Place the orange juice and sugar in a saucepan over medium heat and stir until the sugar dissolves. Bring to a boil, then reduce the heat

to medium-low and simmer until reduced and slightly thickened, about 10 minutes. Remove from the heat, cool for 10 minutes, then stir in the orange-flower water.

◆ Pour the orange syrup slowly and carefully over the cake until absorbed.

◆ To make the rhubarb purée, cut the rhubarb stalks into 2 inch (5 cm) pieces.

◆ Combine the water and sugar in a nonreactive saucepan over medium heat. Bring to a boil and cook, stirring occasionally, until the sugar is dissolved, about 2 minutes. Add the rhubarb, cover and bring back to a boil. Reduce the heat to mediumlow and simmer gently until tender, 8 to 10 minutes.

◆ Cool the rhubarb for 5 to 10 minutes. Using a slotted spoon, transfer the rhubarb to a blender or food processor. Add ½ cup of the cooking liquid and process until smooth, stopping and scraping down the sides as needed. Reserve the remaining cooking liquid for another use.

◆ Pour the rhubarb purée into a serving bowl or pitcher.

◆ Cut the semolina cake into 8 wedges and serve with the rhubarb purée.

NUTRITION NOTES

PER SERVING—Custard Pie with Strawberry Purée (Analysis uses monounsaturated margarine): 268 calories/1127 kilojoules; 10 g protein; 5.2 g fat, 17% of calories (1.4 g saturated, 4.6% of calories; 2.7 g monounsaturated, 8.8%; 1.1 g polyunsaturated, 3.6%); 46 g carbohydrate; 1.6 g dietary fiber; 187 mg sodium; 1 mg iron; 97 mg cholesterol.

PER SERVING—Semolina Cake and Rhubarb Purée (Analysis uses monounsaturated margarine spread): 454 calories/1908 kilojoules; 9 g protein; 10 g fat, 20% of calories (1.6 g saturated, 3.2% of calories; 6 g monounsaturated, 12%; 2.4 g polyunsaturated, 4.8%); 84 g carbohydrate; 5.6 g dietary fiber; 172 mg sodium; 1.1 mg iron; 56 mg cholesterol.

GRANITA DI LIMONE

Lemon Ice—Italy

*T*he *flavored ice or* granita *of Italy is far more refreshing than* gelato *(Italian ice cream). Signor Tortoni of Naples, whose son created the famous sweet cookie* tortoni, *claims the ice as his invention. Served as the final course, this lemon ice is low in calories and has a superb cooling effect on the palate, especially in hot weather. Lemons are a good source of vitamin C and soluble dietary fiber which assists in lowering blood cholesterol.*

TOTAL TIME: 3 HOURS

SERVES 12

Select lemons with thin skins—thick-skinned lemons usually have less juice. Granita glasses, like sorbet glasses, are similar to champagne flutes.

zest of 4 lemons, cut into long thin strips
4 cups (32 fl oz/1 liter) water
2 cups (1 lb/500 g) sugar
2½ cups (20 fl oz/600 ml) freshly
*   squeezed lemon juice, 10 to 12 lemons*
mint sprigs, for decoration
rose petals, for decoration, optional

◆ Combine the lemon zest, water and sugar in a nonreactive saucepan over medium heat and stir gently until the sugar dissolves. Bring the mixture to a boil, then reduce the heat and simmer until syrupy and slightly thickened, about 10 minutes. Set aside to cool, about 30 minutes. Remove and discard the lemon zest.
◆ Strain the lemon juice through a fine mesh sieve and stir into the syrup.
◆ Cover the mixture and chill in the refrigerator for at least 1 hour.
◆ Place the chilled mixture in an electric ice-cream maker and mix, according to manufacturer's instructions, until a thick icy texture with small, even crystals forms, about 30 minutes. Working quickly, spoon the mixture into a rigid freezer container. Cover and chill in the freezer for at least 30 minutes before serving.
◆ Spoon the lemon ice into glasses or onto dessert plates. Decorate with the mint sprigs and rose petals, if using, and serve at once.

NUTRITION NOTES

PER SERVING: *176 calories/739 kilojoules; 0.3 g protein; 0 g fat; 43 g carbohydrate; 0.1 g dietary fiber; 3 mg sodium; 0.1 mg iron; 0 mg cholesterol.*

BORTUKAL MAGHRIBE

Moroccan Oranges—Morocco

Moroccan cuisine is very colorful and bursting with flavor. This typical dessert is quick and easy to prepare. It's a refreshing choice to serve after a hot spicy main course. Fresh oranges are one of our best natural sources of vitamin C. Navel oranges are one of the many popular varieties of citrus fruit that are cultivated to be seedless. The simple yogurt sauce adds protein, calcium and phosphorus to the dessert.

TOTAL TIME: 1¼ HOURS

SERVES: 6

Orange-flower water is available from pharmacies and health food stores. If dried dates are used they must be the best quality.

YOGURT SAUCE

½ cup (4 oz / 125 g) superfine (caster) sugar
½ cup (4 fl oz / 125 ml) water
1 vanilla bean, split in half lengthways
1 cup (6½ oz / 200 g) low-fat, plain yogurt
1 teaspoon orange-flower water

6 navel oranges
2 tablespoons confectioners' (icing) sugar, sifted
½ teaspoon ground cinnamon
2 teaspoons orange-flower water
6 fresh dates, stoned and thinly sliced, or dried dates, coarsely chopped

◆ To make the sauce, combine the superfine sugar, water and vanilla bean in a small saucepan. Bring to a boil over medium heat, stirring until the sugar is dissolved, then reduce the heat to medium-low and simmer until the syrup is slightly thickened, about 5 minutes.

◆ Strain the syrup through a cheesecloth-lined sieve and set aside until cool, about 30 minutes.

◆ Place the yogurt in a medium-sized bowl. Add the strained syrup and the orange-flower water and whisk until the mixture is evenly combined.

◆ Cover and chill in the refrigerator for at least 1 hour or overnight, if preferred.

◆ Meanwhile, use a sharp serrated knife to carefully remove the peel and all the white pith from the oranges. Cut the oranges into ¼ to ½ inch (5 to 10 mm) slices, reserving any juice.

◆ Arrange the orange slices in a single layer on one or two plates; sprinkle with the confectioners' sugar, cinnamon, orange-flower water and any reserved juice.

◆ Cover the oranges with plastic wrap and place in the refrigerator to macerate for 1 hour, turning the slices after 30 minutes.

◆ Arrange the orange slices attractively on dessert plates, dividing equally. Sprinkle the dates over the oranges. Serve immediately, while the oranges are still slightly chilled. Serve the sauce separately.

NUTRITION NOTES

PER SERVING: 199 calories / 836 kilojoules; 4 g protein; 0.2 g fat, 1% of calories (0.1 g saturated, 0.5% of calories; 0.1 g monounsaturated, 0.5%; 0 g polyunsaturated, 0%); 46 g carbohydrate; 5 g dietary fiber; 33 mg sodium; 0.9 mg iron; 2 mg cholesterol.

JAZAAR SAMSON, KOSHOFF

Carrot and Sesame Halva and
Dried Fruit and Nut Salad—Lebanon

This halva recipe features carrots and milk, making it much healthier than the traditional version. A good harvest of dates and almonds signifies prosperity and long life in Lebanon. Both are used in this lovely Dried Fruit and Nut Salad. Rose water gives an elegant and exotic flavor to the syrup. Dried fruit is a good source of iron, potassium, B-complex vitamins and fiber.

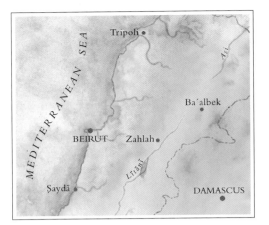

JAZAAR SAMSON

Carrot and Sesame Halva

TOTAL TIME: 1 HOUR 50 MINUTES

SERVES 10

It is important to use a heavy-bottomed saucepan, preferably of enameled cast iron, to prevent sticking.

vegetable oil cooking spray
1½ lb (750 g) carrots, peeled and grated, about 3½ cups
4 cups (32 fl oz/1 liter) skim milk
10 cardamom pods
3⅓ oz (100 g) fat-reduced margarine spread or unsalted butter
½ cup (4 oz/125 g) superfine (caster) sugar
⅓ cup (1 2/3 oz/50 g) shelled pistachio nuts, finely chopped
⅓ cup (1½ oz/45 g) sesame seeds, toasted
1 cup (6½ oz/200 g) low-fat, plain yogurt, for serving

◆ Lightly spray the base of a large, heavy-bottomed saucepan with vegetable oil cooking spray.
◆ Combine the carrots, milk and cardamom pods in the prepared saucepan and bring to a boil over high heat, stirring frequently. Reduce the heat to medium and cook, uncovered, stirring often, until the liquid is absorbed, 50 to 60 minutes.
◆ Melt the margarine spread in a large frying pan over medium heat. Add the carrot mixture and cook, stirring frequently, until the milk evaporates, about 5 minutes.
◆ Add the sugar, half the pistachio nuts and half the sesame seeds. Cook, stirring constantly, until the mixture thickens sufficiently to come away from the sides of the pan, 8 to 10 minutes. Remove from the heat and discard the cardamom pods. Cool.
◆ Transfer the mixture into dessert dishes or long-stemmed glasses. Spoon about 1½ tablespoons of yogurt on top and sprinkle with the remaining pistachio nuts and sesame seeds.

KOSHOFF

Dried Fruit and Nut Salad

TOTAL TIME: 2 HOURS 20 MINUTES

SERVES 8

For variation, add fresh fruit, such as orange segments, sliced peaches, seedless grapes or cubes of melon. Refrigerate for 1 hour longer. Rose water is available from pharmacies, health food stores and in gourmet sections of good food stores.

¼ cup (1 oz/30 g) whole almonds
1 cup cold, brewed herbal or Indian tea
½ cup (4 fl oz/125 ml) freshly squeezed orange juice
2 tablespoons honey
2 tablespoons rose water
1 cup (4 oz/125 g) dried apricots
⅔ cup (4 oz/125 g) dried figs, quartered
⅔ cup (4 oz/125 g) pitted prunes
⅓ cup (2 oz/60 g) golden raisins (sultanas)
16 dried dates, halved and pitted
orange zest, for garnish, optional

◆ Place the almonds in a heatproof bowl; pour over boiling water to cover and let stand for 5 minutes.
◆ Drain, then cover with cold water. (This is known as "blanching" and helps to loosen the almond skins.) While the almonds are immersed in the water, remove the skins and discard.
◆ Combine the tea, orange juice, honey and rose water in a large bowl and mix well until the honey is dissolved and the liquids are well combined.
◆ Add the apricots, figs, prunes, golden raisins, almonds and dates to the orange syrup and stir gently.
◆ Cover with plastic wrap and chill in the refrigerator until the dried fruit is softened, about 2 hours.
◆ Serve in a glass bowl or individual dessert bowls.

PINE NUTS

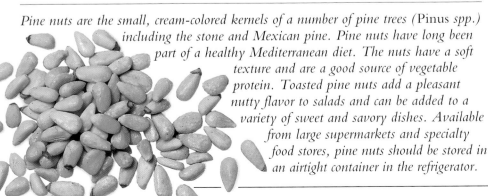

Pine nuts are the small, cream-colored kernels of a number of pine trees (Pinus spp.) including the stone and Mexican pine. Pine nuts have long been part of a healthy Mediterranean diet. The nuts have a soft texture and are a good source of vegetable protein. Toasted pine nuts add a pleasant nutty flavor to salads and can be added to a variety of sweet and savory dishes. Available from large supermarkets and specialty food stores, pine nuts should be stored in an airtight container in the refrigerator.

Carrot and Sesame Halva (top) and Dried Fruit and Nut Salad

MELON EN SALSA DE OPORTO

Melon in Port Wine—Spain

*S*ucculent melons grow around Madrid and in the dry sunny climate of Catalonia. While many varieties are available, the casaba, which is similar to a honeydew, is one of the most popular. When this fresh fruit is combined with the sweet wine of Oporto, on the neighboring Portuguese coast, it makes a quick and simple but memorable dessert. Melon is a source of carbohydrate, vitamin C and folate.

TOTAL TIME: 1 HOUR 15 MINUTES

SERVES 6

If you do not have a melon baller, halve the melon and remove the seeds as directed, then remove the skin and cut the flesh into attractive cubes.

1 large casaba or honeydew melon
2 tablespoons superfine (caster) sugar
1½ cups (12 fl oz/375 ml) port wine
2 tablespoons coarsely chopped walnuts, optional
mint sprigs, for garnish

◆ Cut the melon in half lengthwise and discard the seeds.
◆ Use a melon baller to scoop out balls of melon and place them in a bowl.
◆ Sprinkle the sugar over the melon, then pour over the port wine.
◆ Cover the bowl with plastic wrap and chill in the refrigerator for about 1 hour.
◆ Carefully spoon the melon balls and their liquid into individual dessert glasses or serving bowls, dividing equally. Sprinkle each serving with the chopped walnuts, if using. Decorate with the sprigs of mint and serve immediately.

NUTRITION NOTES

PER SERVING: 176 calories/740 kilojoules; 2 g protein; 0 g fat; 27 g carbohydrate; 2.2 g dietary fiber; 103 mg sodium; 0.8 mg iron; 0 mg cholesterol.

APFEL UND QUARK STRUDEL

Apple and Cheese Strudel—Switzerland

Strudel is claimed by Hungarians, Austrians and Yugoslavs as their own. Such is the "melting pot" of cuisine in Central Europe! However, the original idea comes from the Greek-Turkish baklava *pastry. Strudel may be made with savory or sweet fillings. This Swiss recipe uses cottage cheese, apples, golden raisins and pumpernickel enclosed in light phyllo pastry. The strudel provides protein, calcium, phosphorus, iron, fiber and vitamins B and C.*

TOTAL TIME: 1 HOUR 10 MINUTES

SERVES 6

If you do not have a food processor, push the cottage cheese through a fine mesh sieve to make smooth.

1 cup (8 oz/250 g) low-fat, reduced-sodium cottage cheese
1 lb (500 g), about 3 medium, tart, green cooking apples, preferably Granny Smith
2 teaspoons finely grated lemon zest
1 tablespoon freshly squeezed lemon juice
⅓ cup (2 oz/60 g) golden raisins (sultanas)
¼ cup (2 oz/60 g) sugar
1 teaspoon ground cinnamon
8 sheets phyllo pastry dough
2 tablespoons margarine or unsalted butter, melted
2 tablespoons freshly squeezed orange juice
3 slices pumpernickel bread, coarsely crumbled
1 tablespoon confectioners' (icing) sugar, for sifting

◆ Preheat the oven to 375°F (190°C).
◆ Place the cottage cheese in a food processor and process until smooth.
◆ Quarter the apples. Peel, core and cut the quarters lengthwise into ½ inch (1 cm) slices. Combine the apples, lemon zest and lemon juice in a large bowl and gently mix until the apples are well coated.
◆ Add the golden raisins, sugar and cinnamon to the apples and mix well.
◆ Add the cottage cheese and stir gently to combine.
◆ Carefully unroll or unfold the phyllo pastry. Cover with a sheet of waxed (greaseproof) paper, then cover with a cold damp cloth.
◆ Place a sheet of phyllo pastry on a cool, dry work surface. Lightly brush with a little of the melted margarine. Working quickly, place a second sheet of phyllo on top, brush with orange juice and sprinkle with a quarter of the pumpernickel crumbs. Repeat

these processes three more times until the eight sheets of phyllo are layered.
◆ Place the apple and cottage cheese mixture over the bottom third of one of the short sides of the layered phyllo and spread it to level.
◆ Starting at the filling end, roll up firmly jelly-roll (Swiss-roll) style.
◆ Carefully transfer the strudel to a large baking tray, seam side down. Brush with the remaining melted margarine.
◆ Bake until the pastry is crisp and golden brown, about 30 minutes.
◆ Stand the baking sheet on a wire rack until

the strudel filling is slightly set, about 10 minutes.
◆ Sift the confectioners' sugar over the strudel. Serve warm or cold, cut diagonally into thick slices.

NUTRITION NOTES

PER SERVING (Analysis uses monounsaturated margarine): 286 calories/1200 kilojoules; 10 g protein; 4.9 g fat, 15% of calories (1.4 g saturated, 4.3% of calories; 2.3 g monounsaturated, 7%; 1.2 g polyunsaturated, 3.7%); 51 g carbohydrate; 5.2 g dietary fiber; 445 mg sodium; 1.8 mg iron; 5 mg cholesterol.

CARROT CAKE AND OATMEAL COOKIES

The United States

Carrot Cake is easy to make, has a moist texture and doesn't break the budget. Carrots are an excellent source of beta-carotene and a good source of dietary fiber. Blueberries, orange wedges and a spoonful of low-fat, plain yogurt make good accompaniments. Old-fashioned recipes, like this one for Oatmeal Cookies, are a reminder of the days when all cookies were home-made. These are rich in complex carbohydrate and dietary fiber and low in fat.

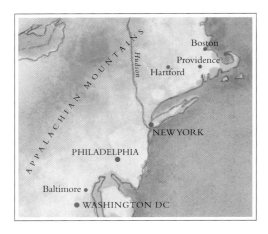

Carrot Cake (top) and Oatmeal Cookies

CARROT CAKE

TOTAL TIME: 1½ HOURS

SERVES 8

Here is a tip for turning a warm baked cake out of the pan, without indenting the moist top with the pattern of the wire rack. Place a clean kitchen towel over the top of the cake, then an upside down wire rack over the cloth. Hold the rack and cake pan together and invert quickly. Remove the pan. Place a second rack upside down over the bottom of the cake and quickly turn the two racks over. Remove the top rack and the cloth.

1 cup (12 oz/325 g) light corn syrup or honey
3 large, free-range eggs
½ cup (4 fl oz/125 ml) macadamia nut oil or canola oil
1 teaspoon vanilla extract (vanilla essence)
1½ cups (6 oz/185 g) wholewheat (wholemeal plain) flour
1½ teaspoons baking powder
1 teaspoon ground cinnamon
2 cups (6 oz/185 g) grated carrot
½ cup (3 oz/90 g) golden raisins (sultanas)
¼ cup (about 1 oz/30 g) poppy seeds
confectioners' (icing) sugar, for sifting, optional

◆ Preheat the oven to 350°F (180°C).
◆ Line an 8 inch (20 cm) springform pan or deep cake pan with parchment (non-stick baking) paper.
◆ Combine the corn syrup and eggs in a medium-sized bowl and beat with an electric mixer, until frothy, about 2 minutes. Add the oil and vanilla. Beat on low speed, until evenly combined, then set aside.
◆ Sift the flour, baking powder and cinnamon into a large bowl and add any bran left in the sieve to the flour mixture.
◆ Add the grated carrot, golden raisins and poppy seeds to the flour mixture and stir until mixed. Make a well in the center.
◆ Pour the egg mixture into the well. Incorporate the carrot mixture and stir well to combine.
◆ Pour the batter into the prepared cake pan and spread the top to level.
◆ Bake until a skewer inserted in the center of the cake comes out clean, 50 to 55 minutes.
◆ Cool in the cake pan on a wire rack for 10 minutes. Remove the sides and base of the pan and turn out onto the wire rack and cool.
◆ Sift the cake with confectioners' sugar, if using. Serve the cake cut into 8 wedges.

POPPY SEEDS

The opium poppy (Papaver somniferum) was a favorite with the Ancient Greeks and Romans for its medicinal properties and its bright flowers. Poppy seeds are the ripe seeds of the poppy, but they contain no narcotic substances. The plants are cultivated in the temperate regions of the world, and the bluish black seeds have long been featured in the cooking of central Europe, the Middle East and North Africa. The nutty flavor of poppy seeds enhances breads, cakes and pastries when added either for decoration or baked in with the other ingredients. They are also sprinkled on salads. Their flavor will be more prominent if the seeds are lightly toasted. In India it is the white poppy seed which is used in spice mixtures for curries. Poppy seeds also yield oil, which is used in much the same way as olive oil. The seeds, which are available in most supermarkets, must be stored in an airtight container out of the light, and should be used within a year.

OATMEAL COOKIES

TOTAL TIME: 1 HOUR 15 MINUTES

MAKES ABOUT 20

Use non-stick baking trays, if you have them, otherwise line the trays with parchment paper (non-stick baking paper). Fine-ground oatmeal, soy grits and steel-cut oats are available in health food stores. The cookies will store for up to 3 weeks in a cookie tin—avoid storing in a plastic container as the cookies will soften.

1 cup (about 5 oz/155 g) wholewheat (wholemeal plain) flour
½ teaspoon baking powder
1 cup (4 oz/125 g) fine-ground oatmeal
2 tablespoons soy grits
4 oz (125 g) reduced-fat margarine spread
1 cup (6 oz/185 g) dark brown sugar, firmly packed
¼ cup (2 oz/60 g) superfine (caster) sugar
1 large, free-range egg, lightly beaten
1 tablespoon skim milk
1 teaspoon almond extract (almond essence)
¼ cup (1⅔ oz/50 g) steel-cut oats
2 tablespoons turbinado (raw) sugar

◆ Preheat the oven to 350°F (180°C).
◆ Line 3 large baking trays with parchment (non-stick baking) paper, or use non-stick baking trays.
◆ Sift the flour and baking powder into a medium-sized bowl. Add any bran left in the sieve to the bowl. Add the oatmeal and soy grits and mix well.
◆ Place the margarine spread and the brown and superfine sugars into a bowl. Beat until the mixture is light and creamy, about 3 minutes.
◆ Add the egg, skim milk and almond extract and mix until evenly combined.
◆ Add the flour mixture to the creamed ingredients and stir until well combined.
◆ Use a tablespoon to form 6 to 7 cookies on each baking tray, allowing room for the cookies to spread—each will be about 3 inches (8 cm) in diameter when cooked.
◆ Sprinkle each cookie with the oats and turbinado sugar, dividing equally.
◆ Bake each batch of cookies until firm around the edges, about 15 minutes.
◆ Place the baking trays on a wire rack and cool until the cookies start to firm, about 5 minutes. Transfer the cookies to the rack and cool before serving.

NUTRITION NOTES

PER SERVING—Carrot Cake:
378 calories/1588 kilojoules; 7 g protein; 16 g fat, 38% of calories (2.4 g saturated, 5.7% of calories; 9.1 g monounsaturated, 21.6%; 4.5 g polyunsaturated, 10.7%); 54 g carbohydrate; 3 g dietary fiber; 111 mg sodium; 3 mg iron; 84 mg cholesterol.

PER SERVING—Oatmeal Cookies (Analysis uses monounsaturated margarine spread): 146 calories/612 kilojoules; 3 g protein; 5.1 g fat, 32% of calories (0.9 g saturated, 5.6% of calories; 2.9 g monounsaturated, 18.2%; 1.3 g polyunsaturated, 8.2%); 23 g carbohydrate; 1.6 g dietary fiber; 39 mg sodium; 0.8 mg iron; 11 mg cholesterol.

BANANA MOUSSE WITH KIWI FRUIT COULIS

The United States

Bananas are puréed for babies, made into sandwiches for toddlers, mixed into milkshakes for children and sliced into muesli for teenagers. In this dish the fruit is made into an elegant dessert mousse for adults! Bananas are rich in complex carbohydrate and a good source of dietary fiber and potassium. Here, low-fat, plain yogurt replaces the cream used to make traditional fruit mousses.

TOTAL TIME: 2 HOURS 20 MINUTES

SERVES 8

Small ½ cup (4 fl oz/125 ml) capacity molds, such as soufflé dishes, custard cups and ramekins, are ideal for this recipe. See Glossary for information concerning raw eggs.

1 cup (8 fl oz/250 ml) banana purée,
  about 3 small bananas
⅓ cup (3 fl oz/90 ml) freshly squeezed lime
  juice
2 teaspoons finely grated lime zest
2 large, free-range eggs, separated
¾ cup (6 oz/185 g) superfine (caster) sugar
1¼ cups (7½ oz/235 g) low-fat, plain yogurt
1 tablespoon plus 1 teaspoon gelatine
¼ cup (2 fl oz/60 ml) water
4 kiwi fruit, peeled and sliced, for serving

KIWI FRUIT COULIS

1 lb (500 g) kiwi fruit
2 tablespoons kirsch
3 tablespoons confectioners' (icing) sugar, sifted

◆ Combine the banana purée with 1 tablespoon of the lime juice in a small bowl to prevent it from turning brown. Cover with plastic wrap and set aside.
◆ Place the egg yolks and sugar in a large bowl and beat until thick and creamy, about 2 minutes.
◆ Add the banana purée, lime zest, the remaining lime juice and the yogurt. Mix well to combine.
◆ Combine the gelatine and water in a small heatproof bowl and stir well. Place the bowl in a medium-sized saucepan and add enough water to reach halfway up the side of the bowl. Bring the water to a simmer over medium-low heat and stir the gelatine mixture until dissolved.
◆ Remove the bowl from the water-bath and set aside to cool to lukewarm.
◆ Working quickly, pour the gelatine mixture into the egg yolk and banana mixture, whisking constantly.

◆ Rinse eight ½ cup molds with cold water and set aside.
◆ Whisk the egg whites in a medium-sized bowl until stiff peaks form. Fold the egg whites into the banana mixture until well combined.
◆ Spoon the mixture into the molds, dividing equally. Chill in the refrigerator until set, about 2 hours.
◆ Meanwhile, make the coulis. Peel the kiwi fruit and cut into quarters. Place the fruit in a blender or food processor. Process until almost smooth, stopping and scraping down the sides as needed.
◆ Transfer the purée to a medium-sized bowl. Add the kirsch and the confec-

tioners' sugar and stir until well combined. Cover with plastic wrap and chill in the refrigerator until ready to serve.
◆ To serve, unmold the mousses onto dessert plates, spoon a small amount of the coulis beside each one and garnish with slices of kiwi fruit.

NUTRITION NOTES

PER SERVING: 263 calories/1106 kilojoules; 8 g protein; 1.9 g fat, 7% of calories (0.6 g saturated, 2.2% of calories; 0.9 g monounsaturated, 3.3%; 0.4 g polyunsaturated, 1.5%); 52 g carbohydrate; 5 g dietary fiber; 58 mg sodium; 1.1 mg iron; 58 mg cholesterol.

FRESH FRUIT SALAD

The United States

Nutritionists recommend we eat several portions of fresh fruit and/or vegetables, each day for optimum health. The following fruit salad is a great way to put this advice into practice. Fresh fruits are high in important dietary fiber, a very good source of vitamin C and provide a range of other vitamins and minerals. Fresh Fruit Salad makes a colorful dish and is a healthy alternative to rich desserts for those who crave sweets at the end of a meal.

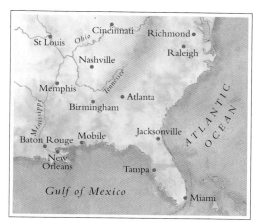

TOTAL TIME: 1 HOUR

SERVES: 8

It is important to select fresh fruit carefully and to store it correctly. Some fruits continue to ripen after harvesting, such as bananas, and others, like melons and oranges, do not. Some fruits, like apples and pears, benefit from refrigeration. Others, such as pineapple and passionfruit, do not. Use a stainless steel knife when preparing fruit: steel knives can stain. Fruit salads often require a sugar syrup to keep the fruit moist, but this recipe uses a natural fruit syrup which is more refreshing.

1 cup cubed pineapple
1 cup cubed cantaloupe melon (rockmelon)
1 cup papaya (pawpaw) cubes
1 mango, cut into cubes (see page 86)
2 peaches or nectarines, pitted and sliced
*   into wedges*
½ cup blueberries
½ cup halved seedless, green grapes
½ cup halved seedless, red or black grapes
1 cup freshly squeezed orange juice
1 cup passionfruit pulp or 1 cup watermelon
*   balls*
1 cup halved small strawberries
1 cup raspberries
mint sprigs, for decoration

◆ Place the prepared pineapple, cantaloupe and papaya in a large bowl. Add the mango, peaches, blueberries and grapes.
◆ Pour the orange juice and the passionfruit over the fruits and fold together gently to mix. Do not bruise the fruit.
◆ Carefully fold in the strawberries and raspberries. Stir gently until the fruits are evenly combined.
◆ Cover the bowl with plastic wrap and refrigerate until slightly chilled, about 30 minutes. If the fruit salad is chilled for much longer, let stand at room temperature for at least 30 minutes before serving, to develop its flavor.

◆ Serve the fruit salad in a large glass bowl or in individual dessert bowls. Spoon over any accumulated juices. Decorate with the mint sprigs.

NUTRITION NOTES

PER SERVING: 76 calories/321 kilojoules; 2 g protein; 0 g fat, 0% of calories (0 g saturated, 0% of calories; 0 g monounsaturated, 0%; 0 g polyunsaturated, 0%); 16 g.carbohydrate; 5.2 g dietary fiber; 11 mg sodium; 0.7 mg iron; 0 mg cholesterol.

PUMPKIN PIE AND LIME AND BUTTERMILK CHEESECAKE

The United States

Eggs, sugar, milk and vanilla combine with pumpkin purée and spices to produce an all-American pie! Wholewheat flour and wheatgerm give an unusual texture to the low-fat pastry. This cheesecake recipe is a delicious and healthy dessert. The buttermilk provides calcium; the lime juice is an excellent source of vitamin C; and the muesli crust provides carbohydrate, fiber and B vitamins.

PUMPKIN PIE

TOTAL TIME: 2 HOURS 10 MINUTES

SERVES 8

You will need about 13 oz (410 g) peeled and seeded raw pumpkin to render 1 cup of cooked purée. Dried beans are used to line the pastry case so that it will keep its shape during "blind" baking. Serve with fresh fruit, like sliced oranges, lychees or poached fresh apricots.

FILLING

*13 oz (410 g) peeled, seeded pumpkin,
    cut into 1 inch (2.5 cm) pieces
⅔ cup (3⅓ oz/100 g) light brown sugar,
    loosely packed
1 teaspoon ground cinnamon
½ teaspoon ground ginger
¼ teaspoon ground nutmeg
1 large, free-range egg plus 1 egg white
5 fl oz (150 ml) evaporated skim milk
1 tablespoon plus 1 teaspoon brandy
vegetable oil cooking spray
1 tablespoon confectioners' (icing) sugar,
    for sifting, optional*

PASTRY

*1 cup (about 5 oz/155 g) wholewheat
    (wholemeal plain) flour
1 cup (1⅔ oz/50 g) wheatgerm
3 oz (90 g) reduced-fat margarine spread,
    chilled
about ¼ cup (2 fl oz/60 ml) iced water*

Pumpkin Pie (top) and Lime and Buttermilk Cheesecake

◆ Bring water to a boil in a medium-sized steamer. Add the pumpkin, cover and steam over medium-high heat until tender, about 20 minutes.

◆ Meanwhile, to make the pastry, combine the flour, wheatgerm and margarine spread in a food processor. Process until the mixture resembles fine bread crumbs.

◆ Add the iced water, 1 tablespoon at a time, and process for 10 seconds each time, adding more water only as needed, until the mixture forms a stiff dough. The dough should leave the sides of the bowl and come together to form a ball around the center when ready.

◆ Turn the dough out onto a cool, lightly floured work surface. With cold hands, lightly pat the dough into a round. Wrap the dough in waxed (greaseproof) paper, transfer to a plate and chill in the refrigerator for 30 minutes.

◆ Meanwhile, transfer the pumpkin to a blender or food processor. Process until puréed, then pour out 1 cup of the pumpkin purée. Set aside any leftover purée for a future use.

◆ Combine the sugar, cinnamon, ginger and nutmeg in a large bowl and mix well. Combine the egg, evaporated milk and brandy in a small bowl and whisk well. Add the egg mixture to the sugar mixture and mix well. Fold in the pumpkin purée.

◆ Whisk the egg white in a small bowl until

stiff peaks form. Fold the egg white into the pumpkin mixture.

◆ Preheat the oven to 425°F (220°C). Lightly spray a 9 inch (23 cm) fluted tart pan (with a removable bottom) with vegetable oil cooking spray.

◆ Use a lightly floured rolling pin to roll the dough out on the floured surface to make a 10 inch (25 cm) round.

◆ With cold hands, gently ease and press the pastry into the pan, starting from the center and working out to the edges. Trim away the edges and prick the bottom of the pastry well with a fork.

◆ Line the pastry case with a square of waxed (greaseproof) paper. Add a single layer of dried beans. Bake for 10 minutes, then remove the paper and beans.

◆ Reduce the oven temperature to 350°F (180°C). Pour the pumpkin mixture into the pastry case. Bake until the filling is set, 45 to 50 minutes. (To test, press the center gently with the back of a spoon—the texture should be firm.)

◆ Transfer the tart pan to a wire rack to cool, about 10 minutes, then remove the pie from the pan.

◆ Sift with confectioners' sugar, if using, while still warm but not hot. Serve warm or cool on a large serving platter.

LIME AND BUTTERMILK CHEESECAKE

TOTAL TIME: 2 HOURS 35 MINUTES

SERVES 12

Allow 15 minutes additional time if the Muesli is not already prepared. Alternatively, use a commercial untoasted muesli. This cheesecake is also delicious served with raspberries or strawberries. The cheesecake can be made up to 2 days in advance. For best results, wipe the knife clean after cutting each slice.

CRUST

vegetable oil cooking spray
2 cups Muesli (see page 37)
½ cup graham crackers (wholemeal biscuit) crumbs
1 tablespoon dried skim milk powder
1 teaspoon ground cinnamon
1 teaspoon ground nutmeg
5 oz (150 g) reduced-fat margarine spread, melted

FILLING

¼ cup (1 oz/30 g) wholewheat (wholemeal) flour
½ cup (6 fl oz/185 g) honey or corn syrup

BUTTERMILK

Buttermilk was originally the residue of turning cream into butter. If the cream was unripe, the buttermilk would be sweet; otherwise the buttermilk would be slightly sour. Today buttermilk is a cultured milk product made from pasteurized skim milk which means it is actually fermented skimmed milk. (True buttermilk, marketed as "churned" buttermilk, is made from full cream milk and is not often available.) Buttermilk has a creamy, mildly acidic, tangy taste with a thick consistency. It is low in fat and provides protein, calcium, vitamin B and phosphorus. It is used as a drink on its own, combined with fresh fruits and as an ingredient in soups. It is also used as a sour milk substitute in breads, cakes and some frozen desserts. Usually sold in cartons, buttermilk can be kept in the refrigerator for up to 2 weeks if unopened. However, once opened, it should be used within a week. Buttermilk should not be shaken or frozen, since both processes ruin its texture.

2 tablespoons reduced-fat margarine spread or unsalted butter
2 large, free-range eggs, separated
1½ cups (12 fl oz/375 ml) buttermilk
finely grated zest of 2 limes
3 tablespoons freshly squeezed lime juice
1 cup (6½ oz/200 g) low-fat, plain yogurt, for decoration, optional
¼ cup passionfruit pulp, for decoration, optional

◆ Preheat the oven to 325°F (160°C). Adjust the rack to the middle position.

◆ To make the crust, lightly spray the inside of an 8 inch (20 cm) springform pan with vegetable oil cooking spray.

◆ Combine the muesli, cracker crumbs, milk powder, cinnamon and nutmeg in a large bowl. Add the melted margarine spread and mix well until crumbly. Transfer the mixture to the springform pan.

◆ Line the bottom and three-quarters of the way up the sides of the pan with the crumb mixture. Press in place with the back of a metal spoon and cool fingertips, shaping until the crust is smooth and even. Chill in the refrigerator until needed.

◆ To make the filling, sift the flour into a small bowl. Add any bran left in the sieve to the flour.

◆ Combine the honey and margarine spread in a bowl. Using an electric mixer, beat well until the mixture is light, creamy and lemon colored.

◆ Add the egg yolks, one at a time, and beat well after each addition.

◆ Stir in the flour. Add the buttermilk, lime zest and lime juice and stir until combined. Do not over-mix or the whites will deflate.

◆ Beat the egg whites in a medium-sized bowl until stiff peaks form.

◆ Stir a quarter of the beaten egg whites into the buttermilk mixture. Add the remaining egg whites and gently fold in until combined.

◆ Pour the batter into the prepared crust. Bake until the filling is firm and golden brown and a skewer inserted into the center comes out clean, 45 to 50 minutes.

◆ Transfer the pan to a wire rack and cool for at least 10 minutes.

◆ Remove the sides of the springform pan carefully, loosening the crumbcrust from the sides with a round-bladed dinner knife or small palette knife, if necessary. Cool on the wire rack, then chill in the refrigerator for at least 30 minutes before serving.

◆ Transfer the cheesecake to a serving platter. Arrange spoonfuls of the yogurt around the top edge and drizzle with passionfruit pulp, if using.

NUTRITION NOTES

PER SERVING—Pumpkin Pie (Analysis uses monounsaturated margarine spread): 232 calories/ 975 kilojoules; 8 g protein; 8.7 g fat, 33% of calories (1.8 g saturated, 6.8% of calories; 4.9 g monounsaturated, 18.6%; 2 g polyunsaturated, 7.6%); 31 g carbohydrate; 3.8 g dietary fiber; 86 mg sodium; 1.8 mg iron; 29 mg cholesterol.

PER SERVING—Lime and Buttermilk Cheesecake (Analysis uses monounsaturated margarine spread): 233 calories/978 kilojoules; 5 g protein; 14 g fat, 53% of calories (3 g saturated, 11.4% of calories; 8 g monounsaturated, 30.2%; 3 g polyunsaturated, 11.4%); 24 g carbohydrate; 1.2 g dietary fiber; 130 mg sodium; 0.8 mg iron; 42 mg cholesterol.

NUTRITION & YOU

NUTRITION FOR LIFE

The pyramid approach to eating (pages 18–19), which is based on the major food groups, can be applied from the time a baby is ready for solid foods. It continues all through one's lifetime.

INFANCY

For the first five months of an infant's life, breast milk and infant formula provide completely adequate sources of all nutritional requirements. Breast milk is the ideal source as it contains the correct proportions of nutrients, is sterile, is maintained at the right temperature, provides immunity from infections and is easily digested. However, there are some cases when breast milk may not be suitable; babies with lactose intolerance (galactosemia) may not tolerate breast milk. An infant formula is recommended in such cases.

At four to six months the baby is ready to eat some solid foods. These consist of rice cereal, vegetables, fruit, meat, chicken and fish. They must be pureéd or strained to attain a smooth consistency. Salt and sugar are not necessary in baby food.

Babies develop their first teeth at seven to eight months of age. Continue breast or formula feeding and introduce bite-sized pieces of food. These foods include toast, zweiback (rusks), pieces of fruit, vegetables and cheese. At ten to twelve months the infant can consume foods from the major food groups. Establish the principles of a balanced diet now for a healthy life.

CHILDHOOD

At the age of two, the child's growth rate slows and the appetite decreases. Give your child healthy snacks: include bread, muffins, fresh and dried fruit, vegetables, milk yogurt and cheese.

From about five to twelve years of age, children are growing rapidly and their appetite increases. It is important that nutritious foods be eaten to supply the necessary energy, protein, vitamins and minerals essential for growth.

ADOLESCENCE

From thirteen to eighteen, both girls and boys grow rapidly. More food is needed to meet the body's increased energy requirements. Teenagers involved in sports need

FIND YOUR IDEAL CALORIE LEVEL

WOMEN

HEIGHT	FRAME SIZE	DESIRABLE WEIGHT (RANGE)	VERY LIGHT	LIGHT	MODERATE	HEAVY
5'0"	Small	106 (102–110)	1400	1600	1800	2100
	Medium	113 (107–119)	1450	1700	1900	2250
	Large	123 (115–131)	1600	1850	2100	2450
5'1"	Small	109 (105–113)	1400	1650	1850	2200
	Medium	116 (110–122)	1500	1750	1950	2300
	Large	126 (118–134)	1650	1900	2150	2500
5'2"	Small	112 (108–116)	1450	1700	1900	2250
	Medium	119 (113–126)	1550	1800	2000	2400
	Large	129 (121–138)	1700	1950	2200	2600
5'3"	Small	115 (111–119)	1500	1750	1950	2300
	Medium	123 (116–130)	1600	1850	2100	2450
	Large	133 (125–142)	1750	2000	2250	2650
5'4"	Small	118 (114–123)	1550	1750	2000	2350
	Medium	127 (120–135)	1650	1900	2150	2550
	Large	137 (129–146)	1800	2050	2350	2750
5'5"	Small	122 (118–127)	1600	1850	2050	2450
	Medium	131 (124–139)	1700	1950	2250	2600
	Large	141 (133–150)	1850	2100	2400	2800
5'6"	Small	126 (122–131)	1650	1900	2150	2500
	Medium	135 (128–143)	1750	2050	2300	2700
	Large	145 (137–154)	1900	2200	2450	2900
5'7"	Small	130 (126–135)	1700	1950	2200	2600
	Medium	139 (132–147)	1800	2100	2350	2800
	Large	149 (141–158)	1950	2250	2550	3000
5'8"	Small	135 (130–140)	1750	2050	2300	2700
	Medium	143 (136–151)	1850	2150	2450	2850
	Large	154 (145–163)	2000	2300	2600	3100
5'9"	Small	139 (134–144)	1800	2100	2350	2800
	Medium	147 (140–155)	1900	2200	2500	2950
	Large	158 (149–168)	2050	2350	2700	3150
5'10"	Small	143 (138–148)	1850	2150	2450	2850
	Medium	151 (144–159)	1950	2250	2550	3000
	Large	163 (153–173)	2100	2450	2750	3250

MEN

HEIGHT	FRAME SIZE	DESIRABLE WEIGHT (RANGE)	VERY LIGHT	LIGHT	MODERATE	HEAVY
5'5"	Small	129 (124–133)	1700	1950	2200	2600
	Medium	137 (130–143)	1800	2050	2350	2750
	Large	147 (138–156)	1900	2200	2500	2950
5'6"	Small	133 (128–137)	1750	2000	2250	2650
	Medium	141 (134–147)	1850	2100	2400	2800
	Large	152 (142–161)	2000	2300	2600	3050
5'7"	Small	137 (132–141)	1800	2050	2350	2750
	Medium	145 (138–152)	1900	2200	2450	2900
	Large	157 (147–166)	2050	2350	2650	3150
5'8"	Small	141 (136–145)	1850	2100	2400	2850
	Medium	149 (142–156)	1950	2250	2550	3000
	Large	161 (151–170)	2100	2400	2750	3200
5'9"	Small	145 (140–150)	1900	2200	2450	2900
	Medium	153 (146–160)	2000	2300	2600	3050
	Large	165 (155–174)	2150	2500	2800	3300
5'10"	Small	149 (144–154)	1950	2250	2550	3000
	Medium	158 (150–165)	2050	2350	2700	3150
	Large	169 (159–179)	2200	2550	2850	3400
5'11"	Small	153 (148–158)	2000	2300	2600	3050
	Medium	162 (154–170)	2100	2450	2750	3250
	Large	174 (164–184)	2250	2600	2950	3500
6'0"	Small	157 (152–162)	2050	2350	2650	3150
	Medium	167 (158–175)	2150	2500	2850	3350
	Large	179 (168–189)	2350	2700	3050	3600
6'1"	Small	162 (156–167)	2100	2450	2750	3250
	Medium	171 (162–180)	2200	2550	2900	3400
	Large	184 (173–194)	2400	2750	3150	3700
6'2"	Small	166 (160–171)	2150	2500	2600	3300
	Medium	176 (167–185)	2300	2650	3000	3500
	Large	189 (178–199)	2450	2850	3200	3800
6'3"	Small	170 (164–175)	2200	2550	2900	3400
	Medium	181 (172–190)	2350	2700	3300	3850
	Large	193 (182–204)	2500	2900	3300	3850

LEVEL OF PHYSICAL ACTIVITY

Eating, sleeping, writing, sitting and standing are classified as very light activity, and use less than 2.5 calories per minute. Cooking, driving, housework and table tennis are classified as light activity, and use 2.5–4.9 calories per minute. Aerobics, dancing, golf, cycling (up to 10 miles per hour), cricket, gardening and walking are classified as moderate activity, and use 5.0–7.4 calories per minute. Basketball, hockey, skiing, squash, tennis, jogging, skipping and swimming are classified as heavy activity, and use 7.5–9.9 calories per minute.

even more energy. Girls need more iron, as menstruation commences around this age. Now, teenagers are likely to take responsibility for their own eating habits. Peer pressure and the media exert enormous influence regarding food preference. Weight problems often occur during adolescence. Teenagers often choose foods high in fat, salt and sugar, but low in complex carbohydrate and dietary fiber. If weight gain is a problem, a healthy, balanced weight reduction diet combined with increased exercise is the answer.

ADULTHOOD

Maintaining a healthy body weight and balanced nutritional intake is desirable throughout a healthy adulthood. Follow the dietary guidelines and the pyramid approach to eating to meet nutrient and energy requirements. Women should be particularly careful to obtain enough calcium to prevent osteoporosis later on.

Use the tables below to determine your ideal daily calorie (kilojoule) intake level.

PREGNANCY

During pregnancy, the mother is eating for two. The requirement for many nutrients increases, including the B-complex vitamins (including folate), vitamins C and E, calcium, iron, phosphorus, iodine, magnesium, selenium, zinc and protein. Energy requirements (measured in calories/kilojoules) do not increase greatly, so foods should be nutrient dense. An iron and folate supplement is usually recommended during pregnancy. The average weight gain by a healthy pregnant woman is about 22–28 pounds (10–13 kilograms). The pyramid approach to eating discussed in the first chapter should still be used during pregnancy, although the daily number of servings eaten from the milk, yogurt and cheese group should be increased to at least three.

Pregnant women should avoid alcohol. Large amounts of alcohol are associated with damage to the fetus. Those trying to conceive should also abstain from alcohol, since damage to the fetus occurs in the first few weeks, often before the woman is aware that she is pregnant. Avoid coffee as well. Water, milk, herbal tea and fruit juice are preferable beverages during pregnancy.

FIND YOUR IDEAL KILOJOULE LEVEL

WOMEN

HEIGHT	FRAME SIZE	DESIRABLE WEIGHT (RANGE)	VERY LIGHT	LIGHT	MODERATE	HEAVY
153 cm	Small	48 (46–50)	5860	6700	7540	8790
	Medium	51.5 (49–54)	6070	7120	7950	9420
	Large	55.5 (52–59)	6700	7750	8790	10,260
155 cm	Small	49.5 (48–51)	5860	5230	7750	9210
	Medium	52.5 (50–55)	6280	7330	8160	9630
	Large	57 (53–61)	6910	7950	9000	10,470
158 cm	Small	51 (49–53)	6070	7120	7950	9420
	Medium	54 (51–57)	6490	7540	8370	10,050
	Large	59 (55–63)	7120	8160	9210	10,890
160 cm	Small	52 (50–54)	6280	7330	8160	9630
	Medium	56 (53–59)	6670	7750	8790	10,260
	Large	60.5 (57–64)	7330	8370	9420	11,100
163 cm	Small	54 (52–56)	6490	7330	8370	9840
	Medium	57.5 (54–61)	6910	7950	9000	10,680
	Large	62.5 (59–66)	7540	8580	9840	11,510
165 cm	Small	56 (54–58)	6700	7750	8580	10,260
	Medium	59.5 (56–63)	7120	8160	9420	10,890
	Large	64 (60–68)	7750	8790	10,050	11,720
168 cm	Small	57 (55–59)	6910	7950	9000	10,470
	Medium	61.5 (58–65)	7330	8580	9630	11,300
	Large	66 (62–70)	7950	9210	10,260	12,140
170 cm	Small	59 (57–61)	7120	8160	9210	10,890
	Medium	63.5 (60–67)	7540	8790	9840	11,720
	Large	68 (64–72)	8160	9420	10,680	12,560
173 cm	Small	61 (59–63)	7330	8580	9630	11,300
	Medium	65.6 (62–69)	7750	9000	10,260	11,930
	Large	70 (66–74)	8370	9630	10,890	12,980
175 cm	Small	63 (61–65)	7540	8790	9840	11,720
	Medium	66.5 (63–70)	7950	9210	10,470	12,350
	Large	72 (68–76)	8580	9840	11,300	13,190
178 cm	Small	65 (63–67)	7750	9000	10,260	11,930
	Medium	68.5 (65–72)	8160	9420	10,680	12,560
	Large	74 (69–79)	8790	10,260	11,510	13,610

MEN

HEIGHT	FRAME SIZE	DESIRABLE WEIGHT (RANGE)	VERY LIGHT	LIGHT	MODERATE	HEAVY
165 cm	Small	58 (56–60)	7120	8160	9210	10,890
	Medium	62 (59–65)	7540	8580	9840	11,510
	Large	67 (63–71)	7950	9210	10,470	12,350
168 cm	Small	60 (58–62)	7330	8370	9420	11,100
	Medium	64 (61–67)	7750	8790	10,000	11,720
	Large	68.5 (64–73)	8370	9630	10,880	12,770
170 cm	Small	62 (60–64)	7540	8580	9840	11,510
	Medium	66 (63–69)	7950	9210	10,260	12,140
	Large	71 (67–75)	8580	9840	11,100	13,130
173 cm	Small	64 (62–66)	7750	8790	10,000	11,940
	Medium	67.5 (64–71)	8160	9420	10,680	12,560
	Large	72.5 (68–77)	8790	10,000	11,510	13,340
175 cm	Small	66 (64–68)	7950	9210	10,260	12,140
	Medium	69.5 (66–73)	8370	9630	10,880	12,770
	Large	74.5 (70–79)	9000	10,470	11,720	13,820
178 cm	Small	67.5 (65–70)	8160	9420	10,680	12,560
	Medium	71.5 (68–75)	8580	9840	11,300	13,190
	Large	76.5 (72–81)	9210	10,680	11,930	14,230
180 cm	Small	69.5 (67–72)	8370	9630	10,890	12,770
	Medium	73.5 (70–77)	8790	10,260	11,510	13,610
	Large	79 (74–84)	9420	10,890	12,350	14,650
183 cm	Small	71.5 (69–74)	8580	9840	11,100	13,190
	Medium	73.5 (72–79)	9000	10,470	11,930	14,030
	Large	81 (76–86)	9840	11,300	12,770	15,070
185 cm	Small	73.5 (71–76)	8790	10,260	11,510	13,610
	Medium	78 (74–82)	9210	10,680	12,140	14,240
	Large	82 (76–88)	10,050	11,510	13,190	15,490
188 cm	Small	75.5 (73–78)	9000	10,470	10,890	13,820
	Medium	80 (76–84)	9630	11,100	12,560	14,650
	Large	85.5 (81–90)	10,260	11,930	13,400	15,910
190 cm	Small	76.5 (74–79)	9210	10,680	12,140	14,240
	Medium	82 (78–86)	9840	11,300	13,820	16,120
	Large	88 (83–93)	10,470	12,140	13,820	16,120

LEVEL OF PHYSICAL ACTIVITY

Eating, sleeping, writing, sitting and standing are classified as very light activity, and use less than 10.4 kilojoules per minute. Cooking, driving, housework and table tennis are classified as light activity, and use 10.4–20.5 kilojoules per minute. Aerobics, dancing, golf, cycling (up to 16 kilometers per hour), cricket, gardening and walking are classified as moderate activity, and use 20.9–30.9 kilojoules per minute. Basketball, hockey, skiing, squash, tennis, jogging, skipping and swimming are classified as heavy activity, and use 31.3–41.4 kilojoules per minute.

LACTATION

More nutrients are needed during breast-feeding than in pregnancy. Add one or two extra servings for each of the food groups in the food pyramid. The lactating mother's own appetite is a good guide to the quantity of food needed, but it is important that the foods chosen be rich in nutrients. Fat gained during pregnancy is usually lost during lactation. There should be no other large changes in weight during this time. The mother should increase her fluid intake (especially of water and milk) according to the amount of milk consumed by the baby.

MENOPAUSE

Menopause, the cessation of menstruation, is a natural transition period in women's lives. During menopause, which usually occurs between 45 and 55 years of age, women gradually stop producing the female hormones progesterone and estrogen. For some women declining hormone levels are barely noticeable, but for others symptoms such as hot flashes (flushes), night sweats, mood swings, headaches and low energy levels make life difficult. Evidence suggests symptoms may be relieved by regular exercise and a healthy balanced diet in accordance with the pyramid approach to eating (pages 18–19). However, there is an increased calcium requirement after the menopause—approximately one extra serving per day—to help prevent osteoporosis. Supplements are also reputedly therapeutic, particularly vitamins C, E and B-complex (containing niacinamide). Vitamins C and B-complex heighten the effectiveness of E. Nevertheless, a healthy balanced diet is preferable to supplementation.

OLD AGE

Growing older does not mean nutrient requirements change a great deal. The two major changes are the need for increased calcium in older women to prevent brittle bones (osteoporosis) and a decrease in calorie (kilojoule) intake if physical activity is reduced. Consume a diet of nutrient-rich foods according to the guidelines given in the first chapter. Many older people, especially those who live alone, do not eat an adequate diet for various reasons, including loneliness, depression or lack of interest in cooking. Physical factors like an inability to chew and swallow food may also contribute to an inadequate diet. Consult a dietitian or nutritionist regarding these problems.

Below: *Typical dairy-farming country in the Gippsland area in southeastern Australia.*

SPECIAL DIETARY NEEDS

Sometimes people need to emphasize a particular element in the diet to deal with a special requirement like lowering fat, cholesterol or sodium levels or increasing dietary fiber. These diets will be dealt with in the following pages along with the issues of weight reduction, diabetes, cancer, lactose intolerance, gluten sensitivity, allergies and eating disorders.

LOW-FAT DIET

A diet low in fat may be prescribed for various health problems including excess weight, heart disease, hypertension, diabetes, gallstones and certain types of cancer. Fat should be reduced to 20–30 percent of energy intake (calories/kilojoules), with no more than 10 percent derived from saturated fat and the remaining 10–20 percent from polyunsaturated and monounsaturated fats.

Ways to limit fats

- Choose low-fat or skim milk, yogurt and cheese.
- Buy lean cuts of beef such as round, rump, tenderloin (fillet) and lean veal and lean pork.
- Have two meat-free days per week.
- Cut off any visible fat from meat, and remove the skin from chicken before cooking.
- Broil, grill, bake, microwave and steam; use non-stick pans when possible.
- If using oil, apply it to the pan with a brush or use a spray.
- Avoid high-fat take-out foods, such as pies, French fries, pastries, deep-fried fish and chicken, and commercially prepared foods such as cookies (biscuits), cakes and potato chips.

CHOLESTEROL-REDUCING DIET

Special diets may be prescribed for those with a blood cholesterol level above 240 mg/dl or 6.5 mmol/liter to lower the risk of heart disease. Most experts believe that reducing the intake of fat, particularly saturated fat, is more important than reducing the intake of dietary cholesterol.

Ways to reduce high blood cholesterol levels

- Reduce the total fat intake, with particular emphasis on saturated fat.
- Restrict the intake of dietary cholesterol, such as that found in meat, dairy products, egg yolks, liver, kidney and brains.

- Eat more soluble dietary fiber such as oats, legumes, fruits, citrus peel and certain vegetables.
- Keep body weight within an acceptable range.
- Participate in moderate regular exercise such as walking, cycling, gardening, golfing, dancing or aerobics.

Diet and exercise alone are not enough to lower blood cholesterol for a small percentage of people. This is usually due to an inherited genetic disorder. Medication is usually prescribed for these people, in combination with a low cholesterol diet.

Above: *A young Russian boy proudly showing his fresh catch of the day.*
Above left: *Duck is often served at traditional Chinese banquets for special celebrations.*
Top: *Organic farming in California; buy fresh organic produce whenever possible.*

Above: *A Colorado cornfield after the harvest; corn is a good source of fiber and vitamin C.* Left: *Indonesian peasants drying rice in the age-old fashion.*

LOW-SODIUM DIET

Reduced-sodium intake may be prescribed for hypertension (high blood pressure), which can lead to a stroke or heart attack. Diet used in combination with medication can lower high blood pressure significantly. In some cases, medication may not be required at all.

Salt is a chemical compound consisting of approximately 40 percent sodium and 60 percent chloride. Sodium in salt causes problems and for this reason salt should not be used in cooking or at the table. A small amount of sodium is needed by the body each day for healthy functioning and there is enough sodium present naturally in foods. A daily balanced diet which consists of the major food groups depicted in the food pyramid will contain sufficient sodium to meet the body's requirements.

Ways to reduce sodium intake

- Do not add salt to food during cooking or at the table.
- If you must add salt, gradually reduce the amount used, to lose the taste for salt. The palate will slowly adjust, allowing the natural flavor of foods to come through.
- Flavor foods with fresh herbs and spices such as basil, tarragon, curry and chili powder in place of salt. Garlic, onions, leeks and shallots are great ways to add lots of fresh flavor to food.
- Avoid highly processed foods such as dried and canned soups, canned vegetables, processed cheeses, commercial sauces and take-out packaged foods as they are generally quite high in sodium. (Sodium is used in processed food as a preservative.)
- Use salt-free, no-salt-added, reduced- and low-sodium products such as cheese, bread, cereals and canned foods. Read food labels; many products advertised as reduced- and low-sodium may still contain quite a lot of sodium.
- Avoid salty snack foods such as potato chips, corn chips, salted nuts and salted savory crackers (biscuits). Substitute fresh and dried fruit, fresh vegetables, unsalted seeds, nuts and popcorn as low-salt snack foods.
- Avoid monosodium glutamate (MSG), baking powder, baking soda, meat tenderizer, some mineral waters, antacids and saline powders as they are all high in sodium.
- Avoid sea salt, rock salt, vegetable salt, garlic salt and celery salt; all contain large amounts of sodium. Salt substitutes such as potassium chloride may be of benefit to some people when they are first reducing salt intake.

HIGH-FIBER DIET

Increased fiber intake may be prescribed for those suffering from constipation, irritable bowel syndrome, diverticulitis, obesity, gallstones, diabetes (Type II) and certain cancers, such as breast cancer. An intake of approximately 30–40 g dietary fiber per day is recommended for a high-fiber diet.

Ways to increase dietary fiber (both insoluble and soluble)

- Eat wholegrain cereal and wholegrain or wholewheat bread. Check the food label for the dietary fiber content per serving of cereal. If the cereal provides 5 g or more of dietary fiber per serving, it is suitable for a high-fiber diet. Extra dietary fiber can be added with unprocessed bran from wheat, barley or rice, if required. Wholewheat (wholemeal) bread contains more than twice the amount of dietary fiber as standard white bread.
- Eat more unpeeled fresh fruit and vegetables (like apples and potatoes) as fiber is contained in the skin.

- Use wholewheat (wholemeal) flour and pasta and brown rice; they have more dietary fiber than the white varieties.
- Use more dried peas, beans and lentils (a good source of soluble dietary fiber).
- Add bran from wheat, barley or rice to hot dishes such as soups and casseroles as well as desserts, including yogurt, cakes and cookies (biscuits).
- Snack on fresh and dried fruit, fresh vegetables such as carrot and celery sticks, nuts, seeds, wholewheat (wholemeal) bread and wholegrain dry cereal.

Note: Drink at least 6–8 glasses of water or other fluid each day on a high-fiber diet, to prevent dehydration. Dietary fiber can absorb a lot of fluid.

WEIGHT-REDUCTION DIET

The Body Mass Index (BMI) (see discussion on page 17) can be used as a guide to determine if an individual is overweight (BMI greater than 25) or obese (BMI greater than 30). Excess weight generally results from eating more food (taking in more energy) than the body uses for metabolism and physical activity. To lose weight, less food (energy) must be taken into the body. Expend more energy through exercise. A safe weekly rate of weight loss is 1–2 pounds (0.5–1 kilogram). Achieve this loss on a diet of approximately 1200 calories (5000 kilojoules) every day for women and of 1500 calories (6300 kilojoules) per day for men. Seek the advice of a qualified dietitian for an individualized weight-reduction meal plan and exercise regime. When dieting, continue to eat a balanced variety of food based on the food pyramid.

General guidelines to achieve weight loss

- Reduce fat intake.
- Reduce sugar intake.
- Drink less alcohol (limit this to an occasional social drink) and drink more water and sugar-free soft drinks.
- Eat more cereal, bread, fruit, vegetables and grain, to supply complex carbohydrate and dietary fiber.
- Exercise daily—at least 20–30 minutes of exercise each day will increase the heart and metabolic rates.

DIABETES AND DIET

Diabetes is a condition in which the pancreas fails to produce enough insulin. Glucose is the main form of sugar in the blood, which is obtained from the digestion of carbohydrate. Insulin allows glucose (in the blood) to enter body cells for use by the body as energy. If there is insufficient

Bottom: *Selling vitamin-C-rich melons in the market in Shufu, a small oasis city in China close to the border with Kazakhstan.*
Below: *Stirring milk curd in a large container; northern India.*

insulin, or it is not working correctly, glucose builds up and excess amounts are lost in the urine. The body then begins to break down its own fat and muscle tissue to fuel itself. If not treated, this results in physical deterioration, which may lead to a coma.

There are two types of diabetes, insulin-dependent diabetes (IDDM), or Type I, and non-insulin dependent diabetes (NIDDM), or Type II. IDDM, or Type I, is controlled by daily insulin injections, in conjunction with appropriate diet and exercise. This type commonly occurs in children and young adults. With NIDDM, or Type II, insufficient insulin is produced by the body but this can be remedied by diet alone or diet plus medication. Typically, this type occurs in overweight adults.

Diet for the treatment of diabetes is not very different from the healthy pattern of eating detailed in the food pyramid. The food should be low in fat (especially saturated fat), sugar and salt. Food high in dietary fiber is recommended. Eat bread and cereal, fruit and vegetables. A healthy balanced diet will help control blood sugar levels, weight and the development of heart disease. If you are diagnosed with diabetes, see a dietitian for an individualized meal plan.

CANCER AND DIET

Cancer occurs when cells grow in an uncontrolled manner. The causes of cancer are not yet clear, but environmental factors such as smoking, pollution and ultraviolet radiation are known to play a contributing role. Diet is also related to the development of cancer, particularly in the throat, esophagus, mouth, stomach, colon, liver, bladder, pancreas and breast.

Ways to reduce the risk of cancer

◆ Choose a wide variety of foods.

◆ Maintain a healthy weight.

◆ Limit intake of saturated, monounsaturated and polyunsaturated fats. Use lean meat and low- and reduced-fat dairy products.

◆ Include food that provides vitamin C and beta-carotene, such as carrots, sweet

Left: *An exotic array of healthy take-away food; Nara, Japan.*
Below: *A fine assortment of produce, so beloved of Italians; Rome, Italy.*

potatoes, broccoli, spinach, oranges and cantaloupes (rockmelons). There is some evidence that these foods provide protection against cancer.

◆ Eat more wholegrain cereal, vegetables and fruit. These major sources of dietary fiber may protect against bowel cancer.

◆ Drink only small quantities of alcohol, 1–2 standard drinks a day (see page 18).

◆ Limit intake of salt-cured, smoked and pickled food. These are linked to a risk of stomach cancer.

These recommendations do not guarantee protection against cancer but they may reduce the risk. They are suitable for healthy people and will assist in the prevention of other diseases linked to diet such as heart disease. The recommended diet for those diagnosed with cancer will depend on the type and stage of cancer. Consult a dietitian for an individualized meal plan and advice.

LACTOSE INTOLERANCE AND DIET

Many people experience some difficulties in digesting lactose, which is the milk sugar found in mammalian milks, including breast milk, cow's milk and goat's milk. If lactose is not digested in the small intestine it passes into the large intestine, and diarrhea, bloating and flatulence may then occur.

Lactose intolerance occurs in a high proportion of the world's population although the degree of intolerance varies greatly. It is best to see a medical practitioner for a correct diagnosis if suffering from bloating, diarrhea and flatulence. A diet which limits lactose may curb the symptoms. If you are diagnosed with lactose intolerance, contact a dietitian so that a diet can be designed to meet your food preferences, nutrient requirements, lactose tolerance level and symptoms.

GLUTEN SENSITIVITY AND DIET

People who are genetically predisposed to gluten sensitivity can suffer damage to the lining of the small intestine, causing nutrients to be poorly absorbed. This is also known as coeliac disease. It can occur in both children and adults. Symptoms include diarrhea, lethargy, vomiting and bloating. A biopsy of the bowel lining is required for diagnosis. Gluten is the major protein found in wheat, triticale, barley, oats and rye. Foods containing gluten must be avoided to eliminate the symptoms.

On a gluten-free diet, avoid food such as bread (unless made from gluten-free flour), cake, cookies (biscuits), pastries, pancakes, flour and pasta; most breakfast

cereal or baby cereal (unless marked gluten-free); many processed foods such as canned and dried soups, sauces, and foods canned in sauces, which contain small amounts of wheat flour or gluten, often as a thickener.

If you are on a gluten-free diet and there is doubt over the gluten content of a particular product, contact the manufacturer or a dietitian for more information.

FOOD ALLERGY AND DIET

A food allergy is an adverse reaction to a particular food or ingredient which stimulates the body's immune system and forms potentially harmful antibodies in the body. True food allergies are common in infants and young children who exhibit symptoms such as eczema, colic, diarrhea, hives or an itchy rash.

Foods which children are commonly allergic to include eggs, milk, wheat, fish and peanuts. If an allergy is suspected, the offending food should be removed from the diet for at least two weeks and then slowly reintroduced. Follow this procedure with guidance from a qualified dietitian. If you are diagnosed with a food allergy, avoid the offending food.

Some individuals react to natural and artificial chemicals in food, but this reaction is not a true food allergy as antibodies are not formed. Natural food chemicals which an individual may react adversely to include salicylates, amines and monosodium glutamate (MSG). Artificial food additives such as preservatives, colorings and flavorings may also cause adverse side effects in some individuals. Avoid the offending food or food additive in your diet. If an individual is extremely sensitive to certain foods or food additives, seek advice from a qualified dietitian.

VEGETARIANISM

Vegetarianism may be adopted for various reasons including cost, religious beliefs, ecological concerns, health or fashion. Most vegetarians fall into one of the following four main categories.

Vegans eat no animal products—neither meat, fish, poultry, dairy products nor eggs. Their diet consists of foods of plant origin only (fruit, vegetables, legumes, nuts, seeds, bread, wholegrain cereal and cereal products).

Lacto-vegetarians eat only dairy products such as milk, yogurt, cheese and foods of plant origin.

Lacto-ovo-vegetarians eat dairy products, eggs and foods of plant origin.

Ovo-vegetarians eat only eggs and foods of plant origin.

Olives and olive oil are an integral part of a healthy Mediterranean diet; Fes, Morocco.

Research indicates that people who follow a vegetarian diet, which is generally low in fat, salt and sugar and high in dietary fiber and complex carbohydrate, experience lower rates of heart disease, cancer, obesity, hypertension, disorders of the bowel and diabetes. They achieve greater longevity as well. One of the main concerns with a vegetarian diet is an adequate intake of protein. Sufficient protein can be obtained from plant foods as long as a variety of food is eaten. Animal protein foods such as meat, fish, eggs, milk, yogurt and cheese each contain all the essential amino acids. Individual plant foods do not contain all the essential amino acids and this is why a variety of plant food is necessary. The essential amino acid missing in one plant food will be provided by the essential amino acid in another; many experts have suggested eating complementary foods together, such as rice and beans; corn and beans; and rice and chickpeas. However, studies have recently shown that it is not necessary for vegetable protein sources to be eaten at the same time. If the daily diet consists of a variety of plant foods, it is likely the body is obtaining the essential amino acids it requires.

Nutrients which may be lacking in a vegan diet include iron, zinc, calcium and vitamin B_{12}. Lacto-vegetarians and lacto-ovo-vegetarians obtain calcium and vitamin B_{12} from their diet, but may lack iron and zinc. Ovo-vegetarians obtain vitamin B_{12} but may lack calcium, iron and zinc. It is therefore important to consume a variety of plant food, paying particular attention to food sources of the nutrients which may be lacking. (See the first chapter for further information on sources of vitamins and minerals.)

EATING DISORDERS (ANOREXIA NERVOSA AND BULIMIA NERVOSA)

Eating disorders are common among females between the ages of twelve and twenty-five years, although they can also occur in males. Anorexics and bulimics both have a desire to reduce weight or maintain a slim figure. Anorexia (meaning "loss of appetite") is concerned with a total avoidance of food, often combined with severe exercising. Bulimia is typically expressed by bouts of binge eating of large amounts of food, which can last for several days, followed by starvation, severe dieting and/or vomiting. Laxatives or diuretics are also often abused by those suffering from eating disorders. Counseling from a qualified psychologist and dietitian can play a primary role in treating an individual who suffers from an eating disorder.

Nutmeg and mace harvested in Indonesia.
These aromatic spices belong to the same plant.

GLOSSARY

ARROWROOT

Arrowroot is a powder obtained from the underground stem of the *Maranta* plant, which grows in the tropics. It is particularly useful as a thickening agent as it dissolves into a clear liquid and cooks at a lower temperature than other starches. It is flavorless and easily digested. Buy it in powder form at any supermarket, and store it in an airtight container out of direct light.

BULGHUR

A staple grain of the Middle East and eastern Europe, bulghur is widely used in many Middle Eastern and Mediterranean dishes. It is used in soups, salads, meat and vegetable dishes. Bulghur is whole wheat that has been steamed, dried and then cracked. It is not to be confused with cracked wheat, which is uncooked. If cracked wheat is substituted for bulghur, the cooking time must be extended. Bulghur has a tender, chewy texture and can be either light or dark in color and fine, medium or coarse in granulation. It is available at health food stores, specialty food stores and some supermarkets and is sold under a variety of names, the most common being bulghur, bulgur and burghul. Store it in an airtight container in a cool, dark place.

CHINESE FIVE-SPICE POWDER

The five spices that make up this powder are star anise, Szechwan pepper, fennel, cloves and cinnamon. A favorite in Chinese cooking, it imparts a fragrant aromatic flavor with a hint of anise. Use sparingly. It is available at most supermarkets and Asian food stores.

COCONUT MILK

Native to the tropics, the coconut is the fruit of the coconut palm *(Cocos nucifera)*. Coconut milk and coconut cream are the liquids obtained by simmering equal quantities of shredded or desiccated coconut flesh with water or milk, then straining the liquid from the flesh. Sweetened coconut milk products like cream of coconut are used mainly in rich desserts.

EGGS (RAW)

Some of our recipes call for raw eggs. The cook must decide if he or she is willing to take a risk with these. A bacteria called *Salmonella enteritidis* is causing concern among some consumers. Elderly people weakened by illness and people with weakened immune systems are particularly vulnerable to this bacteria and may need to avoid eating raw eggs. Washing and sanitizing eggs does not rid them of the virus. The best protection is to use eggs that have been stored under refrigeration. Other helpful procedures to follow include: washing your hands with hot, soapy water before and after handling; using only Grade A or higher eggs; avoiding cracked or leaking eggs; and never leaving raw eggs at room temperature.

FENUGREEK

Fenugreek *(Trigonella foenum-graecum)* is a bitter-sweet, aromatic herb native to southern Europe and Asia. While the plant is normally used as animal fodder, fresh young leaves may be added to salads. However, the seeds are used to spice curries, pickles, chutneys and confections in many recipes. Their flavor is similar to celery. Fenugreek seeds are available at Asian and Middle Eastern food shops and at some supermarkets. Store in a cool, dark place for up to 6 months.

FISH SAUCE

Fish sauce is indispensable to many Southeast Asian cuisines. It is made by placing salt with small fish like anchovies, or shellfish such as shrimp, in jars or barrels to ferment over a few months. The mixture is then strained and bottled. Varying in color from golden to dark brown, fish sauce is known by different names in different countries; for example, *nam pla* in Thailand, and *nuoc cham* or *nuoc mam* in Vietnam, Laos and Kampuchea. Use it as a condiment in a similar manner to soy sauce or anchovy essence.

There is no substitute for its distinctive salty flavor. Look for it in Asian food stores. Once opened, it will keep for several months in the refrigerator.

LEMONGRASS

Also known as citronella, lemongrass is an aromatic herb that grows in most tropical countries. The lower tenderer part of the stem is pounded to release its strong lemon flavor. This gives a dish the sharp freshness that is so characteristic of Thai and other Asian cuisines. The bulbous base is cut up and used in curries. Lemongrass stalks are readily available fresh from Asian food stores and should be kept in the refrigerator. Commercially prepared lemongrass is not as flavorful as fresh lemongrass; look for fresh whenever possible.

MIRIN

Mirin is a sweet sherry-like cooking wine. When heated, the alcohol content evaporates and the flavor concentrates to create a unique sweetness. It is one of the traditional flavors in Japanese cuisine. Mirin is available at Asian food stores. Although it keeps very well once opened it should be stored in the refrigerator in hot humid weather.

MISO

Protein and vitamin-B-rich miso is an essential ingredient in Japanese cuisine. There are several varieties of miso, all made from a fermented mixture of soybeans and other grains. The mixture is then aged anywhere from 6 months to 3 years, depending on the desired flavor. The three most popular varieties of this versatile ingredient in the West are soy miso, barley miso and rice miso. Miso varies in flavor from relatively sweetish to savory to quite salty (low-salt varieties are also available). The enzymes in miso reputedly aid digestion, provided they are not destroyed by boiling in the cooking process. Miso is available at Asian food stores and at some supermarkets. It will keep indefinitely if stored in an airtight container in the refrigerator.

MULTI-GRAIN RICE

While there are a number of rice blends available, the one used in these recipes is a brown rice and wild rice blend in a ratio of about 7 to 1. It has a strong nutty flavor that complements a wide range of full-flavored dishes including salads. Multi-grain rice blends are available in specialty food stores and at some supermarkets. Experiment by combining different varieties and quantities of rice; always remember to choose varieties that have the same cooking times.

NONREACTIVE COOKWARE

Nonreactive cookware is made from materials that do not react with acidic fruit or vegetables. If acidic ingredients like tomatoes are cooked in reactive materials such as cast iron and aluminum, they and other ingredients combined with them may become discolored and taste metallic. Nonacidic vegetables can also be affected when cooked in cast-iron pans. The best nonreactive cookware is stainless steel, glass or ceramic-coated cast iron.

OILS

Oils contain a mixture of monounsaturated, polyunsaturated and saturated fats. The oil is defined by the type of fat present in the greatest quantity. Monounsaturated oils like olive, peanut and canola oils are considered the healthiest choice. Polyunsaturated oils like safflower and corn oils are the next healthiest, while saturated oils like coconut and palm oils should be avoided as they have been linked to heart disease.

ORANGE-FLOWER WATER

Also known as orange-blossom water, this is distilled from the flowers of the bitter Seville orange. Used for centuries in the Middle East for flavoring confections, it is also used in the perfume industry. Orange-flower water is available at Greek or Middle Eastern food stores, and should be kept tightly sealed in a cool area away from direct sunlight.

PHYLLO PASTRY

These paper-thin sheets of pastry are widely used in Greek and Middle Eastern cooking and are sometimes spelled filo or fillo. Made with a high-gluten flour and little fat, the pastry is very pliable and is ideal for wrapping ingredients into small, individual parcels. It is also used for traditional pies. Phyllo pastry is used to make both savory and sweet dishes. It is difficult to make, but it can be purchased chilled or frozen at most supermarkets.

PICKLED GINGER

Pickled ginger is made by marinating fresh young roots (rhizomes) from the ginger plant in vinegar, salt and sugar. After twenty-four hours they are shaved into fine slices or finely shredded and returned to the pickling liquid. Red food dye is sometimes added to obtain a bright red color. Pickled ginger is available in plastic tubs, jars or packets at Asian food stores and at some supermarkets. It will keep indefinitely if transferred to a glass jar with a non-metallic lid and kept in the pickling liquid.

REDUCED-FAT MARGARINE SPREAD

Reduced-fat margarine spread is a relatively new product on the market. It is lower in fat and salt than margarines. As the bulk of the oil used in the spread is canola oil, most of the fat content is monunsaturated.

SEAWEED

Seaweed, a valuable part of many Asian diets, is a rich source of minerals including calcium, iron, iodine, zinc, nickel, copper, cobalt and chromium. Two kinds are used in this book. *Hijiki* is usually dried and resembles short, thin sticks of coarse black tea. It should be soaked for 15 to 20 minutes before using. Kelp has thick, brown leaves and is most commonly found in a powdered form. Use small amounts of kelp to flavor dips, soups and stews. Seaweed imparts a subtle spinach-like flavor.

SHIITAKE MUSHROOMS

Originally from Japan and Korea, shiitake mushrooms (also known as golden oak mushrooms) are now grown in many other areas of the world including California. Fresh and dried shiitakes are available at Asian food stores. The dried ones must be rehydrated for 30 minutes before using.

SOY SAUCE

Soy sauce is a thin, dark sauce made from fermented soy beans. Indispensable in Asian cooking, it comes in different flavors and is enjoyed by many of the world's cuisines. Thick, dark and salty soy sauce is traditionally preferred by the Chinese. It goes well with hearty dishes and is a wonderful condiment. Light brown, thin and mildly salty soy sauce is commonly preferred by the Japanese. Called *shoyu*, this Japanese-style soy sauce is used with chicken and seafood, in soups and some salad dressings. *Tamari* is thick, dark Japanese soy sauce with a strong flavor and generally used as a dip or condiment. *Kecap manis* is an Indonesian soy sauce with added thickeners and palm sugar. Synthetic brands of soy sauce are produced but are inferior in taste due to artificial flavoring. Reduced-sodium sauces with excellent flavor are available under various labels.

SUGARED BERRIES

Sugared berries make colorful and attractive garnishes. You will need: 1 egg white; 1 pound of berries (for example, blueberries, raspberries or strawberries); and 1 cup of superfine (caster) sugar. To prepare the berries, lightly whisk the egg white until foamy. Dip several berries into the egg white, then roll in the sugar to coat. Place on a wire rack lined with waxed (grease-proof) paper and leave until the sugar dries, about 1 to 2 hours.

VANILLA SUGAR

Vanilla sugar is inexpensive and easy to make. Place 2 cups of superfine (caster) sugar into a screw-top glass jar. Add a split vanilla pod to the sugar, cover and set aside for 5 to 7 days or longer. Use the sugar in desserts and cakes.

WASABI

Wasabi, the root of *Wasabia japonica*, is a plant native to Japan and similar to the horseradish root. Hence, wasabi is sometimes known as Japanese horseradish. The root has a brown skin and pale green flesh. Its flavor is more fragrant and less pungent than horseradish. Hotter than even the hottest chilies, wasabi is served sparingly as a condiment with a number of Japanese dishes. The Japanese pickle, *wasabi-zuke*, is made by pickling wasabi in sake. To prepare fresh wasabi to use as a condiment, peel and grate the root. Although the fresh root is not readily available in Western countries, wasabi is usually available in both paste (in tubes) and in powdered form at Asian food stores. Mix powdered wasabi with a little cold water and let stand for about 10 minutes to allow the flavor to develop before using. Once wasabi paste is opened, store it in the refrigerator. Store the powder in a container with a tight-fitting lid in a cool, dry place.

YEAST EXTRACT

Yeast extract is one of the best available sources of thiamin, riboflavin and niacin. It is made by processing brewer's yeast and combining it with vegetable extract. This popular product is used to flavor soups and casseroles and as a healthy spread. Yeast extract is sold in the United States as Savita, in the United Kingdom and South Africa as Marmite, and in Australia and New Zealand as Vegemite.

ZEST

The colored thin outermost peel of oranges, lemons and other citrus fruit is called zest. It contains fragrant oils and has a strong, tangy flavor. To obtain the zest, use a potato peeler, a very sharp knife, a grater or a special zester to separate it from the pith (the bitter white part of the skin). If using a peeler or a knife, cut the zest into julienne strips and then mince; if using a grater or zester, do so over the dish you are preparing to capture the oil spray. Zest is used to flavor both sweet and savory dishes and as a garnish.

INDEX

Page numbers in *italics* refer to
illustrations

A field of immature corn. This nutritious and versatile cereal is best cooked the day it is picked.

Picturesque farmlands in Catalonia in Spain.